A POSSIBLE PEACE
BETWEEN ISRAEL AND PALESTINE

A POSSIBLE PEACE
BETWEEN ISRAEL AND PALESTINE

An Insider's Account of the
Geneva Initiative

By Menachem Klein

Translated by Haim Watzman

COLUMBIA UNIVERSITY PRESS
NEW YORK

Columbia University Press
Publishers Since 1893
New York   Chichester, West Sussex
Copyright © 2007 Columbia University Press
All rights reserved

Originally published as *Yozmat Z'enevah: Mabat mibi-fenim*
(Jerusalem: Carmel, 2006).

Library of Congress Cataloging-in-Publication Data
Klein, Menachem.
[Yozmat Z'enevah. English]
A possible peace between Israel and Palestine :
an insider's account of the Geneva initiative / Menachem Klein ;
translated by Haim Watzman.
p.   cm.
Includes bibliographical references and index.
ISBN 978-0-231-13904-5 (cloth : alk. paper) — ISBN 978-0-231-51119-3 (e-book)
1. Arab-Israeli conflict — 1993 — Peace. I. Title.

DS119.76.K5213 2006
956.9405'4—dc22
2007013143

Columbia University Press books are printed on
permanent and durable acid-free paper.
This book is printed on paper with recycled content.
Printed in the United States of America

c 10 9 8 7 6 5 4 3 2 1

CONTENTS

Introduction   *vii*

Maps   *xi*

1   The Road from Taba to Geneva   1

2   Dividing Divided Jerusalem   81

3   Geneva in Perspective   145

    Epilogue   209

    Bibliography   213

    Index   223

INTRODUCTION

Just before boarding a bus in front of the Mövenpick hotel on Jordan's Dead Sea coast, a group of people paused to have their picture taken. The date was October 13, 2003, and the group was made up for the most part of men and women in their forties, fifties, and sixties, although it also included some children. Nothing about them suggested that they were anything but tourists. Neither did anything in the way the people related to each other suggest that they represented two peoples who at that very moment were fighting a bloody war, the latest phase in a conflict that had begun 120 years before. Two hours previously, they had signed a letter to the foreign minister of Switzerland, to which they attached a fifty-page document. It was the Geneva Draft Peace Initiative, a detailed model Israeli–Palestinian peace agreement, negotiated over the course of two years.

The participants gathered for the signing ceremony with mixed feelings, notable in the way they dressed. A Palestinian cabinet minister stood stiffly in a brown suit. Others were in casual vacation attire, looking as if they had had been caught on their way to the pool. Most of the men wore pressed shirts that gave some air of formality, even though they were without ties and jackets. There was a sense of achievement, but not euphoria. Was it a breakthrough? It was. But a long road remained before the initiative would become policy, and the policy reality. Aware that they had done something unprecedented, the people in the room also wondered how long that road would be.

The Geneva process was more than simulated negotiations under laboratory conditions. Among its participants were officials who had continued to negotiate from the point where they had stopped in authorized formal negotiations. The role they assigned themselves went beyond signing the document. They were committed to do what was necessary to turn it into an official treaty.

I did not predict this. In 2000, I was overly optimistic about the ability of the Palestinians and Israelis to achieve a permanent agreement. My naïveté was the product of bureaucratic inexperience and a lack of information about what was happening behind the scenes. Learning from my experience, I entered the Geneva process without preconceptions. As this book shows, my position changed; so did the positions of other negotiators. And so did Israeli and Palestinian public opinion. Therefore, this is book bears a hopeful message. It is possible to change, and positions must be changed.

I am a scholar, but one who was an involved witness and a participating observer in the events I write of here. Therefore, this book may be seen as a work of political anthropology, in which a scholar turns his gaze on himself, and not just on others. It is my personal gaze, one not necessarily identical to that of other members of the Geneva initiative team. I am aware of the difficulties implicit in the fact that the Geneva document was signed only four years ago. That is too little time to provide the perspective necessary for evaluation of the process, and certainly too little time to measure its outcomes. Nevertheless, few will dispute my claim that the Geneva plan has become the principal reference framework in the discourse on Israeli–Palestinian relations and as the principal model of a permanent agreement between the two peoples. The Geneva initiative stands against the unilateral moves that Israel is imposing on the Palestinians, and against the approach that the conflict is to be managed instead of resolved.

This book examines the Geneva initiative simultaneously from the inside and from the outside. It recounts the ups and downs from the point of view of a participant, and also offers an analytic view that compares the process with similar instances of civil diplomacy that have been studied in the professional literature. At the same time, I also make a clear statement about Israel's relations with the Palestinians under its rule, and about the way in which that may be changed. One person's name appears on this book, but it really has two writers: a professional expert and an involved citizen. Both relate and analyze the process in which they were involved. As the author of this book and a researcher, I am aware of the problem presented by this dualism, and of the impossibility of distinguishing sharply between the two authors. The most I can do is to acknowledge this and to present this dual role to my readers for their judgment.

Although I was a participant and observer of the process by which the Geneva document was produced, my own observations and experiences were hardly my sole material. I also made use of video recordings that were made of the two negotiating meetings of the complete teams, near London in February and on the Dead Sea shore in October 2003. The camera helped where my memory was deficient. There were also cameras at discussions I did not attend. I am grateful to my colleagues at the Geneva headquarters in Tel Aviv, who made the recordings available to me. I am also deeply grateful to Dr. Yossi Beilin and Colonel (Res.) Shaul Arieli, who read large parts of this manuscript and offered helpful and important comments. I also owe much to the wise comments and broad writing and editing experience of Professors Gabi Sheffer and Baruch Kimmerling of the Hebrew University of Jerusalem, Joel Migdal of the University of Washington in Seattle, and Dr. Motti Golani of the University of Haifa. Without their help, I would not have been able to provide my readers with this text. It goes without saying that all responsibility for errors of fact, judgment, and faulty analysis are mine alone.

The translation into English has been accomplished, professionally as always, by Haim Watzman.

The maps were drawn by the talented Vered Shatil, based on the work of Shaul Arieli and Sharry Motro, and I thank all three.

The Rich Foundation for Education, Culture, and Welfare helped produce this book, so I owe thanks to its director, Avner Azoulai. Ambassador Philip Wilcox and his Foundation for Middle East Peace provided a generous grant that assisted in the translation of the manuscript from Hebrew to English. This is part of their longstanding professional and personal involvement in advancing peace between Israel and the Palestinians. They devotion to and investment in this issue are worthy of great praise.

I previously published some sections of this book as articles, and some sections appeared in previous books of mine. All these sections were re-edited and reworked for their inclusion here.

Menachem Klein
June 2007

MAP 1. The Disputed Area

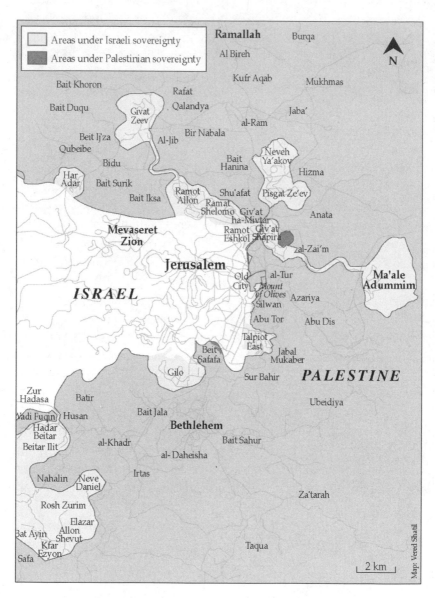

MAP 2. Jerusalem

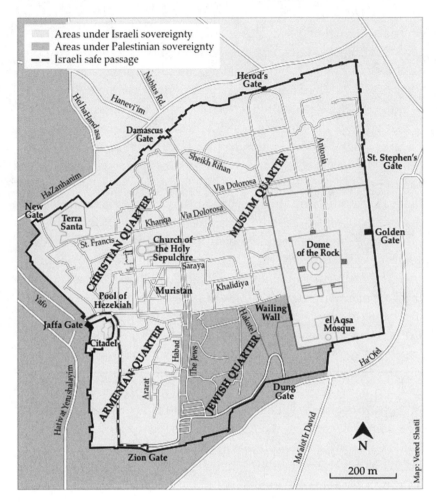

MAP 3. The Old City

A POSSIBLE PEACE
BETWEEN ISRAEL AND PALESTINE

1

THE ROAD FROM TABA TO GENEVA

GOING PUBLIC

Minister of Justice Yossi Beilin emerged from the Taba talks of 2001 feeling that an opportunity had been missed. His party chief and prime minister, Ehud Barak, had come into office in 1999 promising the Israeli public that he would achieve peace with Israel's Arab neighbors and with the Palestinians before the completion of his four-year term. But both direct contacts with the Palestinians and the attempt to achieve a brokered agreement at Camp David in the summer of 2000 had failed. In October, frustration and distrust between Israel and the Palestinians broke out in another bloody uprising, the second, or al-Aqsa, Intifada.

In December 2000, Israeli and Palestinian negotiators gathered in the resort of Taba, in the Egyptian Sinai Peninsula, just over the border from Israel. The Taba negotiations were a last-ditch effort to reach an Israeli–Palestinian peace treaty before Barak's impending electoral defeat by Ariel Sharon, who had denounced the Oslo peace process. In the end, the Taba talks did not produce an agreement. But Beilin was convinced that, with a bit more effort, the Israelis and Palestinians could have achieved an agreement on the principles for a permanent status agreement.

Had Barak had his way, Beilin would not have been in Taba. Meretz, the junior party in the Labor-led coalition, had forced Barak to send him. Yair Tzaban, head of Meretz's strategic team, and the party's chairman, Yossi Sarid, met with Barak and informed him that Meretz would support his rival, Shimon Peres, for prime minister in the elections scheduled for February 2002, unless Barak met three conditions:

Israel must participate in the Taba talks, the Israeli delegation to the talks would be expanded, and an inner cabinet for peace would be established. As often happens in politics, the politics of persons and of statecraft were intermixed. A peace cabinet was set up with Peres as a member. Furthermore, Sarid and Beilin, whom Barak had shut out of active and effective participation in talks with the Palestinians during the decisive period of negotiations, arrived in Taba as part of the Israeli delegation. Accompanying them was Minister of Transportation Amnon Shahak. Unlike Beilin and Sarid, Shahak had taken part in the principal talks with the Palestinians, including those at Camp David the previous summer. But Shahak had virtually no influence on Barak.

The Taba talks produced progress on only two issues: the borders of the state of Palestine and the status of the Palestinian refugees of 1948. While there had already been progress on the territorial issue during the previous year, it was only at Taba that the Israelis and Palestinians actually exchanged maps on an official basis (the maps appear in Klein 2003b:112–13). The differences between the maps were not as great as at earlier negotiating stages, when the two sides had exchanged unofficial maps. While the subject of refugees had been addressed at Camp David, the impressive rhetoric of Foreign Minister Shlomo Ben-Ami, Member of the Knesset Dan Meridor, and Attorney General Elyakim Rubinstein did not constitute negotiation. Taba was the first venue where the two sides talked seriously about the Palestinian refugees. Beilin headed the Israeli negotiating team that addressed this issue. He presented the Palestinians with new ideas and an experienced political team that included his assistants Daniel Levy and Gidi Grinstein. Levy and Grinstein had worked intensively on the refugee question in unofficial talks and in the Economic Cooperation Foundation (ECF), a think tank Beilin founded in 1990 to pursue track-two negotiations (see chapter 3) for a permanent status agreement between Israel and the Palestinians. The veteran negotiators, headed by Ben-Ami and Gilad Sher, chief of Barak's bureau, had been worn out by the exhausting contacts they had conducted beginning in April 2000, and bore with them the disappointments of these earlier stages. Gilad Sher even believed that Barak erred in consenting to enter the Taba negotiations; as a lame-duck prime minister facing election, Barak, Sher argued, did not have a mandate to make critical decisions with long-term implications. Barak had lost his majority in the Knesset when the Shas party bolted his coalition in June 2000, and was trailing in the polls behind his opponent, Ariel Sharon.

Beyond gaining Barak's agreement to enter the Taba talks with a broader negotiating team, Meretz's influence on the prime minister was minimal. Barak himself has said that he did not intend to reach final agreements on the issues at Taba. He even instructed Gilad Sher, who headed the Israeli delegation, not to hold meetings to coordinate the positions of the members of the sub-teams. Sher also told the Palestinian delegation that only he was authorized by Barak to make concessions. Just before leaving office, Barak had the cabinet decide that all proposals made to the Palestinians during the negotiating process were no longer on the table. President Bill Clinton did the same with regard to his proposals of December 2000 (Agha and Malley 2002a, 2002b; Arieli and Pundak 2004; Beilin 2001; Beilin 2004; Ben-Ami 2004; Enderlin 2003; Hanieh 2001; Klein 2003; Matz 2003; Meital 2004; Morris et al. 2003; Pressman 2003; Pundak 2001; Rabinowitz 2004; Ross 2004; Rubinstein et al. 2003; Shamir 2005; Sher 2001; Swisher 2004).

Officially, the proposals discussed at Taba did not obligate anyone, but thanks to two people—the European Union's delegate, Miguel Moratinos, and Yossi Beilin—they were inscribed as political facts that can hardly be expunged. Moratinos is an energetic man and a great believer in the possibility of peace between Israel and Syria and Israel and the Palestinians. In August 2001, he, along with participants from both sides, summed up the points of agreement and disagreement in the Taba talks. For all intents and purposes, Moratinos's document reviews all stages of the official negotiations for a permanent status agreement. Its importance is that it maps the geological strata of the contacts between the two sides. During a flight out of Antalya, Turkey, one of the Palestinian participants loaned the document to Akiva Eldar, a journalist at *Ha'aretz*, on condition that it be returned before arrival in Tel Aviv. Eldar, who immediately realized its importance, took advantage of the fact that his informant had made no other conditions, photographed the document with a digital camera, and published it on February 15, 2002. While the Moratinos document can be read as a requiem, it can also serve as a starting point for a continuation of the effort to reach a final agreement. Yossi Beilin was interested in just that, and Yassir 'Abd-Rabbu, the Palestinian minister of information, was of the same mind.

There is a reason that the Geneva understandings are not called the Beilin-'Abd-Rabbu understandings. The Geneva document is not the work of one person on each side but rather of large and heterogeneous teams. The document testifies to the fact that Beilin learned a lesson from the Beilin–Abu-Mazen understandings of 1995, a behind-the-scenes attempt by Beilin and Yassir Arafat's close associate, Mahmoud Abbas (Abu-Mazen is his nom-de-guerre), to draw up a permanent status agreement. From the start, he brought together a broad group of people and adopted a different plan of action from the one he pursued in 1994–1995. In November 1999, Beilin tried to persuade Prime Minister Barak, to use the Beilin–Abu-Mazen document as a framework for talks on the final agreement that Barak had declared he intended to reach. Barak refused, because he thought that the document had gone too far in offering Israeli concessions. Because Beilin was identified with that document, Barak prevented him from taking any significant part in the permanent status talks. In fact, Barak rejected the document several times during the first half of 2000. Once it was in response to Abbas, who proposed that the two of them open a secret channel of talks through personal delegates. Ahmad Khalidi and Hussein Agha, two Palestinian scholars living in London, who served Abbas as negotiators, had been involved in drafting the Beilin–Abu-Mazen agreement six years earlier. They contacted Gilad Sher in London and asked that the document be used as the basis for open or secret negotiations. At Barak's direction, Sher rejected the request out of hand (Sher 2001:63; Ben-Ami 2004:32; Ahmad Khalidi to the author, Jan. 2004).

The document also came up in talks between Abbas and Amnon Shahak, Barak's delegate, and in Abbas's own talks with Barak. None of this was to any avail. Barak's positions were very distant from those of the Beilin–Abu-Mazen document. In the spring of 2000, Barak's tactical preference was for opening secret talks with the chairman of the Palestinian Legislative Council, Ahmed Qurei (Abu-'Ala), Abbas's political rival, in the hope of obtaining more than Abbas had been willing to concede. To these talks he sent his minister of internal security, Shlomo Ben-Ami, who was the major political rival of Beilin and of Barak's foreign minister, David Levy. Barak's gambit achieved a secondary political goal—he obtained Ben-Ami's loyalty—but he failed to achieve his major objective. There was no breakthrough toward a permanent status agreement. As a result, Barak worked to shape the Camp David summit as means of placing heavy, concentrated, and direct Israeli and American pressure on the Palestinian leadership. Here, too, Barak achieved only a tactical success. President Clinton adopted the tactic that Barak suggested, abandoning his original ideas about the conduct of the conference and the proposals he had planned to place on the table shortly after its opening. They both succeeded in marketing the argument that Arafat had caused the failure, but this did not bring peace.

A document in the same spirit as the Beilin–Abu-Mazen understandings was meant to await both sides at the Camp David summit. The original document was sent to the White House in June 2000, while the summit was being prepared. President Clinton wished to table a compromise proposal of his own, based on the document, at the opening of the conference. But in the end he adopted the strategy that Barak proposed. We can only wonder what might have happened had Clinton stuck to his original plan. According to his aides, Clinton backtracked because he appreciated the political risk that Barak was taking—the Israeli prime minister came to Camp David in July 2000 with a decaying coalition and a tight schedule. Open talks on a permanent status agreement with the Palestinians had begun in July 2000, while secret talks commenced the previous April. Neither channel produced significant breakthroughs.

Negotiations with the Palestinians had not begun at the start of the Barak administration, because Barak had given priority to talks with the Syrians. Among other reasons, he believed that if Israel reached an agreement with Syria, the Palestinians would be left isolated. Israel would then be able to broker a better agreement on the West Bank and Gaza Strip. But Barak's refusal to cede sovereignty over a strip of territory on the northeastern shore of the Sea of Galilee brought the talks with Syria to an end in March 2000. Barak was under pressure to produce results on the diplomatic front. Arafat announced that, if he did not achieve a state through negotiation with Israel, he would issue a unilateral declaration of the establishment of the state of Palestine on September 13. The American presidential elections in November threatened to take Clinton out of action (Agha and Malley 2002a, 2002b; Rubinstein et al 2003; Shamir 2005).

In retrospect, Clinton's deferral to Barak's tactics was a mistake and led to a dead end. With the benefit of hindsight, it is clear that Clinton should have taken advantage of Barak's dependence on him in order to force him to accept the compromise he had proposed. Furthermore, a few months previously Barak had reneged on his promise to Clinton that he would accept a full Israeli withdrawal from the Golan Heights. In doing so, Barak prevented Clinton from achieving a breakthrough with Syrian President Hafez al-Asad that apparently would have led to the signing of a peace treaty between them. Barak's excuse for his sudden case of cold feet was his coalition difficulties. Clinton had not forgotten the difficulties Barak had given him at the end of 1999 and beginning of 2000 during the talks with Syria, and said so quite sharply in moments of anger and frustration at Camp David. But Barak's political position that summer was even weaker, after his coalition disintegrated. Clinton could have used Barak's weakness to apply pressure in favor of the American ideas, but instead the president decided to be considerate of Barak's problems. Unfortunately, only American coercion could have brought Barak around to the American ideas, and Clinton did not want to coerce.

Citizens and historians may look back and ponder "what if." But leaders must look to the future. Clinton did this, belatedly, in December 2000, when he presented a set of guidelines for further negotiations. Clinton's guidelines were based closely on the Beilin–Abu-Mazen understandings, and were the starting point for the Taba talks the following month. The Beilin–Abu-Mazen understandings thus traveled a long and winding path before they began to influence policy. They were never published officially, and there was no campaign to gain public support for them. Neither did they have the official support of Israel and the Palestinian Authority.

In planning the Geneva initiative, Beilin and 'Abd-Rabbu sought to avoid the pitfalls that the Beilin–Abu-Mazen understandings had encountered. Rather than keeping this new informal peace effort shrouded in secrecy until they could be presented to the leaders on each side, the two men planned from the start that the Geneva accords would be placed before the public. Neither did they seek to keep their contacts out of the public eye. Instead, they tipped off journalists and ensured that, during the two years the Geneva talks were underway, several Israeli newspaper columnists would write that Beilin and 'Abd-Rabbu were trying to produce a detailed model of a permanent status agreement.

In accordance with Israeli practice, this began with a leak. Leaks to the press are part of the political process, a way of staging a political event and a way of marketing a political campaign. The leak was not meant to protect the patriotic images of Beilin and 'Abd-Rabbu. Neither were they meant to overshadow other negotiating channels or to protect them by diverting attention to an "open" channel while leaving the "real," secret one undisturbed. Such tactics are not unknown (Agha et al. 2003:186–88), but these were not the motives for the Geneva initiative leaks. In this case, the initial leak produced a period of tranquility. The fact that the contacts were publicized prevented harmful prying and minimized the media's urge to unmask a secret process.

The managers of the Geneva channel made no secret of the contacts and their goal. Drafts of the agreement were shown to journalists and senior politicians. Beilin even outlined the talks to Dov Weisglass, Prime Minister Sharon's chief of staff. The length of the talks, and the disagreements between the two sides, minimized the interest of the press, which sought bigger headlines. Furthermore, many reporters who knew about the contacts were doubtful that the effort would achieve full agreement on all issues, and even scoffed at some of the Israeli participants and their optimism. Beilin and those around him passed out "tips" to selected journalists in exchange for promising them the story when the agreement was ready to sign. The tips helped keep the media and the political arena quiet, and proved their worth when the public campaign commenced.

When the talks reached an advanced stage, advertisers Nissim Duek, Dror Sternschuss, and Kamel Husseini prepared an Israeli–Palestinian campaign, which they presented to both sides at the talks in Woking in south London in February 2003. The marketing package was first designed by the Israelis, with the Palestinians brought in afterward. The marketers convened because there was a sense that an agreement would soon be signed, and that it was necessary to launch a campaign to persuade the public and political leaders to accept it. The campaign's concept was based on an analysis of the agreement's strengths and weaknesses from a marketing perspective with regard to each of the two major target publics. The program was to bring the full document before the Israeli and Palestinian publics in order to create public debate. The marketers' principal fear was that public interest in the initiative would fade quickly and that the public and political leadership would quickly revert to their previous agendas. The campaign thus sought to maintain interest and to ensure that, unlike in previous cases such as the Beilin–Abu-Mazen agreement, the Geneva accords would be fully transparent.

It was clear from the beginning to Beilin, 'Abd-Rabbu, and their associates that marketing was a critical part of the effort and that the director of the public relations campaign would be an essential member of both the Israeli and Palestinian delegations. The decision was to run coordinated Israeli and Palestinian campaigns, to speak in a single voice despite the different expectations of the two target publics, and to reach the maximum number of homes. At the same time, the campaign would seek to create the largest possible circles of support so as to keep those interested in preserving the existing situation from gaining a monopoly over public debate, and to minimize their ability to manipulate it. According to the plan presented at the London talks, the Geneva document would first be concluded; this stage of the campaign was called Geneva I. There would then be two months to organize administratively and to enlist prominent supporters, concluding with a public, international signing ceremony. This would be called Geneva II and would be the beginning of the public campaign. Just prior to the ceremony the entire document would be made public gradually, and would be presented to the heads of the Israeli and Palestinian governments. The agreement would be distributed to every home in the land. There would be an information bank for public inquiries manned by both Palestinians and Israelis. The campaign would come to an end about a month and a half after the signing ceremony. No further public relations plans were presented at London, and it is doubtful whether any existed.

Thanks to Prime Minister Ariel Sharon, the Geneva document came before the public earlier than planned, and with more intensity and success than any of its supporters expected. For reasons that remain obscure, Sharon, at a Likud election rally in Bat Yam on October 8, accused the left of coordinating its actions with the Palestinians at the height of a war, behind the back of the Israeli government. In the early evening of that same day, a few hours before Sharon's speech, the negotiating team gathered for a preparation meeting in the offices of businessman Avi Shaked. In his characteristically dispassionate way, Shaked had done much to flesh out the agreement. As we sat in his office's well-appointed meeting room in a Tel Aviv office tower, we could see the entire churning metropolis spread out below us. It looked very tranquil from there. Tel Aviv's shabbiness is not evident from above, especially at night.

Twenty-four hours later, according to our plan, we were scheduled to set out for a concluding round of talks in Jordan. But when we gathered, we did not know if the Israeli authorities would allow the Palestinian representatives to make the trip to the Dead Sea. Beilin and Amram Mitzna, a Labor member of the Knesset who had been party leader and run against Sharon in the previous election, used all their contacts in the military establishment to ensure that the Palestinians would be allowed to travel. The Jordanians and the initiative's international sponsors, led by Switzerland, seem also to have exerted pressure. The Egyptians may well have been in the picture as well. After hearing on the telephone a report from 'Abd-Rabbu on the planned signing event, Usama al-Baz, political adviser to President Hosni Mubarak, offered to host the meeting in Cairo or Sharm al-Sheikh. Al-Baz wanted to participate personally in the final meeting and signing ceremony. But the Palestinians preferred the Jordanian Dead Sea shore. The Palestinian political system was then in the midst of yet another crisis and senior members of the Palestinian delegation wanted to be able to get back quickly to their political center in Ramallah if necessary. Presumably, Israel intelligence picked up this hum of activity. The central figure in Israeli military intelligence, later coordinator of Israeli activities in the West Bank and Gaza Strip, General Amos Gilad, had little regard for 'Abd-Rabbu (Drucker and Shelach 2005:235, 356), nor for the Israelis involved in the Geneva initiative. However, after two years of drowsiness, during which they failed to appreciate the significance of the Geneva channel, someone at the top woke up and sounded an alarm bell.

This disregard had been useful in the past. So long as the talks had a low profile, Beilin had no difficulty obtaining travel permits and entry into Jerusalem for the Palestinian negotiators. The Israeli military processed hundreds of such requests during the course of the Oslo years. The Geneva talks were only one of myriad sets of contacts between Israelis and Palestinians, encompassing people as diverse as teachers, water experts, economists, journalists, students, and young people. Even members of Sharon's Likud party and the ultra-Orthodox Shas party met with members of Fatah and Palestinian social activists (Adwan and Bar On 2004; IPCRI 2002; Klein 2003b:23–31; Konrad Adenauer Foundation et al. 1998). Apparently the intelligence agencies found it difficult to separate the wheat from the chaff. Only at a late date, it seems, did they realize that the Geneva channel was different from these other sorts of meetings. By then it was already too late to halt the process. It may also be possible that Sharon vented his anger and frustration spontaneously. But many observers believe that Sharon always acted deliberately and that he intended to delegitimize the initiative.

Whatever the case, his attack was ineffectual. In fact, the initiative's Israel public relations strategists were able to use the prime minister's attack to good advantage. Sharon's outburst was first reported, that same evening, on Ynet, the website of Israel's largest newspaper, *Yediot Aharonot.* Immediately thereafter, Ynet also reported the first leak about the gathering in Jordan and its participants. The leak apparently came not from the Geneva initiative's leaders or public relations staff but rather from one of the Israeli politicians who was involved. The leaks proved to be an unexpectedly successful media strategy. The next day other media outlets also reported the news—in particular, the Voice of Israel, the government-run radio network. The Voice of Israel may have been encouraged to play up the story by Sharon's office, to which the network's top administrators had close ties.

From this point onward, the leaks that came from the public relations staff in Jordan—Dror Sternschuss, Nissim Duek, and Uri Zaki, Beilin's spokesman—were partial and fragmentary. This was not always intended. They had trouble keeping up with the pace of the talks and with the changes being made to the draft of the agreement. Furthermore, the embargoed information that the Israeli press possessed, and that they were permitted to publish after the signing, was not up to date and did not include last-minute changes to the agreement. For example, Nadav Eyal of *Ma'ariv* had a draft of the document and published it after the signing. But it was not the full text and did not include changes that had been made during the discussions. The press reports cited as participants some people who, for various reasons, had at the last minute been unable to attend the gathering in Jordan. Sometimes rumors preceded reality. Early on Saturday night, October 11, 2003, Palestinian members said that there were reports circulating in Jordan that the document had been signed—even though at the time there were still points of dispute between the two sides. The rumor produced a sharp response from Hani al-Hasan, a member of the Fatah central committee and a former Palestinian minister of the interior. He called the members of the Palestinian delegation traitors. The Palestinian members evinced no particular concern about this, however.

The managers of the Geneva channel were not certain that the document would be signed at the meeting in Jordan. Neither were they certain that they could control the media reports if discipline broke. The participants had been inundated with telephone calls since news of the Jordan gathering had appeared in the press. Irresponsible comments could sabotage the entire effort. Therefore, on the bus to Jordan, the Israelis were asked not to grant interviews and not to reveal the purpose of their trip. The cover story was that the trip was for just another meeting in the framework of the peace coalition. They were also told that the Voice of Israel's political correspondent might be staying in the same hotel on vacation and that they should be wary of him. The hotel had set aside a separate wing for the two delegations from which the media were kept out. When the Israelis arrived at the hotel they discovered that the Palestinians' appreciation of them had risen considerably. The Palestinians had seen Sharon's attack as a sign that the Israeli peace camp still wielded influence. If so, it was worth pursuing the joint process with the Israelis. For the first time in three years, the Palestinians said, you in the peace camp have managed to make Sharon lose his self-control.

The advance publicity had another positive effect on the discussions in Jordan. It created expectations and fenced in the participants. The Palestinians may have thought of evading any resolution of the remaining disputes and not signing an agreement. They may have not wanted to make the necessary concessions or to make any decisions at the height of a political crisis in the Palestinian Authority. But now that the talks were public, equivocation became more difficult. The Israeli side also had to consider the price of cutting off the talks because of the failure to agree on the points of dispute that came up in Jordan. Cutting off the talks now that they were public and now that there were expectations of their successful conclusion would have utterly buried any hope of peace. If these two delegations couldn't reach a peace agreement, and if Beilin and 'Abd-Rabbu couldn't reach an agreement, the message would be that no accommodation was possible. Yossi Beilin put it this way: any agreement the Geneva teams reached would be a virtual one because the talks were not official ones. But any failure would be very real.

Failure was indeed possible. The talks in Jordan were not easy ones, and the final compromise was reached only on Sunday morning, a few hours before we were to return to Israel. Before agreement was reached, it was suggested that we meet again two weeks later, even though in that case we would lose Switzerland's support. The Swiss foreign minister, Micheline Calmy-Rey, had a tight timetable. Her country was facing national elections and Christmas followed soon thereafter. She would not be able to offer much help once the election campaign began in mid-October. Just before leaving for Jordan, Beilin and 'Abd-Rabbu received an official letter from the foreign minister confirming her commitment to fund the public campaign and signing ceremony—on condition that the two teams succeed in reaching an agreement this time. The text of the letter, and the message she conveyed orally, made it clear that if the negotiations did not conclude successfully and on schedule, the Swiss foreign ministry in Bern would withdraw its support and not provide any more funds.

The Swiss did not have an easy time of it. They had been hoping for awhile that the parties were on the verge of agreement, but were always disappointed. Again and again, old disputes reopened and new ones suddenly appeared. The Swiss had a hard time understanding the obstacles that Israel raised, after violence broke out in 2000, to the Palestinians' travel outside the country. Similarly, the Palestinians' negotiating culture and work habits were far from what the Swiss had expected. Sometimes the Swiss were also frustrated by matters that were not under the control of the negotiating teams, such as military actions, terrorist attacks, and political crises that prevented the Palestinians from preparing properly for the talks. During the final year, the Swiss imposed a firm timetable, but the two sides were unable to stick to it. Mid-October was the last chance. In the end, this framework, together with the framework created by the media reports, were positive influences and led to the successful conclusion of the negotiations.

Once the agreement had been signed, the Israeli public relations staff initiated a new round of press briefings. They made their first phone calls from the hotel and from the bus back to Israel. A television crew arrived at the Israeli side of the Allenby Bridge over the Jordan River. Former Knesset member Nechama Ronen, who belonged to the Likud party, and Brigadier General (ret.) Giora Inbar went straight from the bus to television studios for interviews. Photographs of the meeting in Jordan were provided a few days later. Ilana Dayan, a popular Israeli broadcaster, devoted two of her shows to the Geneva initiative, one to the negotiations and the second to an interview with the novelist Amos Oz, who had been a member of the Israeli delegation. Her show included short, carefully chosen video segments of the Jordan meeting and from the London talks, taken by Paul Usiskin, a television producer and member of the London chapter of Peace Now. An aide to Ahmend Qurei, speaker of the Palestinian Authority's Legislative Assembly, gave—unintentionally, apparently—a *Ma'ariv* correspondent, Ben Kaspit, a full text of the agreement. However, because of a lack of space on the news pages, *Ma'ariv* cut a few sentences from the document without making note of the fact. Only a week after the signing did *Ha'aretz* publish on its website the full English text of the agreement. *Yediot Aharonot* was incensed when *Ma'ariv* published the document, after Sternschuss forbade Nachum Barnea, a senior political correspondent at *Yediot Aharonot*, to do so. Barnea had been promised that the agreement would be published in all media outlets simultaneously.

Following a week of intensive coverage, *Yediot Aharonot* published very few sympathetic articles and prominent reports on the initiative. Instead, it gave precedence to the principles for a permanent status agreement that had been reached by General (ret.) Ami Ayalon, a former Shin Bet chief, and Sari Nusseibeh, president of al-Quds University (more on these principles below) and printed articles critical of the Geneva document. This caused some damage to the Geneva campaign but it was not a mortal blow. During the campaign's two months, the Geneva agreement proved that it was not just a media bubble but a political fact. It did so on its own merits, and with the help of reports in other media outlets. According to polls conducted by Dr. Ya'akov Shamir and Dr. Khalil Shiqaqi in December 2003, a full 95 percent of the Israeli population and 73 percent of the Palestinian population in the West Bank and Gaza Strip had been exposed to the Geneva agreement's message (Palestinian Center for Policy and Survey Research 2003, 2005; Truman Institute 2005).

The media's interest in the Geneva accords rose out of the changes that had occurred in Israeli public opinion since 2003, and out of the sorry state of affairs into which the Sharon government had led Israel. The Israeli public had begun to understand that Sharon had brought the diplomatic process to a standstill. He was, many Israelis had come to realize, looking out for the interests of the settlers, while society and the economy were in a downspin because of the conflict with the Palestinians. The intense media interest brought on a surge of inquiries to the Geneva team—some three thousand during the initial weeks—both requests for information and offers of assistance. Yet, because the initiative had been made public earlier than expected, the Geneva headquarters had not yet put together a staff and administration to handle the deluge. The initial campaign was handled by Dror Sternschuss's advertising agency and Beilin's ECF. At this point, it was necessary to respond to the public's curiosity through the mediation of the press, and to maintain the momentum—high media exposure, public interest, and the production of events. At the same time, two million copies of the agreement were printed and distributed to every home in Israel by mail. There were also public appearances by those who had participated in the talks.

The Geneva initiative appealed to the public over the head of the government in a way unprecedented in Israel. Nevertheless, most elements of the marketing plan were not carried out. The document was not provided simultaneously to all media outlets; instead, it was publicized bit by bit so as to keep the subject "hot." An Israeli–Palestinian information hotline was not set up. Neither was there a publicity campaign to get across the initiative's message independently of the media, which could have made an emotional appeal that would have created great sympathy for the project. The media commotion confounded the original marketing plan and forced the publicists to try to manage events through the release of information and initiation of interviews. The advertisers and politicians involved in the project were elated by the huge media interest and neglected to implement their original plan.

The Palestinians' room for action was much more limited. The mails did not function properly because of the occupation, and the agreement was thus published twice, in special weekend supplements to the two major daily newspapers, *al-Ayam* and *al-Quds*. Furthermore, printed copies of the agreement were placed in the centers of villages and towns. Since the Israelis restricted the Palestinians in their movements outside their place of residence, it was difficult to distribute the newspapers and copies of the agreement, and the members of the Palestinian Geneva team had trouble coordinating their activities. The Palestinians showed themselves to be poorly organized—in addition to the lack of

coordination, they had no consistent working and decision-making procedures, and no efficient division of labor. Beyond that, it was hard for
them to built public support for the initiative while Israel continued
the occupation and built its security fence—a wall cutting through the
Palestinian territories. During 2004, the Palestinian Geneva activists
ratcheted down their activity and became part of a broader body, the
Palestinian peace coalition.

The media later lost interest, and when Sharon presented his unilateral disengagement plan from the Gaza Strip and northern Samaria,
the Israeli agenda changed. The Israeli side of the Geneva initiative
viewed the security fence as aimed at drawing a border and not as a
method of controlling the Palestinians. It also viewed the prime minister's move to the center and the crisis on the Israeli right as events
of historical significance. Some even reasoned that the precedent of
evacuating settlements in the Gaza Strip would lead inevitably to a massive evacuation of settlements and withdrawal to the lines proposed by
the Geneva agreement. The Geneva leadership was thus faced with the
dilemma of whether to offer unreserved support for Sharon's move.
That would involve waiting on the sidelines until after the evacuation
and then pressuring the government to go "from Gaza to Geneva." The
other option was, with their Palestinian colleagues, to declare support
for the evacuation of settlements while sharply opposing the construction of the fence in the West Bank. For political reasons, and out of fear
of losing public support, most of the Geneva team in Israel chose the
first option. The Palestinians were bitterly disappointed when the Israelis used their own point of view as their only standard, while ignoring
the Palestinian view that Israeli occupation and control were the critical issues. The Palestinian public had no interest in a future that now
seemed more utopian than ever, and demanded that the Palestinian representatives on the Geneva team halt the construction of the fence and
the expansion of the settlements. "Where are your Israeli partners on
this issue?" they asked. The Geneva agreement ceased to be a practical
diplomatic solution and became irrelevant to the Palestinian condition.
Those who managed to keep the Geneva initiative alive in the public
consciousness were the members of the Likud party, who passionately
debated Sharon's disengagement program. Sharon argued that if his
program were not accepted, the left and the international community
would impose the Geneva agreement on Israel. At the same time, his

Likud opponents claimed that he himself was striding rapidly toward the same goal.

HOW DO YOU GET TO GENEVA?

The Geneva accords differ from the Beilin–Abu-Mazen agreement in the way they were achieved, their goals, and the use that was made of them. The Beilin–Abu-Mazen agreement was a private initiative by two people, assisted by two negotiators on each. Their goal was to bring their finished but unsigned product before decisionmakers on both sides. But Shimon Peres and Yassir Arafat, each for his own reasons, rejected the document in November 1995. The proposal was leaked to *Ha'aretz* in August 1996, apparently without the knowledge or consent of Abbas. He subsequently denied, in all official Fatah and PLO forums, any involvement in the talks that produced the document. Apparently, he was deterred because the version of the agreement that was leaked rounded off some sharp corners to make it more palatable to the Israeli public. (The original text was published in full only on September 17, 2000, in *Newsweek*, and appears also in Beilin 2004:299–312.)

In contrast, the Geneva accords were signed by the teams that negotiated them. They were distributed to the populations of Israel and the Palestinian territories. The intention was that leaders on each side would be persuaded to adopt them after they had been accepted by large portions of the public on each side and by international public opinion. The Geneva accords built on the experience acquired in reaching the Beilin–Abu-Mazen accords. Furthermore, they appeared in a different political context, and in particular against the background of the second Palestinian Intifada. At the time of the Beilin–Abu-Mazen agreement, Israel had a Labor-led government that was pursuing the Oslo process to achieve a permanent Israeli–Palestinian agreement. The Beilin–Abu-Mazen agreement was meant to assist the leaderships on both sides to advance along the path that they were already on.

True, Oslo's opponents were seeking to disrupt the process. In February 1994, a settler from Kiryat Arba, Baruch Goldstein, massacred twenty-nine Muslim worshipers in the Tomb of the Patriarchs in Hebron. Subsequently, Hamas decided to change its strategy and send suicide bombers to attack Israeli civilians. But the Likud had not yet come to power. In contrast, the Geneva accords were reached while Israel was ruled by a Likud government that sought to destroy the foundation on which the Oslo accords had been built, along with any possibility of reaching a permanent agreement with the Palestinians. In this context, the Geneva negotiators had to mobilize the Israeli public through extra-parliamentary action to support a detailed peace plan.

Direct public appeals cost huge amounts of money. The project's high cost made it necessary to raise money in Israel and, especially, overseas. It was not only the distribution of the agreement and the mobilization of support that were expensive. So were the negotiations themselves. Putting together a document that presents to the public and to their national leaderships a detailed model permanent status agreement required a long string of Israeli–Palestinian meetings. The Intifada prevented Israelis from entering the Palestinian territories and the Israeli authorities made it difficult for the Palestinian team to receive entry permits into Jerusalem, where some of the meetings of the steering body were held. Outside funding made it possible to meet overseas and to purchase the computer software essential for profes-sional negotiations on territorial issues.

Every time the Palestinian team received Israeli permits to leave its territory, the opportunity was used to advance the negotiations. Shaul Arieli, the Israeli point man on territorial questions, often followed his counterpart Samih al-'Abd to other countries to spend weekends work-ing on the maps. The impossibility of knowing in advance when the Israelis would allow the Palestinians to travel cast a cloud of uncer-tainty over every meeting. The Israelis became accustomed to getting organized on short notice. The large meeting in London in Feburary 2003 was made possible because three members of the Palestinian cabinet—'Abd-Rabbu, Nabil Qassis, and Hisham 'Abd al-Razeq, as well as deputy minister Samih al-'Abd—went to London for talks with the "Quartet" (the European Union, the United Nations, Russia, and the United States) about institutionalization and reform in the Palestinian governing bodies, and the requirements made of the Palestinians in President George W. Bush's "Roadmap to a Permanent Two-State Solu-tion to the Israeli–Palestinian Conflict." Israel also demanded reforms in the Palestinian Authority and thus had to approve the Palestinian delegation's trip. When the talks with the Quartet ended, the Palestin-ians proceeded to London.

The document is called the Geneva agreement because the Swiss foreign ministry lent the most support to the process. But at various stages the governments of Japan, Britain, Canada Sweden, and the EU also provided financing. Funds to establish the initiative's administrative infrastructure came from foundations and private individuals as well.

In initiating the process, Yossi Beilin had to cram his considerable political ego into a tiny bottle. The project would have died on arrival had it been labeled just another dangerous big giveaway by the lunatic radical left. Many Israelis assigned Beilin to that fringe and blamed him for conceding too much during the Oslo process. They also knew him as co-author of the Beilin–Abu-Mazen agreement, which offered the Palestinians even more. As a result, his political star had gone into free fall. Beilin thus had to bring other people into the process, in order to ensure that the initiative was not associated with him exclusively.

In one sense, however, the Geneva accords were Beilin's attempt at a comeback. He bolted the Labor party when it became clear that its leaders considered him a liability. Instead, he took a low spot on the Meretz slate in the elections of 2003. Meretz did badly, winning only five seats in the new Knesset. Beilin was stranded outside parliament. The Geneva initiative helped Beilin persuade Meretz to change its name to Yachad and to elect him its chief. Beilin's success as the leader of the Geneva initiative was greater than his success as the leader of a small opposition party. He failed to craft a successful response to Sharon's unilateral disengagement plan, to the Ayalon-Nusseibeh principles, and to the increasing numbers of Israeli soldiers who refused to serve in the occupied territories. All these developments changed the public's agenda and made it difficult for Beilin to sell the Geneva initiative to his fellow-Israelis. As the separation wall-fence cut through more and more West Bank territory, it grew harder for the Palestinian team to sell Geneva to its public.

Beilin's relationship with 'Abd-Rabbu continued after the failure of Taba talks, throughout 2001. They generally met at the World Bank building in al-Ram. The location was easily accessible. It lay between two Israeli roadblocks on the main highway linking Jerusalem and Ramallah. The Jerusalem municipal boundary, a virtual line established with the Israeli annexation to Jerusalem of a swathe of West Bank territory to the city's north, runs six meters to the east of the highway (the wall Sharon later erected left al-Ram outside Jerusalem). In practical

matter of fact, the border is indiscernible; the neighborhood is Palestinian even if it is by law under Israeli sovereignty. The World Bank building is to a certain extent neutral territory because it houses the offices
of international organizations, and as such it was on occasion used as
a meeting place for small teams of Geneva negotiators. Such talks were
generally held on Fridays or Sundays, when many of the participants
did not have to be at work. In general, each such session lasted no
more than a few hours. Work and family constraints prevented them
from going on longer. Furthermore, they nearly never began on time,
because the Palestinians were usually held up at Israeli roadblocks or
at their offices.

Switzerland's involvement and assistance came unexpectedly. The
talks were not fashioned by the Swiss, nor did the Alpine nation set its
program and goals. As often happens in history, serendipity brought
success. In October 2001, Beilin attended an academic conference at
the University of Geneva. Professor Yitzhak Galnor of the Hebrew University of Jerusalem had been asked to recommend Israeli participants
and suggested Shimon Peres. But when Peres was unable to make the
trip, the organizers went back to Galnor, who recommended Beilin.

At the conference, Beilin told Alexis Keller, a professor of international law at the university, about the idea of bringing to a conclusion
the negotiations that had begun in Taba. Keller was enthusiastic. For
him, it was a challenge to combine his professional interest with the
pursuit of peace. The initiative received initial funding from Keller's
father, a former diplomat, vice-president of the International Red Cross,
and wealthy banker. Keller, who fervently believed that the talks could
produce an agreement, was the intermediary who, at a much later date,
would persuade his country's foreign minister to adopt the project.
As will be seen, until the end of 2002, the Swedish government supported track-two Israeli–Palestinian talks. When Stockholm gave up,
Bern stepped in. Keller received diplomatic credentials from the Swiss
foreign ministry and, in most of his contacts, worked together with
Nicholas Lang, director of the ministry's Middle East desk and a former
Swiss delegate to the Palestinian Authority. They did not have an easy
time with the Middle Eastern style of negotiating and with the local
custom of ignoring schedules. In the end, however, the difficulties and
their patience paid off, in their view. While the negotiations were not
conducted in the Swiss city after which they were named, the term

"Geneva talks" became an international trademark. They contributed to Switzerland's image as a facilitator of peace processes and international understanding, an image that had its beginning in the establishment of the League of Nations in Geneva after World War I.

The origins of the process lay in two closed gatherings conducted in November and December 2000 at the Ma'aleh HaHamisha hotel outside Jerusalem. Ron Pundak and I had closely followed the permanent status negotiations and the Intifada's escalation. We thought it worthwhile to draw to the attention of prominent members of the Zionist left information we possessed and the conclusions we drew from it. These contradicted the misleading information that had been disseminated by Ehud Barak's government about what had happened at the Camp David summit. The negative campaign being conducted by Barak's office had plunged the Israeli left into bewilderment, confusion, and silence. The left's disarray was no less a product of Palestinian terror and the Palestinian Authority's blunders throughout the Oslo process in imposing the rule of law on armed militias, and its failure to institute effective oversight that would prevent personal corruption in the Palestinian government. We thought that publicizing our version of how the official negotiations had proceeded, and of the causes of the Intifada, would arouse those who spoke for the peace camp. In retrospect, we were mistaken. Only in mid-2004 did Akiva Eldar of *Ha'aretz* reveal the fact that Israel's political leaders and media had been misled by the simplistic and harsh analysis of Amos Gilad, head of the research division of Israeli military intelligence. Gilad's evaluations stood opposed to the professional briefs produced by the chief of military intelligence, the military intelligence research staff, and the General Security Services (Shin Bet) (Bar Siman-Tov et al. 2005; Benn 2003; Drucker and Shelah 2005; Eldar 2004; Kaspit 2000; Malka 2004; Stern 2004).

In the meantime, myth was in the ascendant and escalated the conflict. Violence worsened both because of Palestinian terror and because of Israeli actions. As Shlomo Ben-Ami and Gilad Sher noted in their memoirs (Ben-Ami 2004:319–21, 387–88; Sher 2001:318), some of these latter operations were carried out in opposition to government policy. The Israel Defense Forces effectively conducted its own war in contradiction of the orders it received from the government (Benn 2003; Drucker and Shelah 2005; Pedatzur 2004). In 2002 everything spun out of control. In competition with the Islamic organizations and in response to the killing of its men by Israel, Fatah sent out terror bands who attacked Israeli citizens within Israel proper. Arafat spoke of fighting Israel, and atheistic Palestinian leftist organizations cooperated with the radical Islamicists against Israel and used religious rhetoric to enlist public support. Dozens of Palestinian intellectuals issued calls for the cessation of suicide bombings and debated with supporters of the terror campaign on the pages of al-Quds (2002). A significant portion of the Israeli left adopted the military discourse of Sharon and the senior military establishment, and supported reoccupation of the territories and collective punishment against their Palestinian inhabitants. The way forward to mutual accommodation and reconciliation seemed blocked. This lasted longer than we thought—three years passed before the Geneva initiative breathed new life into old hopes.

In November 2000, I told Yair Tzaban that I was concerned that the government's claims about what had happened at Camp David were misleading the Israeli public about the possibilities for peace with the Palestinians. Tzaban decided, in coordination with Ron Pundak, to convene the meetings at Ma'aleh HaHamisha, which he chaired. Among the participants were the writers A. B. Yehoshua, Amos Oz, Ronit Matalon, David Grossman, and Tzvia Greenfield, as well as several university faculty members. Ron Pundak's talk at the first meeting served as a basis for his article "From Oslo to Taba: What Went Wrong," which was published in English and Hebrew (Pundak 2001). After the first meeting, most of the participants signed a statement, published in Ha'aretz on November 17. It called for an end to bloodshed and for negotiations on the basis of the June 4, 1967, borders. Baruch Kimmerling, a sociologist at the Hebrew University, saw this as closing the cycle opened with the manifesto that established the Greater Israel Movement, published over the signatures of Israeli intellectuals in November 1967. "It may be the first shot that heralds that we are in the twilight of the age of Israeli colonialism. The only questions that remain open are how much blood will yet be spilled before this realization penetrates the [consciousness] of the political leadership and before it reaches the consequent operative conclusions" (Ha'aretz Nov. 22, 2000).

The third meeting took place at the end of April 2001, again at Ma'aleh HaHamisha. This one was initiated by Amos Oz and A. B. Yehoshua, who sought to enlist the group's support for the idea of a unilateral Israeli withdrawal from the occupied territories. In their view, unilateral action was necessary because there was no partner on the Palestinian side for a permanent agreement. The meeting took place in surrealistic weather—an especially harsh springtime heat wave, of the kind Israelis call a *sharav*, broke that afternoon. The air was yellow and heavy, saturated with fine grains of sand blown up from the Sahara. A thunderstorm raged outside the meeting room and sheets of rain poured down from the sky. The rain and sand blended into a filthy muck. The weather seemed to have been ordered specially for the debate we held in the hotel's security shelter, which had been made over into a meeting room. Yossi Beilin arrived straight from Ramallah, where he had met with Yassir 'Abd-Rabbu and his associates. Beilin's message was that there were people on the other side to talk to. Many of the participants in the three meetings at Ma'aleh Ha-Hamisha would later become part of the Geneva team and take part in the peace coalition that was formed in the wake of the Geneva accords. (The term "peace coalition" refers to a group of prominent Israelis and Palestinians and of a small group of political leaders on each side that met from time to time. It is not a formal coalition of Israeli and Palestinian peace organizations in regular contact, as was the case in South Africa.)

I and some of my colleagues in the peace coalition had a chance to learn about the South African experience firsthand in January 2002. President Thabo Mbeki invited a group of Israelis and Palestinians to rethink our experiences and to learn from the South African example. The Israeli delegation included members of the Knesset Yossi Beilin, Haim Oron, Avraham Burg, and Naomi Hazan. There were also fellows of the Economic Cooperation Foundation (ECF), Yair Hirschfeld and Daniel Levy, as well as former Mossad official and foreign ministry director-general Reuven Merchav, and myself. Robert Malley, who had been President Clinton's Special Assistant for Arab-Israeli Affairs and Director of Near East and South Asian Affairs on the staff of the National Security Council, also participated. The Palestinians were represented by five members of the Legislative Council—Saeb Erekat, Ziyyaad Abu-Zayyad, Nabil Qassis, Yussuf Abu-Safiyya, and Ghazi Hananiyya—as well as Ra'ith al-'Omari, an aide to Abbas.

President Mbeki remained with us for the entire three days we spent at Spier, a vineyard near Cape Town. He brought a delegation of ten associates who had negotiated with the apartheid regime for the African

National Congress (ANC). Four of them were now government ministers, three deputy ministers, and one was speaker of the parliament. President Mbeki also brought five former leaders of the white regime, among them two former chiefs of intelligence organizations and Pik Botha, who had been foreign minister.

I arrived in Cape Town from Oxford, where I was spending a sabbatical. I received the invitation only thirty-six hours before the meeting; apparently I was meant to replace Amnon Shahak, who did not want to meet officials from the Palestinian Authority. It was only a few days after the IDF had intercepted the Palestinian armaments ship the *Karin A*, which according to Israel was headed for the Gaza port. Israel claimed that one of Arafat's aides, Jamal Shubaki, was behind the arms purchase from Iran. In Cape Town, Haim Oron told us that members of Kibbutz Lahav, where he lived, were upset about his trip, and that even his son opposed it. Yussuf Abu-Safiyya, the Palestinian environment minister, said that he had encountered similar reactions in Gaza, where he lived. His youngest son, he related, dreamed of buying a tank and taking revenge on the hostile and cruel Israelis.

The talks in Cape Town were open and frank. At the request of President Mbeki, we and the Palestinians both engaged in self-criticism alongside criticism of each other. Our critique of the Barak government needs no elaboration, since it can be found in the books and particles we have published. Our critical stance toward our own government impelled our Palestinian counterparts to address not just the injustices committed by Israel but also their own errors. The Palestinians presented the reality in which they lived: governing institutions and services that had collapsed, ruined infrastructure, inability to travel from one city or village to another because of curfews and encirclements imposed by Israel. Extremism was gaining on the Palestinian street, leading many to the conclusion that there were no longer any rules to the game. Israel, in this view, did not want peace, and only armed struggle and terror would convince it to retreat. The Palestinians admitted that they had presented their claims regarding the return of the 1948 refugees to the Israeli public in a distorted way, and that this had played into the hands of the Israeli right. This, and Palestinian terror, had destroyed the Israeli public's belief that there was a Palestinian partner for accommodation. Other mistakes the Palestinians admitted to were allowing the Tanzim, an organization of young activists associated with the Fatah, to organize as a militia, and failure to require that all weapons in private hands, including that of Hamas, be licensed by the Palestinian Authority. Israel was indeed strong, the Palestinians said, but they did not intend to surrender or give up their struggle for independence.

In South Africa, we learned that former adversaries had undergone a process of joining and bonding, while we, the Israelis and Palestinians, wanted to separate from each other. Despite this basic difference, the Israelis and Palestinians at Cape Town reached a consensus on what they could learn from the South African experience. The leaders of the African National Congress had displayed impressive maturity in four areas. First, they understood that a solution would not be imposed from the outside. While they gained impressive international support and sympathy, they accepted that they had to talk to the white regime, not reject it categorically. Second, the leaders of the black majority realized that apartheid and white violence would end only when the talks were concluded. Placing a high bar of preconditions for talks would mean failure. They agreed to talk with the leaders of the racist regime even when all their prisoners had not been released. Contacts between the sides were conducted as bloodshed continued on both sides. The cruelest fighting took place after the ANC announced a suspension of its armed struggle. When that happened, the talks took on a less formal guise, but were not halted. Third, they understood that the blacks had to assuage the fears of the whites and that any agreement would have to guarantee white rights under the new regime. Otherwise, the white minority would eventually renounce the agreement and the blacks would have a problem. In the meantime, they had to help their counterparts gain strength and build majority support for accommodation. The black leadership agreed that the whites could conduct whites-only elections, so that they could gain legitimacy and political empowerment. Fourth, the blacks viewed themselves as the strong side, since they enjoyed a demographic majority and moral force—even though the apartheid regime had power, large quantities of sophisticated weaponry, enforcement mechanisms, and control of the judicial system. The ANC understood that the stronger side had to create a space for the weaker side and to guarantee its rights.

The contacts were conducted on a senior level, but the agreement, when reached, was not dropped on the public out of the blue. Each side deployed a network of organizations and agents to communicate with its sub-communities. Both blacks and whites thus each built coalitions, gained supporters, and reported to its public on the progress of the talks. Beyond the prevention of a mass uprising, these broad circles of discourse began the process of constructing a new national identity. Preparing for the day after was part and parcel of reaching an agreement. The guiding principle in coalescing internal coalitions was that marginal elements could not be given veto power. Instead of seeking wall-to-wall consensus, each produced an "adequate consensus." The process of constructing an adequate consensus on a range of questions helped wear down extremist groups, as talks between the central element in the apartheid regime and the major opposition, the ANC, progressed. Both sides set priorities and put at the top a small number of matters that they considered more important than others. The contacts focused on these principles. Both sides knew how to adjust the agenda of the talks to changing circumstances, and profound disagreements did not block the talks. When there was a serious crisis, the agenda was redefined, and the sides made a common effort to reach a breakthrough. There was not, however, any significant change in the goal. Nevertheless, the negotiating process was not structured and continuous. Mistakes were made. Foreign Minister Botha told us about routine intelligence reports to the cabinet that portrayed the ANC as a Communist front and stressed the frightening quantities of arms in its possession. But none of the intelligence reports, Botha said, ever told us what people of high caliber they are—and he pointed at the president and those sitting before him.

The presidential seminar in South Africa taught all of us that, in the Palestinian-Israeli conflict, it is hard to know who are the blacks and who the whites. Who is the majority, the Israelis or the Palestinians? Who is strongest militarily, morally, and politically? President Mbeki summed up what we had learned from the South Africa experience. The comparison between the PLO and the ANC, and between Israel and the apartheid regime, was not as simple and unambiguous as the PLO liked to claim.

Unlike the case of South Africa, the peace coalition does not function as a central body that maintains intensive contact among Israeli organizations that support peace and accommodation. The peace coalition produces events based on loose ties between elites. The first ties were between intellectuals; thereafter, its meetings came to involve political figures and organizational leaders from both sides. The common activity of Israeli and Palestinian intellectuals in the peace coalition produced two calls to stop bloodshed and return to negotiations. The first was published at the end of July 2001 and the second in October, on the Intifada's first anniversary. On the Palestinian side, some of those who signed one or both of these declarations were among those who signed the Geneva accords two years later—ministers Yassir 'Abd-Rabbu and Hisham 'Abd al-Razeq, the archaeologist Dr. Nazmi Jubeh, political activists Jamal Zakut, Saman Khoury, Su'ad al-'Amiry, Ra'ith al-'Omari, and senior Fatah figures Kadura Fares and Mohammad Hourani.

The first declaration included the classic principles of the Palestinian peace movement and of Israel's Zionist left, which would later be broadened into the Geneva agreements: two states with borders based on the 1967 lines, living peacefully side by side, with two separate capitals in Jerusalem. In the matter of the 1948 refugees and the identities of Israel and Palestine, the wording was awkward, but that was the best that could be achieved: "Solutions can be found to all outstanding issues that should be fair and just to both sides and should not undermine the sovereignty of the Palestinian and Israeli states as determined by their respective citizens and embodying the aspirations to statehood of both peoples, Jewish and Palestinian." It was not easy to reach this wording. At a large meeting in al-Ram, each side submitted a draft, and a long debate commenced concerning the state of Israel being the country of the Jewish people. We reached no agreement, and the sense was that neither side was listening to the other because the forum was too large. The obvious solution was to meet in a smaller framework.

One Friday in the summer of 2001, I drove to Ramallah for a discussion in the office of 'Abd-Rabbu, the Palestinian minister of culture and information, along with Yossi Beilin, Daniel Levy, Professor Galia Golan of Peace Now, and Yair Tzaban. At the Israeli liaison point we transferred into an armored Palestinian police car. The streets of the Palestinian city were empty; its inhabitants were enjoying their weekend rest. 'Abd-Rabbu, was waiting for us at his office along with Ra'ith al-'Omari, Nazmi Jubeh, Salim Tamari (a professor of sociology at Bir Zeit University), and television producer and celebrity George Ibrahim. The meeting lasted about five hours. Our task was to explain to our Palestinian counterparts why the concept of the Jewish state was significant for us and for the Zionist movement. We had to explain the difference between an Orthodox religious state governed by Jewish law and the Jewish state as understood by the secular Yair Tzaban and by me, an Orthodox Jew who nevertheless believes that the state must be nonreligious. Our Palestinian counterparts were anxious to ensure that, in agreeing to the statement that Israel is a Jewish state, or the nation-state of the Jewish people, they would not be consenting to any constraints on the civil rights of Palestinians who were citizens of Israel. Our Palestinian interlocutors were concerned that we would use their agreement to such a wording to impose just such constraints in the framework of Israel's internal debate about the character of the country. Yair Tzaban and I made it clear that, in our view, Judaism would not permit us to do this. As we explained, we were anxious to protect the rights of the minority not only because we were democrats but also because we were Jews. In the middle of our discussion, a delegation representing Hadash, a Knesset faction dominated by the Communist party and one of the major political forces in the Palestinian-Israeli community, arrived for a visit. Among the group were two of the faction's Knesset representatives, Mohammad Barakeh and Issam Makhoul. I do not know if 'Abd-Rabbu planned this in advance.

Between this meeting and the signing of the Geneva accords, our Palestinian counterparts had adequate time to learn more about the importance of the principle of the Jewish state for the Zionist left. We, for our part, were in full agreement with the Palestinians in the occupied territories that we did not want to legitimize discrimination against Palestinian Israelis on the grounds of their ethnic origin. The section of the Geneva document that recognizes the Jewish people's right to a state, without detriment to the civil rights and equality of Palestinian Israelis, was not forced on us. For us, it is a matter of principle that the Jewish democratic state of Israel may not discriminate against its non-Jewish citizens. This section, along with the recognition of Israel as the homeland of the Jewish people, was criticized by Palestinian hawks and by Palestinian Israelis who want to turn Israel into a state of all its citizens or a binational state.

ANOTHER MEMBER OF THE FAMILY: THE AYALON-NUSSEIBEH DOCUMENT

Like the Geneva accords, the joint statement of principles authored by Ami Ayalon and Sari Nusseibeh (Ayalon and Nusseibeh 2002) are an offspring of the parameters laid down by President Clinton. The Geneva initiative and the Ayalon-Nusseibeh declaration seek to arrive at the same end point, but by two different paths. Ayalon and Nusseibeh have put their effort into gathering signatures for their principles, with the intention of placing Israel's leaders under pressure from the grassroots. Both lost confidence that the political system could produce change, and instead sought to appeal directly to the Israeli and Palestinian publics. In contrast, the Geneva initiative does not collect signatures. Instead, it presents a complete model agreement to the public and its leaders and calls on them to adopt it. Second, Ayalon and Nusseibeh offer a statement of principles to guide detailed negotiations by leaders, whereas the Geneva initiative offers a document in which most of the details have been worked out. Third, both Ayalon and Nusseibeh are individualists, rather than coalition builders, in their communities. Ayalon is a former Israeli army frogman and intelligence chief, while Nusseibeh is a professor of philosophy. The Geneva initiative was undertaken by teams that included politicians, generals, and scholars. They call the document they produced an agreement or "accords." Ayalon and Nusseibeh's document does not threaten the government's role as shaper of the outcome of negotiations. It only challenges the governments by showing that the first step is possible and seeks to get the public to force the leadership to take that first step.

As a result, the Israeli establishment ignored their initiative. In the Palestinian territories the initiative was criticized by refugee organizations and senior Fatah figures. Many lower-level Fatah activists signed the principles, but their superiors saw this as a threat to their position and blocked the initiative. Fourth, there is a difference in the structure of the team that manages the initiatives. Ami Ayalon set up a staff with clearly defined roles, modeled on an army command. The Geneva initiative, on the other hand, is based on volunteers and has a loose organizational structure. Finally, the content of the Ayalon-Nusseibeh principles and the Geneva accords differ on two important points. The former view the Temple Mount–al-Haram al-Sharif and the Western Wall as a single unit, and suggest separating the issue of political sovereignty from religious observance. In their proposal, Palestine will not have sovereignty on the Temple Mount–al-Haram al-Sharif, and Israel will not have sovereignty at the Western Wall. The compound will be run jointly by Israel and Palestine. Israel will administer the Western Wall as guardian of the site for the Jewish people, and Palestine will administer the Temple Mount–al-Haram al-Sharif as guardian of the site for the Islamic nation.

While, from a philosophical and theological standpoint, it is correct to separate holy sites from worldly political sovereignty, that is apparently not possible in Jerusalem. Jerusalem and al-Quds are capitals, and the Temple Mount–al-Haram al-Sharif and the Western Wall are at their historical and symbolic center. Neither country nor political system will forgo the opportunity to use the city's central system for their national needs. It is difficult to imagine a situation in which Israel would concede sovereignty on the most salient symbol of its victory in 1967, the Western Wall, and on the right to conduct official national ceremonies there. Withdrawing the country's sovereignty from the site would be more difficult for the Israeli political establishment and Israeli society to accept than withdrawal of sovereignty from the Temple Mount.

On the other side, it is also difficult to imagine that, after the al-Aqsa Intifada, as the Palestinians call their second uprising, Palestine would concede its sovereignty over al-Haram al-Sharif. The catalysts for the uprising were Ariel Sharon's politically motivated visit to the site and the Israeli–Palestinian debate at Camp David about sovereignty there. Neither will Palestine give up a site that turns it from a problematic young country into a crucially important Islamic state. The site compensates Palestine symbolically for its few material resources. What Palestinian leader would give up the possibility of welcoming his Arab colleagues at a national ceremony there? Furthermore, Israeli sovereignty over the Western Wall is complete and unofficially recognized by the entire world. The Wall is the holiest active Jewish site of worship. True, the Temple Mount is holier to the Jews than is the Wall, which is a remnant of the retaining wall of the Second Temple compound. But for the last 1,300 years, the Temple Mount has not been an active site of Jewish worship but rather one of Islamic worship, and since 1967 Israeli sovereignty there has been no more than symbolic.

The Geneva initiative proposes dividing sovereignty in accordance with current practices of worship. The Temple Mount is the holiest active site of worship in Palestine. While the Muslims call the Western Wall "al-Buraq," and in their tradition it is the site where the Prophet Mohammad tied his miraculous horse that brought him from Mecca to al-Aqsa on his way to heaven, it is not used by them as a place of worship. The Temple Mount is Judaism's most holy site, but Jewish religious law forbids Jews to tread there. Therefore, worship takes place at the Western Wall. Extremist Jewish groups have attempted to turn the Temple Mount into an active Jewish holy site, but their motives are tainted with nationalism. Their efforts are horribly dangerous, because they threaten the delicate balance between the religions in Jerusalem and may set off an even greater conflagration. According to the Geneva accords, Israel will withdraw its sovereignty from the Temple Mount, but Palestine will recognize the site's historical, religious, spiritual, and cultural significance for the Jewish people. Palestine also commits itself not to excavate or build on the site without Israel's approval. The document thus guarantees the Jewish-Israeli symbolic interest in the site and anchors it in Palestinian recognition.

On the matter of the Palestinian refugees of 1948, the Ayalon-Nusseibeh document limits the implementation of the Palestinian right of return to the territory of the Palestinian state and rejects any Palestinian return to the state of Israel, as well as any Jewish return to the state of Palestine. The Geneva document makes no mention at all of a Palestinian right of return or of the concept of return, not even in the context of the refugees' repatriation to Palestine. The Geneva document allows the individual refugee to preserve a right of return in his consciousness, but if he chooses Israel as his place of permanent habitation, he will undergo immigration procedures subject to Israel's consent to receive him. This stands opposed to the PLO's classic right of return, which demands that Israel accept unconditionally any Palestinian refugee who wishes to settle within its boundaries. According to the Geneva document, a refugee who wishes to exercise the right of return that he retains in his consciousness will not be able to appeal to international decisions or UN agencies, because they will be dismantled and there will no longer be any recognition of Palestinian refugee status, even if individuals choose to continue to identify themselves as refugees.

Many of those involved in the Geneva initiative also signed the Ayalon-Nusseibeh statement of principles, which was published in June 2002, fifteen months before the Geneva accords. Yossi Beilin kept Ayalon informed about the document taking form in his channel and tried to persuade him to unite their efforts and even head them. Ayalon refused. From his point of view, the qualitative differences between the two channels, and the differences in content of the documents, were too great. He also feared that the publication of the Geneva document would overshadow his own initiative. In fact, the opposite occurred. The Ayalon-Nusseibeh document enjoyed a revival because the Geneva document caused a renewed interest in peace initiatives. Ayalon reestablished his initiative in the Israeli public consciousness. Instead of being identified with the left, he appealed to the center and right. He met with people from the Likud, criticized the Geneva document on the subject of the refugees and for what he saw as the Geneva team's intention of replacing the Likud government. He also traveled to the U.S. with Nusseibeh and met Secretary of State Colin Powell and Paul Wolfowitz, undersecretary of defense and a leader of the neoconservative faction that controlled the Republican Party. In 2004, Ayalon joined the Labor party, and was elected to the Knesset on its ticket in 2006. That has left the Ayalon-Nusseibeh document rudderless. Also in 2004, Sari Nusseibeh left for a sabbatical at Harvard.

THE ISRAELI TEAM

The Israeli team to the Geneva talks was composed with thought to the potential contribution that each member could make to achieving an agreement and to its positive reception by the public. As he gradually put together the negotiating team, Beilin understood that he had to surround himself with people who would make it difficult for opponents to brand the Geneva team as a product of the extreme left. First and foremost, he needed to bring in senior retired military officers. In addition to providing professional expertise, they would provide a "military cover" for the project and squelch the expected charge that Beilin was abandoning Israel to its enemies. Amnon Shahak, Shlomo Brom, Gideon Shefer, Giora Inbar, and Doron Kadmiel, all former senior officers, were thus charged with the agreement's security provisions. Beilin also consulted with jurists, and asked Professor Ruth Lapidot of the Hebrew University, a former foreign ministry official, to scrutinize the section of the agreement that addresses the Palestinian refugees. She praised it highly.

The territorial negotiations were led by Colonel (res.) Shaul Arieli. Arieli had worked on this question for about a decade, from the time of the first Oslo agreement. He planned and monitored the Israeli withdrawals carried out at that time in his capacity as head of the Interim Agreement Administration. He later served as deputy military secretary to the minister of defense, deputy military secretary to the prime minister, and chairman of the Peace Administration in Prime Minister Barak's office. His counterpart on the Palestinian side in the Geneva talks was the same man who had sat opposite him in the official talks, the Palestinian Authority's deputy planning minister, Samih al-ʿAbd. Al-ʿAbd was assisted by his aide, Bashar Jumʿah. At various points during their work, they were joined by Dr. Ron Pundak, Amram Mitzna, and Brigadier General (res.) Shlomo Brom. The drafting was done by political advisers Daniel Levy, a graduate of Cambridge University, and Raʾith al-ʿOmari, who studied at Oxford. Levy works with Yossi Beilin and al-ʿOmari works with Nabil Shaʾath, ʿAbd-Rabbu, and Abbas.

The participants took a pragmatic approach and were able to identify problems and find ways to resolve them. They also had excellent political comprehension, impressive writing skills, and did not need many words to understand each other. Sometimes a glance was sufficient. Arieli and Samih al-ʿAbd, two energetic men, cooperated closely, and spoke candidly and openly with each other. Written drafts focused the discussions. As the details multiplied and the range of agreement increased, the impression the text made on the reader grew stronger as well. Daniel Levy and Raʾith al-ʿOmari not only ironed out the draft that took form in the discussions, but also offered compromises on points of disagreement and sent them on for decision by the broad teams. Both of them applied the technique that characterized the South Africa negotiations, what was called "walking in the woods." At times of crisis, individual representatives of each side who have good relationships go off on their own with the goal of breaking the impasse. Throughout the negotiations, this was done on the top level by ʿAbd-Rabbu and Beilin, and at a lower level by al-ʿOmari and Levy. It should be noted that the each side was aware of the internal disputes and political difficulties of the other side. Each side explained its difficulties, and this was of considerable help in reaching a joint document.

Ψ   Ψ   Ψ

I first became casually acquainted with Yossi Beilin at closed meetings, organized by the Jerusalem Institute for Israel Studies, among members of its think-tank brainstorming team and senior decisionmakers. My field of expertise was the Jerusalem issue. I worked for some time with Shlomo Ben-Ami but had no personal contact with Beilin. I did, however, have dealings with Beilin's ECF. I took part, in a professional academic capacity, in meetings that the ECF conducted with Orient House, which functioned as the PLO's legation in Jerusalem. This happened in the framework of the second-track talks that were known as the London channel, because they were held under the auspices of the British government. During these meetings I established close ties with Ron Pundak, Boaz Karni, Daniel Levy, Yair Hirschfeld, and their colleagues. When he began the Geneva initiative, Beilin asked me if I would take part and I agreed. I believe that he extended the invitation not only because of his previous professional acquaintance with me, but also because I had expressed my opinion on the conflict with the Palestinians and its solution in a series of articles in *Ha'aretz* and in interviews in the media in Israel and overseas. After Camp David in 2000, I expressed my opinion that Israel should concede symbolic sovereignty on the Temple Mount, and this position apparently also played a role in Beilin's invitation. He may well also have been eager to have an observant Jew on his team.

I had in the meantime decided to spend the summer of 2001 at Oxford on sabbatical. I made the decision in June 2000, when I took part in the jubilee celebrations of the university's Saint Anthony's College. It did not take long for me to reaccustom myself to Oxford's green and cultured tranquility, which I had left behind me in the after completing a year there as an Israeli research fellow in 1992–1993. Not long before I left I told Yossi Beilin about my sabbatical plans. I could see that he was horribly disappointed. I had another opportunity to take a measure of his feelings. During my time at Oxford, I introduced myself to Jonathan Friedlander, the senior political correspondent of the left-wing British daily newspaper, the *Guardian*. In June 2002, Friedlander invited me to a public event organized by his newspaper in an impressive conference center across from Westminster, with the participation of Beilin and 'Abd-Rabbu. I also saw Palestinians from the PLO negotiations department and Shaul Arieli there. I realized that the public event was the prelude to another kind of meeting—which I indeed read about three days later in the *Guardian*. It was a seminar, conducted in central England, where Israelis and Palestinians met figures from Northern Ireland who had been involved in achieving the "Good Friday Agreement" that officially ended the conflict in that province. Beilin and 'Abd-Rabbu used the encounter to advance their own negotiating channel.

At the start of the event at the convention center, Beilin surveyed the people sitting in the front rows. When his eyes met mine, he smiled warmly. When the discussion ended I approached him. His expression changed and he berated me: "Why did you leave? When are you coming back? I need you." I promised to make myself available to him after mid-August. As he went out the door, with his back to me, I said: "Would you have acted differently in my place and lost a chance to go to Oxford?" He turned around and gave an honest answer: "No."

I met with Beilin and Daniel Levy on September 3 for a long conversation. At its end, they gave me a draft of the agreement. It had been prepared by Ra'ith al-'Omari during 2002, along with Beilin, Shahak, Shaul Arieli, Ron Pundak, 'Abd-Rabbu, and Nabil Qassis, and with the help of Alexis Keller from Geneva and Robert Malley. My Palestinian counterpart for discussions on the issue of Jerusalem was Dr. Nazmi Jubeh. A number of fine professionals assisted us, first and foremost the architect Ayala Ronal, who drafted maps and contributed her knowledge of urban planning, and the attorney Daniel Seidemann, who closely follows events in East Jerusalem's territory and, together with Ronal, was among the few experts that argued that the Clinton principles could be implemented in Jerusalem as well. The Clinton principles stated that areas of Arab population should be part of the Palestinian state and areas of Jewish population part of Israel. The patchwork nature of Jerusalem, where Jewish and Arab neighborhoods are interspersed among each other, seems on the face of it to make that principle impractical in resolving the future of Jerusalem in a peace treaty. But Zeidman demonstrated that it was indeed possible to partition the city along national lines.

The participants in the Geneva initiative all shared high professionalism and a view that the Clinton principles and the Taba talks were the foundation on which a permanent status agreement could be built. They also were excellent team workers and were prepared to appeal to the public and persuade it to support the final product of the Geneva negotiations. The agreement's target audience was the entire public. This was the public whose consciousness had been shaped by the media spins of the Barak and Sharon governments, and by the psychological effects of Palestinian terror—the same public that had concluded that there was no one to talk to on the Palestinian side.

It was clear to all the participants in the Geneva initiative that they would have to swim against a very strong current. Persuading the Israeli public to accept the agreement would not be easy. Principally for this reason, some in the ECF opposed Beilin's project. They argued that Israeli society would reject any agreement he reached through the process and that they would quickly be labeled radical leftists to whom the public should not listen. In their view, it would be better to reach a partial agreement, which would be easier to use to appeal to the "soft" right wing of Israeli society. The way in which the agreement was accepted by the public showed, however, that their pessimism had been misplaced. Others close to Beilin had reservations about the contents of the agreement, but less so about the possibility of persuading a majority of Israelis to accept it. In their view, Beilin had achieved an agreement that went too far in its concessions. Ehud Barak and Gilad Sher made the same claim, adding that the Palestinians needed to be punished for the violence of the Intifada by giving them less than they would have achieved had they accepted Barak's proposals at Camp David. This approach sought to use Israel's military superiority to impose an agreement on the Palestinians. But Barak and Sher admitted that they had no partner for such a scenario. This led them to support unilateral action.

The Geneva approach was diametrically opposed to unilateralism. It did not ignore the fact that Israel, too, had used excessive force in the Intifada and so had contributed to its escalation (Drucker and Shelah 2005). They believed that Israel was capable of meeting the minimum that the Palestinian public could accept. This option, they believed, was far preferable to unilateral moves that would sustain the violence and even make it worse.

Beilin informed journalists, writers, and politicians about the agreement that was taking shape. He showed some of them drafts of the agreement, and reported to others orally. His purpose was to spark their interest and encourage them to become partners in the initiative and its marketing campaign. At the very least, he sought to prevent them from opposing the agreement simply because they had not been in the know. Writers such as Amos Oz, David Grossman, and Tzvia Greenfield were invited to meetings of the broad forum. At these sessions they sat next to political figures to the right of Meretz, such as Avraham Burg, Dalia Rabin-Pelosoff, and Yuli Tamir, all of the Labor party; Eti Livni of the centrist Shinui party, and Nechama Ronen of the Likud. Beilin kept

Peres informed about the initiative's progress, although he did not consult him on details. Peres spoke in favor of the initiative (although not its specific provisions) in the Knesset, and defended it as a legitimate effort, largely in response to the condemnation of the agreement by Ehud Barak and Ehud Olmert, who now sat in Sharon's cabinet. But the fact that Peres was kept informed certainly contributed to his support.

Naturally, not all the participants acted with the same level of commitment, confidence in the project's success, and investment of energy and time. Some, like Avraham Burg of the Labor party, joined late, just prior to the meeting in Jordan at which the agreement was signed. Until then he had been extremely reluctant to concede Israeli sovereignty on the Temple Mount.

Burg and I were childhood friends. We grew up in the same neighborhood and played street ball together in the lot behind Heichal Shlomo, the seat of the Israeli chief rabbinate, where my mother worked. In 1999, Burg, then speaker of the Knesset, asked me to serve as his political adviser. He told me about his intention of establishing a discussion forum with the speakers of the Egyptian, Jordanian, and Palestinian parliaments, as part of a broader framework of meetings between parliamentary leaders in the Mediterranean region. When I told him about my connections with Ben-Ami, at that time minister of internal security, he said without hesitation that I could contribute more to the peace effort by working with a cabinet minister. We spoke a number of times during 1999 and 2000. In June 1999, Burg invited me to accompany him to Ramallah for a meeting with Arafat and the Palestinian leadership. In 2000, Burg had, as an observant Jew, serious problems with Barak's stand on Jerusalem, and was disappointed with the prime minister's inability to feel deeply the capital city's religious significance. These issues are part of Burg's personality. He hoped that in this capacity he could assist Barak, but was frustrated. Barak did not want Burg to participate in the negotiating effort. That was a great loss, because Burg would have been useful in addressing the religious issue and the issue of the Temple Mount. When Barak negotiated on the Jerusalem issue, Burg sent him a brief warning that he should not go so far as to give up Israeli sovereignty on the Temple Mount. The site was too powerful a symbol, he wrote.

My position was different, so while I was delighted to see him at the meeting in Jordan, I was surprised. I asked him what had brought about his change of mind. His answer was that he had imagined what the religious philosopher Yeshayahu Leibowitz would have said had he been shown a draft of the agreement. He would certainly have roared: "For the worship of a holy site's wood and stone you are prepared to risk lives and thwart the possibility of achieving a peace that will prevent bloodshed?"

Burg reevaluated his priorities, but in the discussions in Jordan he still argued for a somewhat different deal. Not peace in exchange for the Temple Mount, but rather an Israeli concession of symbolic sovereignty on the site in exchange for a Palestinian concession on the symbol of the right of return. The difference between the two ways of thinking expressed his qualms. Tzvia Greenfield also had difficulty giving up Israeli sovereignty on the Temple Mount. Others on the Israeli team, such as Amnon Shahak and Nechama Ronen, were somewhat skeptical about it and waited to see how the map would look and how the refugee problem would be resolved. Amnon Shahak wanted Route 443, the road linking the city of Modi'in with northern Jerusalem, to remain under Israeli sovereignty. He maintained that Jerusalem needed an additional entry route, in addition to the main Jerusalem-Tel Aviv road to the west. Nechama Ronen wanted to annex Givat Ze'ev, a suburb of Jerusalem located in the West Bank, north of Jerusalem. In general, she maintained that the negotiations were too focused on the Palestinians' needs and not enough on Israel's. In fact, most of the signers would have preferred to see certain sections in a different form. They signed because it was a package deal in which these unfavorable aspects were balanced by gains in other areas, because they understood that it was necessary to compromise, and also because they knew that this was not the real thing. The real treaty would emerge from discussions between the two governments, and perhaps in that process the Israeli government would iron out some of the wrinkles in the Geneva agreement. Alternatively, the Geneva accords would be so successful in creating the necessary change in public opinion and in the international arena that the solutions proposed in the Geneva document would become acceptable. It is not inaccurate to say that the approach of the Palestinian side was similar. Many of them also had certain reservations about specific details, yet they signed for the same reasons the Israelis did. During the work on the agreement, all the participants changed their positions. This did not happen easily. They had their hesitations and their misgivings. What in the end decided was the deal as a whole.

Member of the Knesset Eti Livni was an exception. She had taken part in a video conference in September, in which the refugee issue was resolved to her satisfaction; and she participated in a preparation session for the Jordan meeting. But the next day she did not show up to get on the bus. She told the press that she was not going because she did not agree to the wording of the refugee provision. She had come under considerable pressure from the leader of her Shinui party. She continued, however, to try to play both sides of the game. When we gathered in Tel Aviv for the first time after signing the agreement, Livni joined us—but only a half hour after our meeting began, when she was able to ascertain that reporters were no longer present. Some of the participants suggested that she add her signature to the agreement, along with those of some other Israelis who for technical reasons had been unable to attend the Jordan signing session—among them Yuli Tamir and Dalia Rabin-Pelosoff—or others who acceded to the document after it was made public, like Uzi Baram and Haim Ben-Shachar of the Labor party, the novelist A.B. Yehoshua, and industrialist Dov Lautman. But Livni refused.

For an effort that sought to appeal to the public and provide a detailed model of a permanent status agreement, it was essential that political figures enter the picture. In the end, a permanent status agreement would have to be decided on by the political system and not civil society, so the accords had to reflect political realities. Furthermore, politicians have easier access to the media. They seek out the press and it seeks them. Politicians know how to create drama on news and interview shows. They can more easily create a presence for a new product in the public mind because they have a specific public identity and label. But these advantages come at a price. First, when political figures endorse a product, it becomes identified with their party or section of the political spectrum, automatically alienating people who sympathize with another party or viewpoint. Second, the initiative becomes slanted by the political agendas and interests of the figures who are involved in it.

For example, Beilin wanted, for electoral reasons, to go public with the Geneva initiative in Stockholm on December 12, 2002, the day after former President Carter received the Nobel Peace Prize. Carter had accompanied the Geneva talks since October 2001. The plan was for Carter himself to announce the initiative at the prize ceremony in Oslo and to travel immediately to Stockholm for the official launch. The plan went awry, however. It was a month before national elections in Israel. Beilin, then still a senior figure in the Labor party, showed the agreement that was taking form to Amram Mitzna, the party's new leader; Beilin wanted it to become part of the platforms of the Labor party and the left. Mitzna rejected it out of electoral considerations. However, as the Jewish sages said, every delay is for the best. At the time the accords were incomplete, and on several important questions the draft contained two wordings, an Israeli one and a Palestinian one, pending final compromise. At this point in time it was doubtful whether an agreement could be reached. Even if the two sides achieved a resolution, making it public during an election campaign would certainly have ruined its chances of acceptance. It would have been perceived as an election ploy and an attempt to recruit foreign intervention in an Israeli election. Later, in December 2003, political agendas again came to the fore. Labor party politicians grew angry that Beilin was upstaging them in the Geneva campaign and on overseas trips, and using the Geneva accords in his race against Ron Cohen for leadership of the Yachad party, Meretz's new incarnation. Beyond the usual jockeying for prestige within the Geneva group, the others were apprehensive about Geneva becoming identified with a person and a party to the left of Labor. That was liable to encourage Labor hawks to use the Geneva accords to try to brand their own party's Geneva advocates as radicals who should be removed from positions of leadership in Labor. The participation of politicians, Beilin included, in the Geneva initiative thus inevitably turned the project into an issue in political jockeying within and between parties. For example, as noted above, the politicians in the Geneva initiative did not want to come out against the separation fence.

To balance the advantages and disadvantages of their involvement, the politicians in the Israeli team decided that Beilin's initiative should not be identified just with Meretz. From the start, Beilin allowed only one representative of his party to participate. Furthermore, the Meretz representative was not one of those identified with the party's position on relations with the Palestinians, such as party chairman Yossi Sarid or the leader of the parliamentary delegation, Zahava Galon. Instead, it was Haim Oron, whose parliamentary specialization was economics and social policy. Oron held the number two slot in Meretz and had coordinated its transformation into the new Yachad party. Other leading figures in Meretz were angry at being locked out of the project for what they thought were political-personal reasons. Beilin, they charged, did not want to share the glory with his potential opponents for leadership of the new party. But this dispute, unavoidable in any political organization, remained within the party and was not conducted publicly. Oron briefed the Meretz parliamentary delegation on the Geneva contacts, which defused some of the charged atmosphere. The considerable length of the negotiations also helped. Many Meretz members had doubts about whether an agreement could be reached, and since one was not reached quickly there was little pressure to take a stand on the project. By the time the agreement was signed in October, Meretz gave its unanimous and active support.

The same was true of Peace Now, an extraparliamentary peace movement. Peace Now had been represented in the broad forum of the Geneva talks by the economist Arieh Arnon. Other leaders of the movement were resentful at not having been invited to take part despite their years of campaigning for peace. In the end, they demonstrated that peace was more important to them than their personal interests. Peace Now supported the Geneva agreement, and mobilized in the campaign to promote it. Its support for the Geneva initiative owed much to the movement's energetic field activists. Not a few members of Peace Now's leadership had internalized Barak's narrative. They supported unilateral withdrawal because they feared that there was no partner for peace on the Palestinian side. The people in the field, who did not allow protest against the Sharon government to fade away, thought differently. They had gritted their teeth through the difficult years of the Intifada and had staged peace vigils every Saturday night in Jerusalem and Haifa. Only rarely were there more than a hundred at these demonstrations, but they kept the fight alive and the movement's nucleus united.

THE COMPOSITION AND PERFORMANCE OF
THE PALESTINIAN TEAM

Over the course of the Geneva track negotiations, the Israeli team received the impression that the members of the Palestinian team were not coordinated and that detailed information did not flow among them in a routine way. When new people joined the team they were not briefed about all the talks' previous stages, nor were they informed about the details of the official negotiations at Camp David and Taba. At the London talks, we Israelis had to inform the Palestinian minister for prisoner affairs, Hisham 'Abd al-Razeq, about what points of agreement had been reached previously on the Geneva track, and the same was true a few months later when Kadura Fares and Mohammad Hourani of the Tanzim joined. Even if newcomers were briefed, when they sat facing the Israelis they felt themselves free to toss out new ideas that sometimes contradicted previous points of agreement. This kept setting the negotiations back, by reopening issues that had already been resolved with other members of the Palestinian team.

In such cases, the Israeli team had to lead the newcomers to the point where the talks stood. In other words, the Palestinian negotiators should have explained to new members of their team what concessions they had made and why. Instead, the Israeli team found itself performing this task. Israeli military encirclements, roadblocks, and incursions into Ramallah, where most of the Palestinian negotiators lived and worked, created a difficult environment for the Palestinians. But this is not sufficient to account for the Palestinians' conduct. The primary cause was flawed work methods, part of the organizational and administrative culture of the PLO and the Palestinian Authority, developed during the PLO's revolutionary period in Beirut and Tunis. The Palestinian team that negotiated with us did not have a state with properly functioning institutions. Neither did it have a decision-making tradition based on teams to which their leader, Arafat, had devolved authority.

In 1994, the Palestinians had barely managed to create a governing apparatus to exercise the limited internal and external authority that the Oslo accords granted them, and the PLO's way of working was carried over into the Palestinian Authority. The Palestinian leadership had no way of integrating itself into the local administration and learning from it how to manage political institutions in an advanced, modern way. The Jews, in contrast, had learned administration from the British when they—but not the Palestinians—were integrated at high levels into the institutions of the British Mandate. The Palestinians had not undergone a period of "internship" under the British, as had the governing organs of Jordan, Egypt, and Iraq. Neither did the Palestinian administration grow out of the Israeli administration, because the latter employed not Palestinians but Israeli soldiers. The generation that had administered the West Bank under Jordanian rule faded away between the mid-1970s and mid-1980s. The Palestinian Authority in the West Bank and Gaza Strip was thus built out of the PLO establishment and a group of Palestinian professionals who had been educated in the West but lacked administrative experience.

The difficulties caused by Palestinian performance in the negotiations have been chronicled by Shlomo Ben-Ami (2004), Gilad Sher (2001), and Ehud Barak (Morris 2002; Rubinstein et. al. 2003). In the Geneva talks, the Israeli team found ways of coping with this reality. It successfully geared its negotiating strategy to the Palestinians' working procedures, presenting proposals that the Palestinians could accept. This is not to claim that all was orderly and immaculate on the Israeli side. The Israeli team also caused avoidable difficulties that the Palestinians had to address.

The Palestinian team had a hard time fathoming their interlocutors' motives and reasoning. They sometimes failed to understand why the Israelis were making a given demand—was it a real need or an expression of an occupier's mentality? By their own account, some members of the Palestinian team found it hard to treat the Israelis they sat with as partners and not as occupiers. In the face of roadblocks, sieges, and closures that the members of the Palestinian team had to endure on their way to our meetings, it was not easy for them to cross this psychological barrier.

But cross it they did. The Palestinian team decided to help turn the Israelis into partners by deliberately displaying flexibility. In doing so, they sought not just to respond to real Israeli needs but also to provide the Israelis with tools to use in conducting the public discourse on the agreement within Israel. The Palestinian side was sensitive to Israel's real military needs, and also to its psychological needs. They understood that that Israeli needed not only actual security but also a sense of security. When the Palestinians consented to leave certain settlements in place, they did so to assist their partners in the internal Israeli debate, not because the Palestinians accepted the settlements as legitimate.

The Palestinian goals, as the Palestinian team saw them, were first and foremost to sign a model detailed permanent status agreement, the first in the history of their contacts with Israel. They also wanted to prevent the Israeli peace camp from collapse, to rehabilitate it as a partner, and through it to keep open a window into Israeli society. The Palestinian negotiators also sought to maintain contact with Arafat, to receive his sanction and indirectly the legitimacy that their president could grant to the negotiations. They needed this for their own internal reasons, in order to neutralize ideological, political, and personal opposition to their effort. They also needed it as a counterweight to the Israeli government's policy of boycotting Arafat, besieging him, and seeking to destroy him physically (Drucker and Shelach 2005:229–37, 291–97).

It was clear to the Palestinian negotiators, as well as to Yossi Beilin, that nothing could be done without Arafat. Beilin spoke with Arafat about the agreement-in-the-making on three occasions, the last of which was in November 2001. From that time onward, the Palestinian negotiators were in contact with Arafat. The Palestinians were careful to manage Arafat as an internal matter and not to involve the Israelis. Most Israelis viewed Arafat as a Satanic terrorist, so any open association of Arafat with the agreement was taboo. For its part, the Palestinian side was in contention with Sari Nusseibeh's initiative and wanted to prove to him and his supporters that it was possible to achieve a better deal. The Palestinians also had to rehabilitate their side's peace camp, which had been shunted into the sidelines during the armed conflict with Israel. Palestinian peace activists wanted to resume their status as central players, at the expense of the nationalist and Islamic extremists whose status had risen as the conflict spiraled.

To achieve these goals, the Palestinian team determined that the negotiations would be based on mutual gains and not just on fulfilling Palestinian demands. They decided to learn the lessons of the mishandled implementation of the Oslo agreements and the factors that led to the failure of the negotiations over the official permanent status agreement. This meant taking positions in the Geneva talks that differed from the official Palestinian position. By their own testimony, the most difficult concession for the Palestinians to make was in the section addressing the 1948 refugees. Second to it was the recognition of Israel as a Jewish state.

When Tanzim's representatives, Kadura Fares and Mohammad Hourani, joined the negotiations in the summer of 2003, the talks took a positive turn. Tanzim's leaders had been in touch with Ron Pundak and Yossi Beilin throughout the Oslo years. The involvement of Fares and Hourani in contacts with Israelis was not an innovation. The innovation was their participation in the Geneva initiative, which was on the verge of concluding an agreement. It is important to note that 'Abd-Rabbu, who headed the Palestinian team, is not a member of Fatah. Fares was a member of the Palestinian Legislative Council for Ramallah, while Hourani represented Hebron. It was not easy to get them to join the Palestinian team, even though Beilin, Pundak, and Daniel Levy had asked them to do so at a much earlier date. They preferred not to get in a vehicle that was not being driven by a member of Fatah. When the agreement was close to completion, the Israelis contacted them again and told them that by joining they could give the agreement much greater potential. In parallel, the Israelis asked 'Abd-Rabbu to ease their way in. The Israelis and his Palestinian colleagues persuaded him that it was important to broaden the circle of Palestinian participants, and he reached an understanding with the two men that granted them senior status in the Palestinian team.

The two Tanzim representatives joined the Geneva initiative with the knowledge and consent of Tanzim's regional committees and of their leader, Marwan Barghouti, who was serving a prison sentence in Israel. They added a new dimension to the contacts. Even though Arafat had given them a green light, the Palestinian negotiators had no independent standing with the public. 'Abd-Rabbu had been the leader of the tiny FIDA party, which had broken away from the Democratic Front for the Liberation of Palestine in 1991. In 2003, 'Abd-Rabbu clashed with his party's leadership. FIDA demanded that he give up one of his two positions, either as the party's minister in the Palestinian cabinet or as its representative in the PLO's executive committee. They wished to allow other members of the party to enter into the national leadership. 'Abd-Rabbu refused. As a consequence, his party notified Arafat that 'Abd-Rabbu no longer represented them. 'Abd-Rabbu's public standing was thus totally dependent on his relationship with Arafat. He had no base of support of his own.

The decision to broaden the circle of Palestinians involved in the Geneva initiative by bringing in Tanzim's representatives caused some problems, even if it turned out to be worthwhile in the end. Negotiations were delayed because Fares and Hourani were not briefed by their colleagues about the status of the points of disagreement with the Israelis. The Palestinians took it for granted that the Israelis would know how to keep to their red lines and would "school" the newcomers, who would in the end endorse the agreements that had already been reached. Second, Fares and Hourani were not the types to accept without challenge everything their colleagues had done. They wanted to try their own hands at negotiating.

Fares and Hourani attended the meetings at the World Bank building and asked to reopen several issues that had been resolved at the London meeting in February 2003. On the matter of territory, they wanted Israel to give up Ma'aleh Adumim and/or Givat Ze'ev. Alternatively, they suggested that Israel receive one of them, and that the other, most likely Ma'aleh Adumim, pass into Palestinian sovereignty but be leased by Israel from Palestine for several years. On the matter of prisoners, they wanted to move up the date on which the last of these would be released. With some eight thousand Palestinian prisoners in Israeli jails, their release was a vital matter for tens of thousands of their family members. A timetable for prisoner release had been reached at the London talks in February. The talks on this issue had been acrimonious, especially with Hisham 'Abd al-Razeq, the Palestinian minister for prisoners' affairs. 'Abd al-Razeq was a member of Fatah from the Gaza Strip and had himself spent many years incarcerated in Israel. On the matter of refugees, they raised the possibility that Palestine would receive additional territory from Israel, beyond the 1:1 territorial exchange already agreed on, as partial compensation for the nonrepatriation of the 1948 refugees to Israel. This was not a new idea—it had been in the air during track-two negotiations since the Taba talks. The Israeli team called this the 101 percent option, with the additional percentage point being territorial compensation for the Palestinian concession regarding refugees.

Their requests created a dilemma: on the one hand, the Israelis were reluctant to reopen and make further concessions on these issues. On the other hand, they believed it was important for Tanzim's representatives to remain involved in the negotiations. The Israelis thus had to find a golden mean—to make clear the point of view of the Israeli public, which saw the prisoners as actual or potential murderers, and the common interest both sides had in gaining maximum public support. On the other hand, the Israelis understood that the Tanzim representatives needed a gain they could take back to their colleagues as proof that their entry into the Geneva process had been worthwhile.

Fares and Hourani indeed made an important contribution to the initiative. They stood out in their willingness to assume responsibilities, to make decisions, and to reach a win-win agreement, but their involvement was important from another angle as well. Hourani and Fares were part of the up-and-coming generation of the Fatah and Palestinian national leadership. During the first Intifada (1987–1993), the members of this generation were prominent field commanders, and many of them spent years in Israeli prisons. During the Oslo period (1993–2000), they vied with the older generation for positions at the top of Fatah. Some of them were brought into the decision-making leadership, but most were not, and they resented this. Tanzim was a grassroots organization that grew out of their isolation from the Fatah leadership. It had a popular organizational power base but remained without international political experience and without involvement in negotiations with Israel. By taking part in the Geneva process, they were able to gain skills and experience in expectation of their future advancement into more senior positions.

It should hardly be surprising, then, that their participation caused the old-guard members of the Fatah's central committee to oppose the Geneva initiative. Hani al-Hasan, Sahar Habash, and Abbas Zaki did not mince words—they castigated the participants and encouraged verbal and physical violence against the Palestinian signers of the Geneva accords and the participants in the ceremony in December 2003. Refugee organizations and those who opposed any compromise on the refugee issue acted alongside these opponents, as did those who opposed any restriction on sovereign powers and the right of return. The intra-Palestinian debate descended into recrimination and physical threats because of the lack of a central Palestinian governing authority, the destruction of the Palestinian Authority by Israel during the Intifada, and the creation of pockets of anarchy in parts of the West Bank and Gaza Strip. The Palestinian leadership did not have enough tools of government to organize a campaign of support, nor to keep down the flames of violent opposition to the agreement. Furthermore, the Palestinians involved in the Geneva initiative were slow to organize and did not operate a well-oiled public relations campaign. It should not be forgotten that the reality in which the Geneva group operated was a convenient one for its opponents: the Palestinian territories had been cut into pieces by hundreds of roadblocks, and the Israeli army was regularly raiding Palestinian population centers. Israeli forces were arresting, wounding, and killing thousands of Palestinians. The emotional effect of these actions was unambiguously against talking with

Israel and against making concessions to a group of Israelis unassociated with their government.

In addition to Arafat, other Palestinian political figures who supported an agreement with Israel were in the picture regarding the
Geneva initiative. These included cabinet ministers such as Saeb Erekat and Nabil Sha'ath, and prime ministers Abbas and Qurei. They
received reports on the agreement-in-progress from the Palestinian
participants and from Beilin. As was his habit, Arafat took no interest
in the details and provided only general backing. He also lent general
support to the opponents of the Geneva process and to the demonstrations they organized after the signing ceremony. This was Arafat's way
of protecting himself against the initiative's failure. This way, he paid
no price, while at the same time benefiting from the infighting within
the Palestinian leadership. When Arafat learned that Palestinian supporters of the Geneva accords were organizing a conference to explain
the initiative in November 2003, he asked them to come to his office
in the Muqata. The Palestinian Geneva activists demanded of Arafat
that he order the initiative's opponents within Fatah to hold back their
criticism. The discussion at the Muqata was strident and stormy, but
in the end the opponents toned down their campaign.

The political competition at the top of the Palestinian hierarchy prevented 'Abd-Rabbu's competitors from lending him open and unambiguous support. They did not want to give him an achievement; furthermore, some members of the leadership had a different agenda. Erekat,
for example, had for years maintained that preference should be given
to fulfilling signed commitments and implementing the remainder of
the Oslo interim accords that he had labored on, as a way of building
confidence and making progress. He was not enthusiastic about new
agreements that would inevitably be violated just as their predecessors had been, and opposed jumping into talks on a permanent agreement. Furthermore, he preferred to move forward in accordance with
President Bush's roadmap, which enjoyed broad international support,
and to use it as a means of putting pressure on Israel. As an advocate
of closer relations with the United States, Erekat also feared that the
Americans would react unfavorably to an initiative that sought to get
around the Road Map. Nabil Sha'ath, who was in practice the Palestinian Authority's foreign minister, did not appreciate having 'Abd-Rabbu
trespassing into his territory.

The name of the game on the Palestinian side was, therefore, neutralizing obstacles and preventing vocal opposition, rather than seeking to drum up active support. The Palestinian leadership allowed 'Abd-Rabbu to move forward with his contacts with Beilin and the Zionist left. They had an interest in trying to convince the Israeli public that there really was a Palestinian partner for peace negotiations. Having watched with disappointment as the Israeli left shrank, they wanted to extricate the diplomatic wagon from the mud of the Intifada. Furthermore, the Geneva talks gained international support from countries that sent observers to the talks or supported them financially.

Beyond all this was the Palestinian leadership's disappointment with Ariel Sharon. In the elections of 2002, the Likud, under Sharon's leadership, won a stunning victory, larger than that ever won by any other leader of that party. The left was reeling. The Palestinian leadership had believed Sharon's election slogan that only he could bring peace. Sharon expressed his willingness to accept the Road Map, although he made some hundred reservations. The Americans pressured him to reduce these to fourteen preconditions. The Palestinians interpreted this as a signal that he was prepared to talk with them. President George W. Bush's firm support of Sharon also entered into the Palestinian calculus. Prime Minister Abbas tried to speak with Sharon and to move toward him when he, Sharon, and Bush met at the Aqaba summit of June 2003, even without receiving anything from Sharon in exchange.

THE PERFORMANCE OF THE ISRAELI TEAM

The Israeli negotiating team to the Geneva track talks had neither a formal hierarchy nor compartmentalization. Professional areas of proficiency and personal experience created foci of knowledge and expertise, but rather than being exclusive, they were put at the service of all members of the team. A member of the broad team who wished to express his opinion on a given issue and attend the relevant meetings at the World Bank building was welcome to do so. Yossi Beilin conducted team meetings and divided up work democratically. Members expressed their opinions without any time limit, and decisions were made by consensus and not by vote. For example, Yuli Tamir, a member of the Knesset from the Labor party, proposed reversing a decision made in February

2003 to absorb the settlement Alfei Menashe into Israel while leaving the settlement of Efrat outside. Similarly, as noted, Nechama Ronen proposed that the Israelis insist that the settlement of Givat Ze'ev become part of Israel rather than conceding it, as Fatah delegates demanded. In no case did a majority ride roughshod over a minority; each of those involved had an interest in preserving a heterogeneous team where a variety of opinions were represented. At times, a team member brought up an issue that had not come up in talks conducted by a smaller team, or suggested that an issue that had been brought up be handled in a different way. If the point of view won support, he or she was invited to voice the opinion directly to the Palestinians, or the smaller team did so in the name of everyone. These work patterns were possible because the Geneva group was a voluntary and not an institutionalized group. Each member of the team wanted all others to sign the final document and to identify with as many of its provisions as possible. Any resignation from the team could have been detrimental to the campaign and called into question the agreement's legitimacy. Yet there was also a practical reason to run the team in this way. All the issues discussed overlapped to a large extent. Security issues are linked to territory, and both are relevant to Jerusalem and the question of borders. And clearly the refugee issue was of critical importance to all members of the team.

Unofficial meetings between representatives of two warring peoples, called "track two" talks (see chapter 3) do not prevent participants from dividing themselves into "us" and "them" according to national affiliation (Agha et al. 2003:175–81; Davis and Kaufman 2002; Kaufman 2002). The success of track-two meetings depends on the ability to keep the national differences that separate the sides from taking control of the discussions. It requires that participants be able to perceive their common interests and construct coalitions that span the line of conflict.

This is, of course, psychologically problematic in a reality of bloody confrontation. Building bridges over a line of conflict is easier to the extent that each side recognizes the fears, positions, and point of view of the other side. The goal is to come to know the other side as it sees itself. In the case of the Israeli–Palestinian conflict, however, such knowledge has in the past been used by Israel to exploit Palestinian weaknesses, divide the Palestinians internally, and to turn Palestinians who talk with Israel into collaborators who entirely accept Israeli positions. Familiarity with the other side's positions grow out of personal contacts and, in track-two talks, make it possible to find common denominators. This becomes easier as the process progresses and the membership on each side becomes consistent, because relationships of trust and friendship are built between participants. Good and open ties between the participants are also created when the same people take part in the different frameworks that are part of the track-two talks. Often a group will have a common experience that brings its members closer. It is easy for opponents of compromise to charge negotiators with identifying with the other side and with alienation from their own society. But it is important to understand that without mutual confidence and empathy, no compromise is possible in bitter ethnic conflicts like that of the Jews and Palestinians.

Ψ Ψ Ψ

Because of a teaching obligation, I was a few hours late to the talks in London in February 2003. When I entered the hall in which the plenum was meeting, I glanced to the right. The Israeli faces were familiar to me from the newspapers, but I did not know most of them personally. When I looked to the left, I saw Palestinians with whom I had spent untold hours since 1996, in discussions, in security checks at Ben-Gurion airport, on flights, at meals, and on trips between one meeting and another. So, quite naturally, I turned to the left. Nazmi, Samih, Ra'ith, and Yassir 'Abd-Rabbu rose each in turn and embraced me warmly. Only afterward did I reach Yossi, Shaul, and Daniel. I sat down on the left side of the table and felt perfectly comfortable. Daniel Levy also sat on the left side during part of the discussions. Paul Usiskin, who videotaped the meeting, later told me about the astonishment he had seen on the faces of former military men Giora Inbar, Gideon Shefer, and Amnon Shahak. They couldn't fathom the warm welcome that this Israeli, wearing on his head the kippa that marked him as an observant Jew, received from the Palestinians.

I knew the Palestinians not only because the discussions and academic conferences we had attended together. Palestinian politics is also the subject of most of my academic research. I found a common language with my Palestinian colleagues, with whom I exchanged views on Palestinian and Israeli politics and society. I am sure the Geneva talks provided my Israeli colleagues with similar experiences, and that the experience changed them. But I had had such experiences previously, so I had more rapport with my Palestinian interlocutors than did my fellow Israelis—not just those involved in the Geneva talks, but also those involved in other contacts with the Palestinians. Other Israeli participants often suspected me of representing the Palestinian rather than the Israeli position. In their view, the only thing to my left was an abyss. Eli Bar Navi, Israel's ambassador to France, charged me in the summer of 2002 of having crossed the lines to the other side. Indeed, with regard to the Barak and Sharon governments he represented, I had indeed crossed the lines. I was profoundly persuaded of my position and was frustrated by the blindness of my fellow-Israelis. I do not accept a particular position simply because it is the position of the Israeli government. When I form an opinion on a matter of public controversy, I do not automatically accept the Israeli establishment's view, simply because I am an Israeli citizen. Similarly, when I examine the Palestinian position I do not do so from the vantage point of the Israeli position. To the greatest extent that I can, I aspire to see both sides from a neutral perspective. It is therefore easier for me than for others to suggest win-win solutions. Such solutions are vital for any agreement, because negotiations never succeed when they are conducted as a zero-sum game.

Many Israeli Jews have a difficult time shedding a self-righteous attitude that makes patriotism, conformism, and ethnocentrism the measure of all. In this way of thinking, any concession is a sign of weakness. It views the Palestinians either as subservient, or as dangerous terrorists who must be eradicated. Such people see themselves and others through the prism of power relations. Furthermore, too many Israelis find it convenient to accept what they are told by their government. They do not challenge the common wisdom, nor do they bother to cross-check the government's message against information from other sources. As Israeli leaders have published their memoirs on the peace talks and the Intifada, it has become clear that Palestinian reports have often been more accurate than the initial reports issued by official Israeli sources (Arieli 2004; Arieli and Pundak 2004; Ben-Ami 2004; Hanieh 2001; Klein 2003b; Pressman 2003; Sher 2001). Social pressures in Israel push people toward conformism and identification with the collective, and with accepted and dominant views. These pressures are the product of ongoing conflict, and of socialization mechanisms that foster a collective Israeli identity—for example, extended military service—as well as of the collectivist heritage of the Labor Zionist movement and Jewish religious frameworks.

Amram Mitzna came to the Geneva talks after a brief and not particularly successful stint as the Labor party's candidate for prime minister and parliamentary leader. His election campaign, in the winter of 2002, demonstrated that he was not particularly well-versed in the details of the Barak government's permanent status negotiations. Mitzna seemed to have been briefed on what took place in the talks, but he did not assimilate the information he received. His campaign messages were not consonant with the latest developments, and were thus unrealistic. His positions grew out of his desire to appeal to the average voter, and to the center of Israel's political spectrum. But, beyond that, they demonstrated his failure to assimilate the information he had. In mid-2003, after he resigned his post as Labor party chief, he joined the Geneva initiative team, displaying his signature energy and diligence. He studied the issues on the agenda and became a catalyst who pushed the negotiations forward, especially on the matter of territory. In fact, some of his Israeli colleagues thought he was going overboard in his willingness to make territorial concessions.

Mitzna knew the West Bank well from his service as general of Israel's central military command. More important, however, was his determination to find pragmatic compromises at moments of crisis. Despite his position as a former Labor leader, he demonstrated a willingness to immerse himself in details at small team meetings in al-Ram. He had authority, but it was an acquired authority that had nothing of the magnetism and overweening overconfidence that makes those around charismatic leaders afraid to express their own opinions. In debate, he appeals to reason, seeks to persuade—he generally succeeds—and keeps his word. When the talks between Shaul Arieli and Samih al-'Abd ran into serious obstacles, Mitzna, along with Ron Pundak and Shlomo Brom, managed to get them going again. Their approach was pragmatic, and they looked for a fair compromise and for the center of gravity between the different interests, and eventually found it. General (res.) Gideon Shefer and former Chief of Staff Amnon Shahak also made significant contributions to the territorial talks. Shahak had, in the official talks at Taba, supported giving up

Ariel, a settlement city built a considerable distance from the Green Line in the northern part of the West Bank. In the Geneva talks, Shahak supported giving up Efrat, a large suburb of Jerusalem in Gush Etzion, in exchange for keeping the rest of Gush Etzion, along with Givat Ze'ev, Ma'aleh Adumim, and Alfei Menashe, a West Bank settlement that serves as a commuter town for Israel's central region. The Palestinians had agreed to Israel's annexation of these settlements at various stages of the official talks.

Shaul Arieli was the Israeli team's greatest asset. In uniform, he had served in a key position in the prime minister's office. He took the work of national intelligence and diplomatic agencies and turned them into working papers for the interim and permanent status negotiations. This was of particular importance in the territorial talks, where it was necessary to integrate data on Jewish and Arab population, security, topography, and geography in order to draw a border. He thus had unparalleled expertise in these areas. Arieli preferred border and annexation lines different from those Prime Minister Barak suggested at various stages of the negotiations. At the beginning of 2000, he told Barak that, in his view, the map that the prime minister had ordered presented to the Palestinians at the opening of negotiations with them was a nonstarter and would be rejected out of hand. Barak did not accept the recommendation and Arieli deferred. Only in July 2003, at a conference at Tel Aviv University, did he talk frankly about his experiences in the official talks. In a joint conference presentation with Ron Pundak, he showed how, during the official negotiations, Israel's position on the territorial issue, untenable from the start, had been eroded, bringing the positions of the two sides closer together (Arieli and Pundak 2004; Shamir 2005).

Arieli worked days on end with enthusiasm and dedication. His field of expertise, the territorial question, took up more time than any other in the Geneva talks. His brain, heart, and laptop computer served as the talks' organizational memory. As far as he was concerned, the Geneva talks were a continuation of the official talks, and he invested all his professional abilities, time, and emotions in them. The fact that his Palestinian counterpart was the same man he had faced in the official talks—Dr. Samih al-'Abd—had both advantages and disadvantages. Each of them bore within them the disappointments and successes of the protracted and frustrating official talks.

THE NEGOTIATIONS ON PALESTINIAN PRISONERS,
SECURITY ARRANGEMENTS, AND THE 1948 REFUGEES

Nazmi Jubeh first served time in an Israeli jail when he was in his teens, for his activity in the Palestinian Communist Party. He later switched to the Democratic Front for the Liberation of Palestine. At that same time I was a student at a hesder yeshiva—one in which students combine studies with their mandatory military service—in the settlement of Alon Shvut in Gush Etzion. Hisham 'Abd al-Razeq, Kadura Fares, Mohammad Hourani, and Zuhir Manasra were each in turn the most senior of Palestinian prisoners, and thus their leader and representative before the prison authorities. When they demanded the release of Palestinian prisoners as a central issue in our discussions, the issue was not beyond their ken. It was part of their biographies, just as security arrangements related to the biographies of the senior Israeli officers who participated in the talks. Looking at photographs from the talks near London or on the Dead Sea shore, one cannot but compare the number of years that some of the Palestinians spent in Israeli jails and the number of years that Amnon Lipkin Shahak, Giora Shefer, Shaul Arieli, and Giora Inbar spent in the Israeli army. The Israeli officers had met no few members of the Palestinian team in jails and army detention camps.

The Geneva document proposes that all Palestinians imprisoned before it was signed be released in three stages. In the first stage, Israel would immediately release all those imprisoned before the establishment of the Palestinian Authority in May 1994, prisoners in administrative detention who were never brought to trial, and all ailing and female prisoners. In the next stage, over the following eighteen months, Israel would release all those imprisoned from May 1994 to the date of the signing of the permanent status agreement. In neither of these stages, however, would Israel release prisoners of any type it classified as "having blood on their hands" (although this definition does not appear in the agreement). These latter prisoners would be released in a third, final stage, during the thirty months in which Israel would complete its withdrawal from Palestinian territories. In other words, five years after the signing of a permanent status agreement, Israel would hold no Palestinians in detention or in prison for crimes committed before the signing of the permanent status agreement. This timetable was accelerated compared to what was originally agreed, out of a desire to take account of the positions of the Tanzim's representatives.

The compromise on staged release of Palestinian prisoners was achieved at the London talks in February 2003. The settlement followed a difficult and emotional debate, in which Hisham 'Abd al-Razeq, Amnon Shahak, and Yossi Beilin were the chief contenders. 'Abd al-Razeq demanded that all prisoners arrested because of the conflict be released on the day the agreement was signed. He made clear to Yassir 'Abd-Rabbu and Nabil Qassis, neither of whom had ever done time in an Israeli prison, that no leader could go before the Palestinian public and defend neglect of the prisoners. He did not say so explicitly, but it was clear that he was referring to accusations that Mohammad Dahlan leveled against Abbas after the Wye agreement of 1997. Dahlan charged Abu Mazen with negligence in approving the wording of the prisoner provision in that agreement in a way that allowed Israel to release criminals instead of security and political prisoners. Dahlan's charges led to violent demonstrations against Abbas. It was also clear that if the minister for prisoner affairs opposed the agreement stridently, it would not be supported by the public.

Beilin, for his part, said that Israel could not accept 'Abd al-Razeq's sweeping formulation without a real permanent agreement being signed first. The demand would give every terrorist or potential terrorist a guarantee that he would be released as soon as a permanent peace treaty was signed. The shadow of the present, in the form of the Intifada and Israel's countermeasures, lay over the discussion, as did the biographies of its major participants. The biographies made the past present. Against 'Abd al-Razeq's past stood Beilin's term as minister of justice and Shahak's military background. 'Abd al-Razeq categorically refused to accept a general formulation that deferred the subject to the future ("an agreed solution will be found") or by moving it into an appendix that would be written later. At the end of the debate, the two sides reached a compromise under which those imprisoned before the permanent status agreement was signed would be released gradually, but those who committed crimes after it was signed would not be freed. The Geneva document and permanent agreement it proposes does not grant automatic immunity to future perpetrators of terrorist attacks.

The prisoner issue was not the only point of dispute during the final year of negotiations. There were differences, some of them sharp, across the entire spectrum of issues. As a rule, the talks over security arrangements went relatively smoothly. Their parameters did not change to any great extent from what they had been at the Camp David and Taba talks. What did change was the context into which they fit. As the Israeli team to the Geneva talks displayed a willingness to withdraw from more territory and to grant the Palestinians full sovereignty, the Palestinians displayed a greater willingness to move toward Israel on security issues. The guiding principle of the Geneva initiative was security for Israeli individuals and Israel as a whole, without occupation.

The Palestinians faced several dilemmas. First, how could they reconcile the measures Israel needed to meet its real security requirements with the fact that such measures necessarily impinged on Palestinian sovereignty? Second, how could the Palestinians sell to their public, for example, the need for an Israeli early-warning station near Ramallah, deep in Palestinian territory? How could they explain the difference between the station that now exists and that which would exist after the end of the occupation? And there were other questions. For example, would the agreement state explicitly what kinds of arms the Palestinian state could possess? Would the Palestinians have a symbolic presence in the early warning stations, and how many such stations would there be? These were not technical questions. They were perceived as crucial to the issue of Palestinian sovereignty.

The Palestinians came to accept Israel's search for absolute security, even though they did not understand how the regional superpower could feel such insecurity. The Palestinians are the weak side in the conflict, and over the years they have suffered acutely under Israeli rule. Having suffered heavy losses at Israel's hands, they were puzzled at the country's sense of existential insecurity. But they were prepared to come toward Israel. For example, they accepted the premise that Palestine would be a demilitarized state, and that it could have no armed force not explicitly provided for in the agreement. Most important for the Palestinians was, first, to achieve full sovereignty and, second, to put an end to Israel's use of its security needs to justify the occupation and settlements. They agreed to far-reaching security measures, including Israeli training flights at high altitude in West Bank air space, the existence of two early-warning stations, and an Israeli military presence in the Jordan Valley. The Israeli presence in the Jordan Valley would be under the auspices of a multinational force. These security arrangements would be open to reevaluation after a few years. These Palestinian concessions were the subject of much criticism when the Geneva document was disseminated in the Palestinian territories.

The negotiations on the refugee issue were concluded in September 2003 at a video conference conducted by satellite hookup. According to the original plan, the two delegations were meant to meet in Switzerland or at the World Bank building in northeast Jerusalem. The agenda was to reach final agreement on this issue as well as on the remaining territorial differences. However, Beilin's office was unable to obtain permits for the Palestinians to get through Israeli roadblocks. Alexis Keller and Nicholas Lang of the Swiss foreign ministry thus had to come to Israel and conduct the conference by video linkup. At very short notice, six people gathered in the Crown Plaza Hotel in Tel Aviv at the same time that the Palestinians assembled in 'Abd-Rabbu's office in Ramallah. The Swiss officials chose to be with the Palestinians. The video conference lasted for two hours. Although the communication was cold, at a distance, and of a type to which both sides were unaccustomed, the Israelis and Palestinians reached agreement. Both the Israelis and the Swiss were gratified and surprised. They felt that there had been a significant breakthrough, and that all that remained was to close the gap on the remaining territorial disputes, which related to Jerusalem. An agreement seemed to be within reach. That evening, Keller and Lang arrived at Avi Shaked's office in Tel Aviv to meet the Israeli team. They wanted to report how the negotiations on the refugee issue had looked from Ramallah, and to discuss the continuation of the contacts.

The practical aspects of the refugee issue were the easy part of the Geneva initiative. They were based on the parameters that had been proposed by President Clinton and discussed at Taba (on the evolution of the negotiations on the refugee issue, see Klein 2006b, Klein 2007). These issues were concluded at the beginning of the Geneva negotiations and there was no real dispute over them. This was not true, however, with regard to other aspects of the problem. The Palestinian side refused to accept any mention of the Jewish refugees who left Arab countries for Israel, on the grounds that the Palestinians were not a party to any possible Israeli claim against Morocco, Iraq, or Algeria. The Palestinians also refused to promise that they would support the Israeli position if it made a claim against any relevant Arab country on this issue, or to accept any wording that might imply this. The Palestinians also rejected a proposal to include a paragraph stating that the subject could come up in future negotiations that Israel would conduct with each Arab state, and also refused to allow a general reference to the fact that a Jewish refugee problem existed. The Palestinians justified their rejection of the latter on the grounds that such a general formulation had no practical value; their position was accepted. It was also true that the issue had not been included in the Egyptian-Israeli peace agreement, even though some Jewish refugees had come from Egypt. Prime Minister Menachem Begin, of the Likud party, had conceded this point to a country that was directly responsible for part of the problem, so why couldn't the Israelis participating in the Geneva talks do the same in their negotiations with a party that bore no responsibility and had no standing with regard to the issue?

One point of dispute that remained unresolved after the Taba talks was the 1948 narrative. In other words, who bore the "blame" for creating the refugee problem and, consequently, what should the nature of its resolution be, and what would that solution be called? Would its name reflect the Palestinian or Israeli point of view? Both sides learned from the failure of the official talks to agree on a common narrative of what had occurred in the 1948 war. The Geneva initiative assigned this task to the civil societies, with the encouragement of the two governments. There was no serious dispute about this. The decision also included an apology for Israel's part in creating the refugee problem. In the past, Israel had denied categorically that it had any part in the creation of the problem, and insisted that the blame lay with the leaders of the Arab countries and of the Palestinian national movement. In light of current scholarship, for the most part written by Israelis and based on Israeli archival material, it is now difficult to deny the fact that the Israeli leadership indeed played a part in creating and perpetuating the Palestinian refugee problem. The academic argument is no longer about whether Israel created refugees in 1948, but rather about the extent to which this happened, the motives of those involved, and to what extent the phenomenon was centrally planned and controlled. Israel also took action to prevent refugees from returning and from infiltrating back to their original places of residence.

Yet these historical studies remained within the purview of the academic and intellectual communities and did not affect official policy. Neither did they permeate the rest of Israeli society, nor were they accepted by the central actors in the political system, where the dominant narrative continued to be that Israel was founded by force of arms in 1948. Thus, admitting that Israeli forces committed war crimes in 1948, or that central organs of government played a role in turning many Palestinians into refugees, meant admitting that Israel had been founded on an injustice. Such an admission, many Israelis feared, would void their country's moral foundation and legitimacy. In the dominant Israeli narrative, such an admission would lay the groundwork for invalidating Israel's right to exist. In order for the popularly accepted Israeli narrative to change and integrate the findings of academic research, Israelis must be told that acknowledging responsibility for the refugee problem will not reverse the outcome of the 1948 war. When Israel is reassured that its darkest nightmares will not come to pass, the hour will have arrived for Israel to apologize for its role in the refugee problem. This will constitute moral and symbolic compensation for the Palestinians. So long as Israel feels a real or imagined threat to is existence, it will be difficult for most of Israeli society to make the transition from viewing that Israel was founded by force of arms to one in which Israel was founded on the Jewish people's right to self-determination in his historic homeland. In other words, it is difficult for most Israelis to let go of a narrative in which their country owes its existence to military force exercised against foreign invaders. But such a narrative actually puts them in a weaker position, because then any admission of wrongdoing in their war of independence calls into question the moral foundations of the state. To assert, instead, that the Jewish people's right to a state derives from the right of every nation to self-determination is to make the Zionist claim stronger, for this right exists independently of the specific actions of the state and its agents.

The PLO had a similar difficulty. Palestinian society as a whole was reluctant to admit to war crimes that its forces committed during its national liberation struggle, and to apologize for the terror that its organizations used and still use against Israelis and foreigners. Acknowledgement of the immorality of terror and of Palestinian war crimes is restricted to the educated elite. The Palestinian masses believe in the establishment of a sustainable Palestinian state by taking up arms against the Israeli occupation. They also fear that admitting to war crimes and terror will invalidate recognition of their right to self-determination. When the Palestinians are ensured of sovereignty over the territories Israel conquered in 1967, and when they are certain that their confession will not be exploited by Israel to undermine their country, the Palestinians will be able to apologize.

At the Geneva talks on this matter, the Palestinians were not able to persuade the Israeli politicians and military men of the Palestinian public's need to receive "moral compensation" as a surrogate for the actual repatriation of refugees to Israel. Only in February 2005, after the death of Yassir Arafat and the election of Abbas, did the novelist David Grossman publish a series of newspaper advertisements advocating such compensation. The ads, signed by Israeli literary and cultural figures, called on the Israeli government to commence negotiations "by addressing the Palestinian people and acknowledging their suffering, and recognizing that Israel bears partial responsibility for that suffering. We feel that, as Israelis, we today have the ability to make the first necessary step: to look directly at the neighboring Palestinian people and recognize their suffering, out of human sympathy and empathy... . We expect that the new Palestinian leadership will also express its empathy for the suffering that Israelis have known in the years of conflict and recognize its partial responsibility for that suffering (Ha'aretz, February 9, 2005). Signed on the statement were some of the most prominent participants and supporters of the Geneva initiative, such as novelists A. B. Yehoshua, Sami Michael, Yehudit Katzir, and Ronit Matalon. Unfortunately, however, it did not appear at the behest and in the name of the Geneva initiative itself.

Given the failure of official talks to agree on a common narrative, it is better to leave the issue of historical responsibility to civil society. In any case, a formal decision cannot change public consciousness on both sides. Such a change takes a long time, and if it happens at all it will be as a result of complex and long-term processes of reconciliation. True, a formal decision can have an educational effect by pointing the way, but the practical benefit would not be great. It could even cause damage. With all the fundamental differences between the cases, the Jewish attitude toward Germany is proof of this. Germany's apology, and the compensation it paid, did not expunge the past from Jewish hearts. For a long time, many Jews refused to buy German products and to visit the country. This changed to some extent when a new generation of Jews reached adulthood, but even today many Jews who travel to Germany feel some revulsion. The Jewish attitude toward Germany, including by those who did not personally experience the horrors of the Holocaust, is at the least ambiguous. The trauma has not been erased, and in fact public bodies work to maintain it in the Jewish collective memory.

Once the Geneva negotiators agreed that the issue of the 1948 narrative would be left to civil society to resolve, most of the subsequent discussions dealt with a section titled "Return." The Palestinians wanted this section to state that both sides recognize their right of Palestinian refugees to return to their homeland, Palestine. The Israelis, for their part, demanded that the words "the state of" be prefaced to "Palestine"—in other words, to state that refugees could return only to the Palestinian state itself. At the London talks of February 2003, 'Abd-Rabbu, Nabil Qassis, and Hisham 'Abd al-Razeq proposed using the text of President Clinton's proposal of December 2000, or to write "according to President Clinton's parameters." Clinton's text stated that, in the framework of a two-state solution—Palestine as the homeland of the Palestinian people and Israel as the homeland of the Jewish people—Palestine would be the focal point of Palestinians who choose to return to the region. This did not rule out the possibility that Israel would absorb some part of these refugees. Clinton also proposed choosing one of two formulations: either that both sides recognize the right of Palestinian refugees to return to historic Palestine, or that both sides recognize the right of refugees to return to their homeland (Klein 2003b:199–203). The Israeli team rejected this idea because the parameters contained a general recognition of the right of Palestinian return to sovereign Israeli territory. Yassir 'Abd-Rabbu stated this explicitly at the London talks, where he asked for a nebulous recognition of the right of return, with a clear and explicit limit on the extent of its implementation. The Israeli team was not prepared to accept this. On the other hand, the Israelis did not want to force the Palestinians to abjure the right of return explicitly. That would not be accepted by Palestinian society—certainly not in the framework of unofficial and nonbinding talks like the Geneva framework.

Long hours of discussion ended in September with a Palestinian compromise proposal put forth by Nabil Qassis—to eliminate the problematic words "right of return" from the text entirely. The Swiss representatives who took part in the video conference were witnesses to agreement on this issue. At the Dead Sea talks, in an attempt to achieve last-minute Palestinian gains, Nabil Qassis attempted to reinstate the word "return" in the heading to one of the sections, instead of the technical term "permanent place of residence." However, this attempt was categorically rebuffed by Beilin, Burg, and Haim Oron, with Swiss support. The idea of territorial compensation for the refugees, beyond the size of the 1967 territories (the "101 percent option"), in exchange for a Palestinian concession of actualizing the right of return into Israel, was rejected utterly by the Israelis. They believed it essential to adhere to the principle that the 1967 lines were the basis of the peace agreement.

THE TERRITORIAL NEGOTIATIONS

After the 1967 war, the state of Israel turned the settlers into its agents. The settlers did not kidnap the state and coerce it into accepting their messianic world view, as some Israelis think. The grandiose national project began in September 1967 with the establishment of the first settlement in the West Bank, Kfar Etzion. The rationale for this settlement was to effect the right of return of the Jewish refugees from this village, which had been destroyed in 1948. A number of factors came together to effect Israel's settlement policy. There was the classical Zionist ideology and praxis of settling the land, which could suddenly be carried out on an unprecedented scale thanks to Israel's military and technological superiority. Politicians jockeying for prestige and political blindness also played a role, as did the messianic religious theology of Gush Emunim, the settler movement. Looking the other way, dissembling, and sanctimoniousness also played a role. So did refusal to view the Palestinians as a collective that would rebel against the occupation, as did the refusal to enforce legal sanctions against Israeli institutions that committed despicable actions in order to establish facts on the ground at the expense of the local population (Eldar and Zertal 2005; Gorenberg 2006; Segev 2005).

When Likud came to power in 1977, it made an alliance with the religious nationalist movement and its reservoir of motivation and manpower. These were put at the service of the settlement movement and raised the level of expectations. The World Zionist Organization's Settlement Division issued a settlement plan in 1978 that provided for the establishment of sixty new settlements over five years. At the end of that period, in 1983, the Settlement Division submitted a plan to bring 100,000 settlers into the territories within three years, a goal that actually took a decade to achieve. The longer-term goal in that plan—a million Israeli settlers in the territories by 2013—seemed unachievable in 1997, in light of the first Intifada and the impending talks with the Palestinians on a permanent status agreement, within the framework of the Oslo accords. The Settlement Division therefore recommended a change of policy. Instead of Israel seeking to change the demographic balance, it should achieve geographic control by taking possession of roads, lands, water, and commanding terrain by means of its power mechanisms (Eldar and Zertal 2005:136–37, 184–85). This served as the blueprint for settlements and outposts, the latter being the name given to wildcat settlements set up in violation of Israeli law but with the encouragement of the Israeli government. In contradiction of the common wisdom in Israel, there are no isolated settlements and no remote ones. Every settlement is linked to others by roads, by contiguous territory, or by neighborhoods built close to the Green Line. Most of the settlements lie in the heart of Palestinian territory or near populated areas. The distribution of the settlements makes it virtually impossible for the Palestinians to establish a viable Palestinian state in the territories Israel conquered in 1967 (Foundation for Middle East Peace undated; Peace Now undated).

But the national settlement project took revenge on its creators. The evidence can be seen in a report prepared for Peace Now by an economist in the budget division of the ministry of finance, Dror Tzaban, in 2001. The report shows that each settler received an average of NIS 8,600 (about $2,000) more from the government than did Israelis living within the Green Line (*Hu'aretz* undated). This is especially glaring given that the settlers constitute less than three percent of the country's population, and given that the greater part of the settler population is in a strong socioeconomic position. The calculation above does not include the benefits that every settler enjoys through the budgets of the ministries of defense and education and through government support of settler nonprofits. The settlers grew stronger and the citizens of Israel who live within the Green Line became weaker (Swirsky 2005).

To defend the settlements, huge numbers of troops must be deployed. During the second Intifada, each soldier was employed defending four settlers, on the average. This figure does not include the unknown number of General Security Service (Shin Bet) agents who are deployed in the territories, nor the number of soldiers who serve within the Green Line but perform tasks relating to the defense of the territories—for example, air force, intelligence, planning, operations personnel. Even without them, the figure is astonishing. It demonstrates the disparity between security outlays on the settlers and on the other 97 percent of Israel's population. If we add to the equation the fact that the greater portion of the adult male settlers are army veterans who continue to bear arms, in the framework of the regional defense network in the settlements, we end up with some 100,000 armed personnel defending some 100,000 women and children in the settlements. A significant part of the Israeli army has thus turned into a police force. Furthermore, a flourishing private security industry has developed within the Green Line, employed in protecting civilians against Palestinian terror.

According to a report published by *Ha'aretz*, the excess annual budget that goes to the settlements is at least NIS 2.5 billion (about $544 million). This consists only of moneys explicitly allocated to the settlements as special supplements. It does not include the benefits that settlers receive as individuals or funds included in general budget lines that are apportioned to the settlements, numbers that are very hard to deduce from the national budget data (*Ha'aretz* undated). This huge investment in the security of just three percent of Israel's population is a product of the demographic gap between them and the Palestinians in the West Bank and Gaza Strip—200,000 Israeli settlers versus three million Palestinians. Another computation leads to the figure that there is an armed Israeli for every thirty Palestinians in the territories. The lopsided demography has forced the settlers and their allies to tighten their control of the population, and this necessarily led to an uprising on the part of the majority population. The Intifadas, and especially the second one, brought an end to the normal life that the settlers enjoyed in the years of enlightened and inexpensive occupation. To defend the settlements, Israel built in the West Bank, between September 2000 and the end of 2004, a total of 608 unmanned road blocks and 56 manned road blocks that completely disrupt the Palestinians' daily lives (B'Tselem 2004) and show the occupation in its full ugliness: brutal, arbitrary, hostile, manned by a force numerically inferior to the local population that is all to often blind to the civilians who are at its mercy and whom it ought to be serving.

Many soldiers seek to counter their sense of alienation from the hostile locals by tyrannizing the locals in symbiosis with the settlers (Machsomwatch 2004). These measures failed to suppress the Palestinian uprising. Instead, they created a desire to seek revenge and to break free of the Israeli stranglehold through the use of low-technology, high-motivation guerrilla warfare against military targets, and by criminal terror. At the beginning of 2004, the number of immediate terror warnings returned to the level it had been at two years previously, before the Israeli army reoccupied the Palestinian territories in the Protective Wall operation. While this shows that Israel has been able to contain terror, it also demonstrates that Palestinian motivation to attack Israelis has not abated. In other words, Israel can control the uprising in the short term, but it cannot defeat the Intifada with force alone, as the Sharon government claimed it could and as the public demanded. The calm that prevailed at the beginning of 2005 was achieved largely as a result of an agreement between Hamas and Fatah. The agreement sought to give Abbas a chance to achieve the liberation of the 1967 territories by diplomatic means, or at least to allow Israel's unilateral evacuation of its Gaza Strip settlements in August 2005 to proceed undisturbed. It also sought to allow reorganization of the Palestinian Authority's political institutions and other administrative reforms, via local and general elections in which Hamas would participate. The Palestinian factions also sought a respite from Israeli military pressure. They wanted to regroup before resuming combat, if the diplomatic effort was not successful.

The official Israel negotiators did not define territory as a core issue, as it did Jerusalem and the refugees. But the Palestinians did not view the 1967 territories and the settlements that Israel established in them only from the pragmatic point of view. For them, territory had a symbolic dimension—a full cessation of the occupation and the nonexistence of Israeli settlements in sovereign Palestine. This was synonymous with the full sovereignty that for them was a sacred principle and the object of their national liberation struggle. From the beginning of the official negotiations, the Palestinians wanted to reach an agreement in which they would cede the 1948 territories—that is, that part of Mandatory Palestine which became the state of Israel—in exchange for receiving the 1967 territories—the West Bank and Gaza Strip—which constitute less than 23 percent of the territory they view as their homeland. Did not Egypt receive all its territory back in its peace agreement with Israel in 1979? Did not four Israeli prime ministers offer Syria a full withdrawal from the Golan Heights? In 2000, did not Israel withdraw from Lebanon to the international border? Should Israel wish to annex a few settlements, in a way that would not interfere with Palestine's territorial contiguity, the relevant precedent was that set by the Israel-Jordan peace treaty, in which Israel compensated Jordan for territory it annexed by ceding an equal amount of territory to Jordan in a 1:1 ratio. Israel, on the other hand, wanted the compromise to take place on the 1967 territories themselves. That, in a historical nutshell, sums up the geographic negotiations (Arieli and Pundak 2004).

During the negotiations, Israel did not have in mind the other side's interests, sensitivities, and points of views. It was cognizant only of its own interests. When it took into account the desires of the Palestinians, it did so in accordance with an Israeli perception of those desires. Israel tried with all its might to establish that only the Israeli interest and only the limits of Israel's ability to compromise would determine what the other side received. This was part of a strategy of setting "red lines," which inevitably created a zero-sum game in which every Israeli gain was a Palestinian loss (Klein 2003b: 164–79). Israel's decisionmakers characteristically asked government agencies, headed by the defense establishment, to provide lists of vital Israeli interests, without the government providing clear guidelines and definitions of vital interests and how to resolve fundamental contradictions between different vital interests. This was especially notable with regard to the territorial question, including the issues of the settlements and East Jerusalem. This way of working allowed the political leadership to avoid making decisions about the future of the territories and the fate of the settlements in advance of negotiations. The defense establishment, for its part, was not prepared to go any farther than what it estimated the political leadership's position to be. When the political leadership factored the Palestinian position into its considerations, it adjusted the Palestinian position to fit the Israeli position, creating a false belief that the Palestinians would modify their positions in ways that Israel desired. Added to this was the need for Israel to add to its opening positions margins of defense, padding, and reserves that could be conceded during negotiation without giving up what were considered, rightly or wrongly, vital Israeli interests.

The resulting maximalist dynamic produced, of course, a series of harsh disputes and confrontations with the Palestinian delegation. Prime Minister Barak ruled that populated areas should be transferred to the Palestinians—zones A and B in the Oslo agreements—with the addition of territories that Israel did not need. This was done by taking advantage of Israel's asymmetrically strong position in relation to the Palestinians. As a result, the permanent status negotiations opened in January 2000 with an Israeli map in which Palestine was assigned about 60 percent of the West Bank and Gaza Strip, surrounded and divided into pieces by territories that Israel would control or annex. In the spring of that year and at Camp David, Israel's offer rose to about 77 percent of the occupied territories. Even so, the Israeli map still presented a fragmented Palestine surrounded by Israel. Along with insisting that Israel control large swathes of the West Bank, Barak also decreed that land on which 80 percent of the settlers lived must be annexed to Israel, not including the Israelis living in East Jerusalem. Only under heavy pressure from President Clinton did Barak agree to compensate the Palestinians for the annexed territory with Israeli territory—but only at a 1:10 ratio, in Israel's favor, of course. The Palestinians demanded a full Israeli withdrawal and were willing to consider annexation of settlement blocks amounting to 2–4 percent of the territories in exchange for territorial compensation at a 1:1 ratio. The last stage of the negotiations was held on the basis of the parameters that Clinton presented in December 2000. Israeli proposed annexing 6–8 percent and territorial compensation in the ratio of 1:2 in its favor. The Palestinians, for their part, agreed to a 4 percent annexation and equal territorial compensation (Arieli and Pundak 2004, Klein 2003b).

Israel deliberately never defined "settlement" and "settlement block": did these encompass only the built-up areas, which occupied less than two percent of the West Bank's land, and another one percent in Jerusalem? Or the built-up areas plus a security belt? Or a land reserve for future expansion? The jurisdictions of the regional and local authorities? Or perhaps the territory for which a master land use plan had been prepared? If Israel were to define "settlement" and "settlement block" in these last two ways, it could not offer Palestine more than 50 percent of the West Bank. This was where Israel began negotiations. However, as soon as the Israeli offer exceeded this percentage, these definitions could no longer be used. On the other hand, defining settlements and settlement blocks as only the built-up areas would have meant conceding more than the Israeli negotiators at Camp David and Taba were willing to offer. The result was that each settlement block was the subject of separate talks. The problems that arose in regard to each place were identical. First and foremost came the question of which interest should be paramount—those of the small number of settlers, or those of the Palestinians, who were in a majority in each area. As a general rule, the Israeli errors in the territorial negotiations were strategic, while most of the Palestinian mistakes were tactical. Reaching agreement in the Geneva framework thus required a change in Israeli strategy. The Geneva channel was based on a win-win model. The text was formulated from the points of view of both sides, in an egalitarian and balanced way. The Israeli participants understood the implications of the official talks' failure, and took a different tack. This new strategy proved itself when the agreement was signed. A real permanent status agreement will have to proceed along the same lines.

The Geneva territorial negotiations were conducted with the aid of maps and aerial photographs, stored on two laptop computers. The aerial photographs were identical; the maps were similar but based on different sets of coordinates. Samih al-'Abd used the Mandatory coordinates, while Shaul Arieli used those of the Israel Defense Forces. This led to a series of small disagreements. Only during the final stage of the negotiations were the two coordinates united into a single map, on which the proposed border that the sides had agreed to appeared. In fact, the final map was drafted a few days after the Geneva agreement was signed. The participants had not planned to reach a final agreement in Jordan, and up until that Sunday morning no one knew if an agreement would be signed, or whether the negotiators would disperse with the hope of meeting again in the future. Because of time pressures, only three copies of the text were printed, and preparation of a detailed map was left for a later stage, when the technical problems were resolved. Samih al-'Abd and Shaul Arieli drew the agreed line in Jordan, which required a few more days of technical work. Because al-'Abd had to undergo an emergency angioplasty, the technical work could be done while he went overseas for rest and recovery, about a week after he returned from Jordan.

Arieli was well-acquainted with his Palestinian counterpart, and with al-'Abd's methods. He therefore decided to use a classic Israeli tactic, in which he kept territorial assets as bargaining chips, as a reserve for moments of crisis in which he would have to make concessions. Second, Arieli did not want the Geneva agreement to win approbation only from the extreme left, so he sought to annex to Israel a maximum number of settlers. Third, he wanted to reserve some bargaining chips for the real negotiations that would take place in the future between the governments, in light of the Geneva agreement. He thus sought a way to reach an agreement in the Geneva channel without making concession after concession, capitulating to the Palestinians' characteristic salami method of negotiating.

This tactic required Arieli to play tough. The result was two emotionally and physically exhausting years for both Arieli and al-'Abd. Arieli relieved the stress by riding a bike; Al-'Abd chain-smoked. And the combination of tension and nicotine brought him in 2002 to the angioplasty clinic. In the final stage of negotiations, in October 2003, at the Movenpik hotel on the Jordanian Dead Sea shore, the pressure became too great, as the negotiations went on each day until 4 a.m. One Friday night he began to feel ill. He had a medical examination in a hospital in Amman, and was summoned back on Sunday for an additional angioplasty procedure. His doctors forbade him to participate in the discussions until after his treatment was completed.

For the two years in which al-'Abd conducted the territorial negotiations, his position had been that every centimeter of the 1967 territories belonged the Palestinians. If Israel and Palestine wanted to leave certain settlements in place, Israel would have to reduce the relevant territory to a minimum; the same applied to the roads leading to them. Agreeing to leave settlements standing was a Palestinian concession. If restricting their land led the settlements to shrivel in the future, that was all for the better. The difference between the approaches of the two sides led to grueling debates that ended in specific agreements on individual points, which did not prevent the next argument. The Palestinians' way of conducting negotiations made it all the more difficult for us.

Arieli frequently complained that al-'Abd was reopening border issues on which the two of them had already agreed, sending him by e-mail maps displaying lines different from the ones they had drawn at the negotiating table. This caused him no little frustration. Furthermore, a map was drawn and approved by al-'Abd and Yassir 'Abd-Rabbu during the meeting near London in February 2003. It showed the border that had been agreed on as well as those places that still remained in dispute. When talks resumed, the Palestinians abjured the agreements reached in London. Formally, it is true, these agreements were not binding, since one of the ground rules of the negotiations was that nothing was final until everything was final. But this method of negotiating created a negative atmosphere, dragged out the talks, and added to the difficulties.

Beyond the cultural factor, this Palestinian tactic also reflected the need to fight for every centimeter of land against the occupation and the settlements. The Palestinian negotiators were anxious not to be seen as giving up too much. A lack of backing, a lack of authority to make concessions, and doubts about whether superiors in the Palestinian hierarchy would back the plan may also have played a role. Samih al-'Abd was a technocrat who held the position of deputy minister of planning. In other words, he had no political organization or movement behind him. As a result, he had to prove that he was tough and to get as many concessions as possible out of the Israelis. He was burdened, by his own account, by frustrations from the official talks, in which Israel had presented positions that were impossible from a Palestinian point of view. In the official talks, Israel had also frequently padded its proposals with spurious demands for the express purpose of giving them up and thus displaying its willingness to make "concessions." The same was done in the Geneva talks, for the reasons noted above. So, for example, the Israeli team originally insisted that the settlement of Mishor Adumim be included in the territory of Ma'aleh Adumim, and then conceded this point later in the negotiations.

The opening points of the Geneva channel were those that characterized the final stage of official negotiations at Taba. On the territorial issue, this meant that Israel wished to annex some settlement blocks. The Israeli delegation demanded that these blocks be connected to Israel by broad corridors, and not by narrow strings of land meant for access roads, ending in balloons where settlements stood. The Israelis also demanded that the settlements receive modest land reserves. Shaul Arieli argued that the agreement had to prove that those settlements that were left on the ground would remain there in perpetuity. Therefore, they could not be left in a situation in which they would inevitably decline. The Palestinians had a hard time accepting this. From their point of view, the settlements were colonial outposts established by an occupying power and thus utterly unacceptable. Furthermore, most of the settlements lay alongside populated Palestinian areas, creating a contradiction between the interests of the Palestinian inhabitants and those of the settlers whose towns would be annexed to Israel. As a result, the territorial negotiations were conducted in great detail on each hill and road and each settlement. During the two years in which the Geneva agreement was prepared, the negotiations on territory and the border were the longest and most exhausting. Most of the debates were on the following issues: First, where would Palestine receive equal territorial compensation for the West Bank land that Israel annexed? The Palestinians opposed receiving the Halutza sands, in the south, as the Beilin–Abu-Mazen document had proposed. They argued that the territory was distant from and not contiguous with the Gaza Strip, undeveloped and of inferior quality compared to most of the land that Israel would annex. From the beginning of the official negotiations, the Palestinians demanded not only territory of an equivalent size to that annexed by Israel, but also of equivalent quality. In the Geneva talks they also rejected the idea of receiving some pieces of territory in southern Judea, in the direction of Arad, on the grounds that this, too, was desert land. In the official talks from Camp David to Taba, Samih al-'Abd proposed that Israel cede areas in the central West Bank and the northern Jordan Valley, in the direction of the Beit She'an valley. The Israeli team refused, but agreed in the London talks to replace the offer of Halutza with an area bordering on the Gaza Strip. From this point onward the debate was over the size of this territory and what other areas would be given as territorial compensation to the Palestinians, to make the land exchange equivalent in a 1:1 ratio.

The territorial argument was affected by two parameters: the amount of territory and the number of settlers that Israel would annex. Both these quantities shrank during the negotiations. Originally, the Israeli delegation sought to leave 70 percent of the settlers in their homes, not including the Jewish neighborhoods in East Jerusalem. Eventually they agreed to 50 percent. This meant the evacuation of about 140 out of 160 settlements, not including some 100 outposts that were in existence at the time the Geneva agreement was signed. In terms of quantity of territory, this meant annexation of about two percent of the West Bank to Israel, including the built-up land in the Israeli neighborhoods in East Jerusalem. In exchange, the Geneva agreement provides the Palestinians with

full territorial compensation in the form of land now farmed by kibbutzim on the east edge of the Gaza Strip. This would enlarge the Strip by
about 25 percent. Both sides to the agreement here identified a common
interest, since the narrow Gaza Strip was too small for its burgeoning
population, which needed means of production and income. Farmland
whose produce could be exported could help mitigate the plight of the
Strip's inhabitants and prevent an anticipated demographic and economic disaster, from which Israel would suffer. From the point of view of Israeli society, there was an advantage to spreading the sacrifice so that not
just one sector, the settlers, would pay the price of withdrawal. In this way
the kibbutzim could also contribute to acceptance of the agreement and
to the national healing that Israel would require after the storm passed.
Furthermore, both sides agreed to the transfer of land in the Beit Jubrin
area from Israeli to Palestinian sovereignty. This land is not cultivated
and is scattered with the ruins of Palestinian villages that were destroyed
in 1948, such as Tal Bayt Mirsam, Tal 'Itun, and Khirbet Naqiq. The Palestinians would be able to rebuild these villages and settle refugees there,
or make them into memorial sites of the Palestinian Nakba of 1948.

The no-man's land of the Latrun enclave was the subject of an extended debate. At the start, Arieli and al-'Abd agreed that Israel and Palestine would divide this land evenly. At the London talks, the two sides
agreed that Israel would take more than half of the enclave, and would
compensate the Palestinians elsewhere. The uneven division was necessary because of Israel's need to defend the main Jerusalem-Tel Aviv
highway. But a while later the Palestinians reopened this issue. At the
final talks in Jordan there was a bitter debate about each square meter
of the enclave, ending only during the concluding hours of the talks.
The addition of Mitzna, Shlomo Brom, Ron Pundak, Zuhir Manasra,
and Mohammad Hourani to the negotiating teams made it easier to
reach a compromise. The Palestinians agreed to give the Israelis more
than half the land; the Israelis came toward the Palestinians by agreeing that the Palestinian part would include the ruins of the villages
Bayt Nuba, Alu, and half of 'Amawas—villages that Israel had destroyed
during the 1967 war and whose inhabitants it expelled. Compromise
was also reached on the security margin that Israel needed between
the highway and the border. The topographic structure of the land did
not leave much choice. Israel would retain the hills adjacent to the road
near Sha'ar HaGai.

As a general rule, two factors weighed in the decision about which settlements would be annexed to Israel—proximity to the Green Line, the 1948 border; and the size of the Jewish population. The settlements close to the Green Line are for the most part larger and more urban than those deep in the West Bank. Their inhabitants are generally more moderate in their politics and are less ideologically committed than are the Israelis who live in the heart of Palestinian populated areas. These characteristics grant the urban settlements that lie on the Green Line significant demographic and electoral weight. At the London talks, in February 2003, the Israeli delegation made a decision to prefer the annexation of Alfei Menashe to Efrat, two settlements with approximately the same number of inhabitants. Efrat lies to the east of and alongside the main Bethlehem-Hebron road. It has a sausage shape whose northern end borders on al-Hader, near Solomon's Pools and the Deheishe refugee camp. Annexing Efrat would thus create problems. Furthermore, Efrat's population consists primarily of upper-middle-class national-religious Israelis, most of whom are politically moderate compared, for example, to the settlers in Hebron.

In addition, the border that can be drawn without annexing Efrat is much more logical. Some members of the Israeli team nevertheless preferred not to push Efrat's settlers into the arms of the extremists, and sought to include Efrat in the Etzion block, slated for annexation. Beilin and Shahak preferred, however, to annex Alfei Menashe, whose population is primarily nonreligious. This would widen the narrow "waist" that pre-1967 Israel had before it occupied the West Bank. The Palestinians swallowed this only with great difficulty, because Alfei Menashe lies adjacent to the city of Qalqilya and the village of Habala. Ma'aleh Adumim, with almost 30,000 inhabitants, and Givat Ze'ev, with about 11,000 inhabitants, were marked for annexation for demographic-electoral reasons. Both had mayors from the Likud party, and were home to former residents of Jerusalem who had moved out of the city to improve their living conditions and find inexpensive housing. Both these settlements are, in Israeli parlance, part of the "Jerusalem envelope," and there is a broad consensus that they must remain part of Israel in any permanent status agreement. Few Israelis view them as settlements. Their annexation would allow the Israeli side to claim that Jerusalem's border had been expanded to the east and north. This would keep some less ideologically committed Israelis from opposing the agreement.

But Ma'aleh Adumim lies in an area that the Palestinians designate for the development of their capital, al-Quds, and on the road that constitutes the West Bank's north-south axis. It was difficult to persuade the Palestinians that, despite the existence of Ma'aleh Adumim and Givat Ze'ev, with the boundaries suggested by the Israeli team, East Jerusalem and Ramallah still had space for development. They viewed the two Israeli towns with today's eyes. Their perspective was not that of the possibilities the future opened for them if the Geneva agreement were carried out, but rather that of the bitter experience of the Oslo period, in which the number of settlers was doubled. The Palestinians accepted that these two settlements would stand because they had no alternatives. At one stage of the negotiations, they proposed that Ma'aleh Adumim be placed under Palestinian sovereignty and leased to Israel for thirty years. But there was unanimity in the Israeli team that, for demographic and electoral reasons, the inhabitants of Ma'aleh Adumim had to stay where they were. The city lies on a ridge and can be isolated from the surrounding territory. Furthermore, a significant part of the road linking it to Jerusalem is subterranean. Beyond Ma'aleh Adumim's built-up area, there is also an industrial park, Mishor Adumim. As at the Taba talks, the Israeli delegation in the Geneva channel demanded that this be included in the area to be annexed to Israel. At the London talks, Beilin suggested that sovereignty in Mishor Adumim be Palestinian but that the industrial park be managed by Israel. In the end, there was no choice but to give up the industrial park and to retain the residential built-up area, with the addition of a small amount of land for expansion. For the purpose of comparison, the Ma'aleh Adumim territory that Israel demanding to annex at Taba was fifteen times the size of the residential built-up area. Even before the permanent status negotiations began, Israel's planning authorities had approved the E1 plan, aimed at preventing any possible expansion of Arab Jerusalem by creating physical link between Ma'aleh Adumim and Jerusalem. The legal link was established by Israel in the 1990s, when Ma'aleh Adumim's jurisdiction was expanded to make it tangential to East Jerusalem. The map of this plan was presented by Israel at Taba. The Geneva approach was different and produced Palestinian consent to leaving Ma'aleh Adumim in place.

Givat Ze'ev lies southeast of the Ramallah–al-Bireh metropolitan area and constitutes a north-reaching finger emerging from Jerusalem.

Along the road leading to it are places like Givon and Givon HaHa-dasha, which would also be annexed to Israel under the Geneva plan. Closer to Jerusalem lie Nabi Samu'el and a small settlement called Har Shmuel. Nabi Samu'el, identified by both Jews and Muslims as the tomb of the prophet Samuel, is holy to both faiths. The site also topo-graphically commands Jerusalem's Ramot neighborhood. Nabi Samu'el was not included in the territory Israel annexed to Jerusalem immedi-ately after the 1967 war, because the city's planners did not imagine then that Jerusalem would become so large that it might be wise to annex the ridge to the city's northwest. From the official Camp David negotiations to the Taba talks, Israel sought to retain Nabi Samu'el as part of a broad corridor leading from Ramot to Givat Ze'ev. This made the Israeli map unacceptable to the Palestinians. From their point of view, such a corridor would stunt the development of Ramallah and al-Bireh and cut them off from the villages and towns of the two cities' metropolitan area.

During the Geneva talks, the Palestinians proposed, informally, a compromise in which Givat Ze'ev would be moved southward into the space, still in the West Bank, between Ramot and Mevasseret Yerusha-layyim. This would keep the Israeli finger from penetrating deep into the West Bank. The idea seems to be logical and in Israel's interest as well. Israel could offer Givat Ze'ev's inhabitants an opportunity to upgrade themselves into living in a middle-class western Jerusalem suburb, like Mevasseret Yerushalayyim and Har Adar, instead of living surrounded by Palestinian territory. Jerusalem would also gain by broadening its northwest corridor, from Ramot to Ma'aleh HaHamisha, along with broadening its southern corridor with the annexation of Gush Etzion and Beitar Ilit. But this idea was not accepted by most members of the Israeli team, since it would require removing Givat Ze'ev's inhabitants from their homes. That would lower the percentage of evacuated set-tlers to over 50 percent. This deterred most of the Israelis, especially the politicians. They feared that the plan would be opposed no matter what alternative was offered to the Givat Ze'ev settlers.

Some members of the Israeli team proposed giving up Givat Ze'ev and annexing Efrat instead. But this idea was also rejected—Givat Ze'ev has far more inhabitants than Efrat. Many Israelis view Givat Ze'ev as part of Jerusalem, and its population is more varied than Efrat's. Mo-hammad Hourani and Kadura Fares proposed, as previously noted, that

Givat Ze'ev come under Palestinian sovereignty, with Palestine leasing it back to Israel for a number of years. They suggested that delaying the settlement's evacuation would make its loss easier to bear. The Israelis politely refused. Nechama Ronen, the Likud representative on the Israeli team, was the major advocate for keeping Givat Ze'ev, and she sought to persuade the Palestinian delegation on this point. A compromise was achieved by narrowing Givat Ze'ev's link to Israel and giving up the small settlement of Har Shmuel, which lies along the road. The issue of Nabi Samuel was solved by including it in the list of holy sites for which there would be special arrangements under Palestinian sovereignty.

According to the Geneva map, Alfei Menashe, Ma'aleh Adumim, and Givat Ze'ev were connected to their natural hinterland in Israel by roads. The border would run 100 meters (330 feet) on each side of these roads. Even if all went well and the agreement were observed assiduously in these areas, it is reasonable to assume that these settlements would be surrounded by Palestinian construction and that their inhabitants would feel distant and isolated. Those who could do so would probably leave, and the value of property there would decline. It may well be that in the real permanent status agreement between Israel and Palestine, these settlements will require a different solution. The precondition for this is to modify the requirement that 50 percent of the settlers remain in their homes. Instead of being overly concerned about meeting this number, it might be better to consider how settlements will be able to function in the reality created by the map the two sides agree on. This may not be possible. The agreement will be signed by politicians, and there is no guarantee that they will not fear evacuating a large number of settlers. This was one of the principal considerations that shaped the Israeli maps in the official talks, and it also influenced the Israeli negotiators in the Geneva channel. Israel's representatives had difficulty imagining how the map might look twenty or thirty years after the permanent status agreement was signed. The same is true of the Palestinian politicians. They saw the settlements that would remain as invasive and harmful to their rights and freedom of movement, not as isolated islands of Israeli habitation. What the Palestinians viewed as territorial boluses, nearly impossible to swallow, were for the Israelis settlements that could not possibly be evacuated, because they constituted difficult demographic and electoral problems. Both sides read the map of the present and not the map that would come into being "the day after."

Most of the difficulties arose during the last stage of the negotiations. Fatah activists Fares and Hourani joined the initiative and demanded the Israel give up Ma'aleh Adumim and/or Givat Ze'ev, even though the two sides had already agreed that these blocks would be annexed to Israel. The debate dragged on from September to October 2003 and from the discussions in al-Ram to the decisive meeting at Movenpik Hotel in Jordan. Shaul Arieli believed that the Palestinians had already passed the point of decision on whether or not to sign. All they wanted, he reasoned, was to gain something more. He maintained that the decision on Ma'aleh Adumim and Givat Ze'ev should be left for the real negotiations. If there was no choice and it became necessary to give up one or both of them, the concession should be made in the permanent status agreement, with Israel's prime minister conceding them to the Palestinian president at the end of the negotiations. Alternatively, if it was absolutely necessary to make this concession now, in the Geneva framework, it should not be done by the salami method, but rather "cold turkey"—on condition that the concession mean the end of the negotiations. He argued that Israel should not make concessions to Fares and Hourani, with all due respect to these representatives of Fatah and Tanzim, but to Yassir 'Abd-Rabbu, head of the Palestinian delegation. Yossi Beilin should go to 'Abd-Rabbu with the smallest possible concession, to be made on condition that the agreement as a whole be signed.

Amram Mitzna took a different position. Mitzna joined the territorial talks in their final stage and encroached on Shaul Arieli's exclusive position. Mitzna and other members of the Israeli team believed that giving up Givat Ze'ev or Ma'alch Adumim might be worth considering, as a way of roping the Fatah-Tanzim representatives into the Geneva document and of shoring up their position within their own organization. Beyond the benefit to the Geneva initiative itself, it was in Israel's interest that prominent members of the Fatah leadership's younger generation be part of the process. Mitzna sensed that leaving these settlements in place would be a problem for the Fatah delegates because they constituted fingers of Israeli territory sticking deep into Palestinian territory. In October, the problem became acute. Arieli found it emotionally and mentally difficult to continue with the negotiations as they had developed, so it was necessary to change tactics in order to avoid a dead end. Arieli proposed that Mitzna replace him as the principal negotiator on the map. Yossi Beilin and Mitzna made it absolutely clear to Arieli that they were going nowhere without him. It was a difficult moment for the entire Israeli team, but especially for Arieli. The fate of the talks was in his hands. Displaying great character, he acceded to his colleagues' request. He resumed work on the map with Ron Pundak, Mitzna, and Shlomo Brom, and gradually returned to center stage. The Palestinians reinforced their delegation as well. They supplemented Samih al-'Abd with Zuhir Manasra, previously Jabril Rajoub's replacement as chief of the West Bank Preventative Security force and now governor of Bethlehem. Mohammad Hourani of the Tanzim was also added to the team. The final agreement was reached not by giving up the settlements but by reducing the area of the roads leading to Givat Ze'ev and Ma'aleh Adumim. A corridor two kilometers (1.25 miles) long would link Alfei Menashe to Israel, a belt of 2.5 kilometers (1.5 miles) would connect Givat Ze'ev to Jerusalem's Ramot neighborhood, and a territory 3 kilometers (1.9 miles) wide would link Ma'aleh Adumim to the Mt. Scopus tunnel. Each of these roads would have security margins of about 100 meters (330 feet) on each side.

The discussion on the future of Ma'aleh Adumim and Givat Ze'ev touched on several issues related to Jerusalem. Among these were sovereignty over the Old City's Jaffa Gate and the road leading from it to the Zion Gate, and sovereignty over the part of the village of Beit Safafa that lay in the West Bank (see Chapter 2). Would the Israelis have gained full sovereignty over these parts of Jerusalem had they given up Ma'aleh Adumim and Givat Ze'ev? There is no way to be sure, but it is certainly possible. It is also possible that the Palestinians would never have given up sovereignty over these sections of the Old City, even if they received in exchange the largest settlements in the Jerusalem area. The question remained without an answer, as it was not put to the Palestinians, only discussed within the Israeli team.

The issues of territory and settlements thus lead to the issue of Jerusalem. In principle, the Palestinians maintain that the same rule should apply to the far-flung settlements of the West Bank and the Jewish neighborhoods that Israel built in East Jerusalem after the 1967 war. In practice, as had already been proven in the official negotiations, they reluctantly accepted the distinction that Israel made between the Jerusalem neighborhoods and the large satellite settlements on the one hand, and the rest of the settlements on the other. In no other part of the occupied territories did Israel so succeed in changing the demography and geography as it did in its capital. In East Jerusalem, approximately one percent of the West Bank's land, live some 200,000 Israelis, where they constitute about half of the total population, and half of the Jews in Jerusalem.

As a matter of fact, the biggest breakthrough in the official negotiations was on the Jerusalem issue. But the two sides did not know, in 2000, how to complete what they had begun. In practice, what was on the table was not only the territory that Israel had annexed to Jerusalem, but all the central West Bank as well, from the outskirts of Jericho in the East to the outskirts of Ramallah in the north and to the southern edge of Gush Etzion in the south. The Jerusalem issue touches on the symbolic center of both sides, on the location of the border, and on the settlements. Up to this point I have addressed the issues on the city's periphery. Now the time has come to focus on the breakthroughs that took place in the official and unofficial negotiations and to show how the Geneva initiative completed a process that had begun years previously.

2

Dividing Divided Jerusalem

SHATTERING THE MYTH OF THE OPEN CITY

In 1967, Israel declared united Jerusalem to be its eternal capital. For many in Israel and around the world, the city's mayor at the time, Teddy Kollek, was the personification of the enlightened annexationist. Kollek argued, with great conviction, that Jerusalem could be united and open only under Israeli rule. Only as part of Israel could it be a city of many cultures and many religions, in which Jews, Muslims, and Christians could live together in harmony as good neighbors. Kollek and the Israeli establishment depicted themselves as having reunited an urban fabric that had been rent by Jordan nineteen years previously. The two parts of a single, organic entity were now rejoined and open to each other. As proof, Israel pointed to Jordan's violation of section eight of the cease-fire agreement of 1949, which had guaranteed that Israelis would have access to the Jewish prayer site at the Western Wall and to the Jewish cemetery on the Mount of Olives. Israel, unlike Jordan, kept its promise immediately after annexing the Jordanian part of the city. It allowed freedom of worship for all.

After the war, a united and open Jerusalem became an Israeli myth. Questioning it was a social, ideological, and political taboo. The city boundary established by Israel became a sacred symbol and a component of Israel's national identity. Jerusalem Day celebrations, instituted to commemorate the date of the city's unification, institutionalized the symbol and sought to root it in Israeli national consciousness.

The myth was built on two foundations. One was symbolic, experiential, and deeply rooted. The arrival of Israeli paratroopers at the

Western Wall on June 8, 1967, sparked the emotions of every Jew in the world. The sharp transition—from the fear of destruction that overwhelmed Israel, to the crushing victory the country won—also contributed to a mythological view of the war and of Jerusalem. The war was not perceived as a historical drama of this world, but rather as a meta-historical phenomenon. The conquest of Jerusalem provided superb material for this view of events. Photographs of paratroopers at the Wall and of Moshe Dayan and Yitzhak Rabin striding toward it became symbols of the war and of a narrative of identity. For most Israelis this was a constitutive experience, a symbol of the link between the Sabra "new Jew" and his religious and national roots. Israel's national identity changed as a result of this encounter (Segev 2005).

The second foundation is political. The perception of Jerusalem as open and united was meant to justify the annexation of East Jerusalem. When the annexation line was drawn, it was possible to claim that Jerusalem was free and open on all sides. At that time the border between Jerusalem and the West Bank was virtual. There were no roadblocks between Jerusalem and the West Bank. In practice, the city was entirely open, and physically the city ended where the annexation line marked the limit of Israeli sovereignty. Israel could thus emphasize the fact that no international border crossed Jerusalem, and it could fudge the fact that Jerusalem's boundary with the West Bank was, according to Israel, an international border. In other words, East Jerusalem was entirely open to the west, but on the east, south, and north its border was also the end of Israeli sovereignty. The lack of physical barriers between East Jerusalem and the West Bank in the early years after the annexation made it easier to create a myth of open Jerusalem and get it accepted in the country and throughout the world.

The Arabs of East Jerusalem were not parties to this Israeli discourse of identity. Their attitude to the united city was and remains instrumental. Since May 1967, they have enjoyed and appreciated the material benefits and personal rights that the imposition of Israeli law brought in its wake. The occupation of Jerusalem was easier and more tolerant than that of the West Bank and Gaza Strip. In the balance, the economic and personal benefits of Israeli occupation have been greater than those in the rest of the territories conquered by Israeli in 1967.

Despite the annexation, and to some measure precisely because of the benefits it brought to the city's Palestinians, in less than three decades

Jerusalem underwent a physical metamorphosis. As a consequence, Israelis' awareness of it changed. This can easily be seen by examining one of cornerstones of Israeli identity: demography. Demographic considerations have shaped Israeli policy in East Jerusalem since 1967, just as they have shaped the Zionist movement's policies regarding the larger Arab question. In this regard, Jerusalem is a microcosm of the Israeli–Palestinian conflict. Since 1967, the Israeli establishment has invested huge resources to preserve the demographic balance that prevailed at the time of the annexation—74.2 percent Jews and 25.8 percent Arabs—and to ensure that it continue indefinitely. Paradoxically, however, annexation increased the Palestinian presence in East Jerusalem. In 2000, the balance was 68 percent Jews and 32 percent Arabs (Klein 2001:4–18).

During the 1990s, Israel attempted to reverse the demographic trend by confiscating identity cards, stripping Palestinians of resident status, and destroying illegal structures within the city and in its metropolitan area. But this served only to underline how little it could control the balance. Israel confiscated some 4,000 identity cards out of a target population of 50,000 to 80,000 who held resident cards but did not in fact live in the city, and ended up causing a wave of Palestinian resettlement as Palestinians returned to the annexed part of the city. Only four to eight percent of building violations that were identified resulted in demolition orders that were actually carried out (Klein 2001:278–93). After three decades of annexation, the geographic criteria that Israel had used to draw the border were no longer valid. Arab villages that had not been included within the annexation boundaries for demographic reasons turned into suburbs. The annexation line now actually runs straight through some East Jerusalem neighborhoods, dividing them in two. East Jerusalem's expansion has turned it into a municipal and political center that provides income and services to a large population that lives outside its boundaries.

For many years, Israel viewed the residents of East Jerusalem as exotic scenery, an extension of the enchanted oriental landscape of the Old City's alleys and colorful *shuk*, the Arab bazaar (Klein 2004a). This perspective was reinforced by the passivity of the East Jerusalem Palestinians and their invisibility as a collective. In addition, the Palestinians boycotted municipal elections so as not to grant legitimacy to the occupation and annexation. In the absence of political representation, they had neither a public voice nor access to resources.

In contrast to Palestinian passivity, the Jews were hyperactive. The Israeli establishment entrenched its superiority by giving preference to the Jewish sector and creating structural discrimination against the Palestinians of East Jerusalem in the distribution of resources, construction of infrastructure, and supply of services. During the first Intifada, the Palestinians of East Jerusalem turned from a passive to an active factor in the city, and this accelerated the race to grab land through construction and to assert de facto authority. Both Israel and Palestinian institutions acted unilaterally (Klein 2001:4–18, 278–93). Israel, the stronger side, still had a notable advantage in the contest. But the Palestinian presence could not be expunged, nor could it any longer be ignored. The Palestinians in Jerusalem constitute a critical mass; they make up ten percent of the total West Bank population. Their simple presence is a problem for Israel. East Jerusalem's different, Palestinian character is asserted every moment by the day-to-day lives of its residents. The residents themselves express a distinct identity by a variety of means, and there is a gap between the reality on the ground and the formal legal status of the Palestinian part of the city.

The Jerusalem myth was fractured and, at the Camp David summit of 2000, it shattered. The processes in the field were slow and imperceptible. The urban fabric changed slowly. Open Jerusalem turned from a way of life and daily life to no more than a series of events on Jerusalem day. The Jerusalem Day holiday was nationalized in the 1970s. Instead of private observances by the soldiers who had fought in the battles of 1967 and by the Zionist religious subculture, it became an official national observance. The spontaneity with which the day had originally been observed had been lost, and institutionalizing the holiday was meant to give it an established form. Ostensibly, nationalization of the holiday elevated its status. In fact, all it did was keep it from fading away. The Intifada that began in 1987 physically and mentally distanced Israelis from Jerusalem. To preserve the myth, the state raised the volume of Jerusalem Day celebrations and even organized a commemoration of the city's three thousandth birthday. It was no coincidence that the chosen number marked the conquest of the Jebusite city by King David, and not the earliest human habitation of the site. This latter event was observed on a much smaller scale by the Palestinians, who in defiance of the Israeli festivities marked the five thousandth anniversary of the founding of the city by the Jebusites, whom they claim as their ancestors. It is no coincidence that both these celebrations took place in 1995, after the future of the Israeli annexation of East Jerusalem was put on the negotiating table in the Oslo agreement of 1993.

It slowly became clear to the Israeli public that Jerusalem was not the multicultural and multiconfessional city they thought it had become in 1967. It was, rather, a divided city. In a multicultural city, the orientation of the various groups is toward creating a collective "we." With Jerusalem today polarized more than ever, the orientation is toward division. Only in rare cases will an Arab from East Jerusalem and a Jew from West Jerusalem call themselves a "we" or describe Jerusalem as "ours," with both referring to the same collective.

The truth is that the breach in Jerusalem is more profound than that in Belfast. The adversaries in Belfast speak the same language, share a common physiognomy, eat and drink the same things, read the same publications, and even intermarry. All these characteristics, which bring Catholics and Protestants together in Belfast, are polarizing factors in Jerusalem (Klein 2001:9–18; Hepburn 1994). No physical wall divides the city, but the partition is salient. The two populations differ in their nationality, history, mentality, religion, ethnicity, culture, language, political alignment, and representation in organs of government. They live in separate neighborhoods, have separate hinterlands, transportation systems, media, urban centers, industrial areas, educational systems from preschool through higher education, community institutions, health-care systems, and communal leaders. It goes almost without saying that the two groups are separated by discrepancies in income level, employment scale, participation in the labor market, income distribution, access to material resources, and state and municipal investment in infrastructure and services. In all these areas, there is a structural preference for the ruling Jewish sector and discrimination against the subject Palestinian-Arab sector (Klein 2001:18–41).

Jerusalem is not simply a unit of territory. It is a unit of identity. Israeli identity rejects Palestinian Jerusalem (Eran and Gurevitch 1991; Klein 2004a; Klein 2005). Until 1967, the dominant stream of Zionism and Israel preferred "Israeli Jerusalem" to "Jewish Jerusalem"—in other words, it preferred the Jewish western part of the city to the Old City and East Jerusalem (Golani 1998). It is thus hardly surprising that on the eve of the 1967 war, the Voice of Israel's record collection contained fewer than ten modern songs on Jerusalem. There was, of course, no lack of religious songs and songs written for secular ceremonies, but there were next to no "regular" songs about Jerusalem (Almagor 2005). After June 1967, Israel reversed itself and turned to face the eastern city and its Jewish identity, placing Jerusalem's Palestinian inhabitants outside the pale. They were the "other" that threatened the Jewish identity community.

The Palestinians in Jerusalem suffer from double marginality. They are marginal to Israel, inferior even to the Bedouin of the Negev desert, who are the state's most deprived citizens. Yet they are also on the fringes of Palestinian society. Closest to Israel of all Palestinian groups who are not Israeli citizens, and distant from the Jewish and Israeli collectives, they lie in between. Their rejection from Israel pushes them closer to Palestine, but their nearness to Israel pushes them into the Palestinian margins. Their weakness is structural. In the Oslo years, from 1993 to 2000, the Palestinian public in Jerusalem underwent an awakening of sorts and strengthened its ties to Palestinian national institutions in the West Bank (Klein 2001:183–246). But when Israel retook the West Bank in response to the new Intifada of 2000, it destroyed the central institutions of the Palestinian Authority, closed Palestinian institutions in Jerusalem, and commenced the construction of a system of fences and obstacles (Klein 2005). This returned the East Jerusalem Palestinians to their passive starting point. They lack strong local institutions, community organization, and leadership, all of which could overcome the population's atomization. Palestinian collective institutions (central government, parliament, security services) exist outside Jerusalem and are ineffective in the eastern city. Their ties with the Israeli side have never gone beyond them being limited and instrumental and inferior. Even in a situation of no collective activity they present a problem for Israel because of their different identity and their large quantitative presence in a territory that Israel considers a unit of its own identity.

The Geneva initiative proposes to link them to the Palestinian hinterland, and to their primary community of identity and belonging. At the same time, it proposes to create interaction between the two populations in Jerusalem, in particular in the Old City, which will be open. The initiative therefore suggests that Israel should acknowledge that the unification of Jerusalem stands on shaky foundations. Israel has lost its hegemony in the geographic space and in both its own and the Palestinians' consciousness.

There are Israelis who maintain that it is vital to reunify the city's two parts. Some of these believe that, first and foremost, Israel must assert its control vigorously and impose its will on the Arab city by geographic, demographic, and administrative means. According to this group, the demographic balance will be preserved by enlarging the city's territory and adding to its Jewish population. The city will expand to include Jewish satellite towns such as Mevasseret Tzion, Givat Ze'ev, and·Ma'aleh Adumim; new Jewish neighborhoods will be built in East Jerusalem, such as Sha'ar Mizrach; and Har Homa will be enlarged. In addition, they believe, Israel must police the Palestinian population by isolating blocks of Arab neighborhoods, cutting them off from their natural hinterland in the country's interior, and enforcing Israeli law in Palestinian neighborhoods. It is not sufficient, in this view, to develop the Jewish side and grant it structural preference. The Palestinian side should also be hindered. East Jerusalem should not be permitted to serve as a metropolitan area for the central West Bank.

This was the Sharon government's program for Jerusalem. It thus sought to take control of property and buildings in Palestinian neighborhoods, with the aid of the fence and wall it built to achieve its strategic goal of "liberating Jerusalem." As will be seen, the Sharon and Olmert governments have not been willing to allow any Palestinian sovereignty in the area it defined as Jerusalem.

This approach, however, is a desperate Israeli attempt to revive the myth and avoid acknowledging the limits of its power. The myth of a united and open Jerusalem was born in an atmosphere of heroism. In contrast, the Israeli project of constructing walls and fences grew out of an atmosphere of despair. In 1967, Israeli dominance was taken for granted and required no wall. Since 2004 Israel can rule only from behind a barrier.

Others—this was Ehud Barak's approach—prefer the carrot to the stick as a way of uniting Jerusalem. They give priority to investment in Jewish Jerusalem, which they claim will normalize the city and make it an attractive place for Israelis to live and work in. Such investments should not ignore the Arab part of the city, but they must enhance Jewish-Israeli superiority and ensure the dominance of the Israeli side. This approach does not reject reaching a permanent or interim agreement with a Palestinian state, in the framework of which Palestine would enjoy broad powers in East Jerusalem's Arab neighborhoods. But Israel would retain its superiority and supreme sovereignty.

A third position, that of the religious and nationalist right, emphasizes spirituality and ideology. It comes in two versions. One version is religious and mystical, centering on the Temple Mount cult and the construction of a Third Temple. In this view, Israel's loss of hegemony in Jerusalem derives from its disconnection from the source of its spiritual strength. The Jews' physical and spiritual identities derive from the Temple. The physical structure was destroyed, but not its spiritual resources. The contest with Islam for control of the Temple Mount will determine the future of West Jerusalem and the future of the Zionist project, which is itself perceived by this group in religious-messianic terms.

The second version is nationalist, advocating that Jerusalem be shaped in accord with "the vision of generations" and the connection to Jerusalem declared by the Jewish people over thousands of years. At the focus of this vision and obligation are the Temple Mount and the Old City, and no less so the entire territory that Israel annexed in June 1967. Applying this vision to modern reality fails to recognize the profound differences between the past and the present. It also ignores the difference between Jerusalem as a symbol and holy city, to which fealty may be expressed, and the actual situation on the ground. In Jewish history, the memory of Jerusalem has been a stronger force than actual residence in the city. When Maimonides left Morocco, he visited Jerusalem but settled in Cairo. Rabbi Yehuda HaLevy called prayers and the declaration of a commitment to Jerusalem "the speech of the parrot and the chirping of the nightingale"—words spoken without any intention of carrying them out in practice. This gap between they city's symbolic-sacred standing and personal and concrete duty characterized the Jewish attitude toward Jerusalem over many generations. It does today, as well, when it is profoundly a part of the mental and spiritual relationship to Jerusalem and of the fabric of the city (Klein 2003b:1–18).

Since 1967, Jerusalem has developed as two central cities with their backs to each other. Israeli-Jewish Jerusalem faces west, toward its natural hinterland in the state of Israel. Palestinian Jerusalem faces the West Bank. The segregation of these two cities is profound, and the only people who spend significant time in both are an ever-diminishing stream of Palestinian laborers who cross the ethnic boundary for a few hours each day. Such interaction as there is takes place for the most part in functional geographic areas that serve as areas of encounter and interaction. For example, a Jewish resident of Jerusalem may well find that the cab he has flagged down has a Palestinian driver. He will interact with Palestinians who work in construction, automobile repair, and restaurants. Israelis and Palestinians also encounter each other in a limited number of leisure and shopping facilities. These include, for example, Palestinian restaurants located on the seam, the Liberty Bell Park, the zoo, the Jerusalem Mall in Malha, and supermarkets in the Talpiot shopping area.

These areas of contact have become much more limited since the al-Aqsa Intifada of September 2000. Recession, unemployment in both economies, and the sharp drop in tourism are all reasons, as are terror, the militarization of daily life, mutual suspicion, and each society's preference for remaining within its own part of the city. The Jewish-Israeli city in the west rules some 200,000 Palestinian Arabs who live their lives separately in the east. Each of the two ethnic communities has developed, within the bounds of its city, a complex composed of an urban, political, and religious focal point.

There are eight boundaries between the western and eastern complexes (Klein 2004b, 2005):

1. *The demographic boundary.* The residential and living space of each of the two groups. This is a dynamic line that has changed since 1967 in accordance with the construction and habitation of residential neighborhoods. In Jerusalem, there is almost complete segregation of living space between Jews and Arabs. Only about one percent of the residents of the Palestinian neighborhoods are Israeli Jews. This small minority of settlers lives in fenced-off and guarded compounds in Palestinian neighborhoods, and hostility prevails between them and the Palestinian majority in the neighborhoods. There are almost no Palestinian areas of residence in West Jerusalem. The settlers and the Israeli establishment take advantage of the vacuum that has existed in Palestinian Jerusalem since the spring of 2001 (see the seventh boundary, below) in order to penetrate Palestinian areas more deeply in Silwan, Sheikh Jarah, Abu Dis, and Walajeh. Their goal is to prevent the partition of Jerusalem on a demographic-national basis. They are aided by organs of government, using methods

similar to those used to establish settler outposts in the West Bank. The outposts have a similar goal—preventing the establishment of a viable Palestinian state and ensuring Israeli rule and supremacy over the much larger Palestinian population.

2. *Israel's effective boundary of control.* This border goes beyond the demographic border but, for the most part, does not extend deep into Arab territory. So, for example, the Sho'afat refugee camp has never really been under Israeli control. Since the inception of the al-Aqsa Intifada, Israel's effective rule is diminished more than ever in the past. Israeli institutions and services that functioned in East Jerusalem, such as the construction of classrooms by the municipality or branches of Israeli businesses, are no longer in existence. Since 2000, Israel has sought to expand this boundary by taking control of homes and land in Palestinian neighborhoods and transferring them to Israeli settlers (*Ha'aretz* Jan. 30, 2005; Rapoport 2005).

3. *The symbolic boundary of control.* In areas in which effective rule is tenuous, there is limited Israeli symbolic control, for example, by the presence of Israeli road signs or law enforcement agencies. In this area, too, there has been erosion as a result of the al-Aqsa Intifada. Especially prominent in this regard is the Temple Mount. Since 1967, Israeli rule of this site has been symbolic, since it has been administered by the Islamic Waqf. Until 1994, the Waqf functioned under Jordanian sponsorship, and since then it has been part of the Palestinian Authority. Since the beginning of the al-Aqsa Intifada, the Waqf has unilaterally closed the site to visits by non-Muslim tourists and Israelis; this situation prevailed until mid-2004. A tacit understanding between the Waqf and the Israeli police led to the reopening of the site to Jewish Israelis, but with some limitations. The visitors are under the supervision of the Israeli police and members of the Waqf. People of Orthodox Jewish appearance are sometimes not allowed into the compound.

4. *The international border.* The border was established between Israel and Jordan in 1949. Israel broke through it in 1967, when it conquered the Jordanian West Bank. Israel's actions in Jerusalem turned this line into a historical relic, recognized in international but not Israeli law.

5. *The Israeli annexation line.* Israel established this boundary at the end of June 1967. This border is also Jerusalem's municipal border and is considerably larger than the combination of the Israeli and former

Jordanian city. The "united Jerusalem" created unilaterally by Israel includes territories that under Jordan were not part of the city. This line is not recognized by the international community. It should be noted that the urban growth of East Jerusalem and its expansion northward, eastward, and southward has made the line a virtual one. In some places it divides roads, houses, and apartments down the middle. The wall that Israel is constructing (border no. 8) seeks, along some of its contours, to re-create and enforce that boundary. Until the beginning of the 1990s, this boundary was not apparent on the ground. At that time, Israel began, for security reasons, creating a physical wedge between its territory and that of the West Bank. Then, in the early 1990s, the wedge consisted of a number of military roadblocks that severed East Jerusalem from the West Bank for varying periods of time. In 2000, the city was cut off more severely and on a permanent basis. In 2004 the boundary was institutionalized with the construction of fences and walls. Israel's need to defend itself against terror was used to accomplish annexation.

6. *The metropolitan boundary.* The boundary is defined by the function and daily influence of a metropolitan center on the periphery to which it supplies employment and services. East and West Jerusalem constitute two different metropolitan centers, each with its own distinct hinterland. East Jerusalem's metropolitan area spreads beyond the annexation line. It is important to note that East Jerusalem became a metropolitan center unintentionally. Huge Israeli investment in the former Jordanian territory (which resulted in half Jerusalem's Jewish population living there) created a Palestinian center of employment and services. Two processes diminished East Jerusalem's metropolitan influence: first, the establishment of roadblocks and the imposition of closures and sieges of various levels since the first Gulf War in 1991. The ties between the metropolitan center and the periphery became more difficult and detrimental to both. Second, the Oslo agreements created a new political border in Jerusalem and its surroundings. Cities close to Jerusalem, such as Ramallah and Bethlehem, became central cities, under the full control of the Palestinian Authority. As a consequence, they detached themselves from East Jerusalem, except in matters of religion. Jerusalem continues to be a religious and symbolic focal point, even though physical access to it is more difficult than in the past.

7. *The political border.* Until the Oslo agreements, the political border, as far as Israel was concerned, was the same as the municipal border. For the Palestinians, the political border was the line of June 4, 1967. The Oslo agreements, and the January 1996 elections to the institutions of the Palestinian Authority, created a new line. According to these agreements, the Palestinian Authority was forbidden from operating in East Jerusalem, but the Palestine Liberation Organization (PLO) was allowed. This strengthened the collective identity of the Palestinians and Jerusalem and institutionalized the activity of PLO political organs, most importantly Orient House. The political border is based less on the legal status of East Jerusalem as occupied territory and more by the fact that only between two and four percent of the inhabitants of East Jerusalem requested Israeli citizenship (a citizen has political rights on the national level that a resident does not enjoy). The right of East Jerusalem Palestinians to be part of the Palestinian political system on the national level was recognized by the Oslo agreements. The agreements determined that the inhabitants of East Jerusalem, in that area to which Israeli law was applied, could vote for and be elected to Palestinian Authority institutions, but that the election procedures in this area would differ from those in the rest of the Palestinian areas. In addition to the political reality created by the Oslo agreements, there was a change of consciousness regarding the shape of a permanent status agreement in Jerusalem, in the wake of the Camp David summit of 2000. The summit did not end in an agreement, but the Israeli taboo against redrawing Jerusalem's boundaries and against transferring Arab neighborhoods to Palestinian sovereignty was broken. The process of reshaping the political line was halted and perhaps even reversed after the death of Faisal al-Husseini, the senior Palestinian political figure in Jerusalem, who ran a number of Palestinian institutions and organizations. His death, in June 2001, created a leadership and institutional vacuum that was exacerbated when, in August of that same year, the Israeli government shut down these institutions, most notably Orient House. The institutions were forced to relocate from East Jerusalem to its suburbs. The destruction of the Palestinian Authority by the Israeli army during the Intifada of 2000 deepened the political and institutional vacuum in East Jerusalem and its periphery. Israel exploited that destruction in order to establish the next border.

8. *The line created by the system of walls and fences.* This barrier was constructed unilaterally by Israel to cut East Jerusalem off from its hinterland. On the ground, most of this line follows contours approved
by the Israeli government in July 2003 and February 2005. The objective of this program is to produce the most dramatic metamorphosis in East Jerusalem since Israeli conquered and annexed it in 1967.
Geographically, the barrier is a de facto revision of the annexation
border. In June 2005, the government admitted, in a brief filed with
Israel's Supreme Court, that the lay of the fence "gives weight to the
state of Israel's political interests" and that "The political interest is a
relevant consideration in regard to the line that runs within the territory of Israel (Council for Peace and Security 2005; Lein and Cohen-
Lifshitz 2005). How else may the following figures be understood?
The length of the barrier in the Jerusalem metropolitan area is 130
km (81 miles), of which only 4 km (2.5 miles) run along the annexation line and another 12 km (7.5 miles) within a few hundred meters
of the annexation line. Some 12 km (7.5 miles) of the line penetrate
the Israeli side of the annexation line, to a depth of about 2 km (1.25
miles). In this way, Israel places outside its area of annexation Kufr
Aqab, the Sho'afat refugee camp, and Semiramis in the north, as well
as Arab al-Sawahra and part of Sur Baher in the south. But a full 102
kilometers (64 miles) go past the annexation line to the east, south
and north, up to a distance of 10 km (6 miles). In this fashion, the
barrier in East Jerusalem takes in 99,680 dunams (24,920 acres) of
the West Bank (brief submitted to the Supreme Court by the Council
for Peace and Security). In practice, Israel is thus annexing Ma'aleh
Adumim and the vacant land between it and Jerusalem. This vacant
land is the available area for the expansion of East Jerusalem, which
is strangling from housing density and construction restrictions imposed by Israel. Israel has a plan to build up the area between the
Jewish neighborhoods of northeast Jerusalem—Neve Ya'akov and
Pisgat Ze'ev—and the settlement of Ma'aleh Adumim. Similarly, the
barrier takes in, to the south, Rachel the Matriarch's tomb and the
settlement of Har Gilo, at the expense of Bethlehem and Beit Jala;
Israel also seeks to use the fence to link the Gush Etzion settlements
to these areas. In the land to be annexed de facto, next to Har Gilo,
Israel began to build a new neighborhood of thousands of housing
units. In southeast Jerusalem, Israel plans to expand Har Homa in

the area of Kherbet Mazmuriah-Nu'aman. This will cut East Jerusalem off from its natural hinterland to the south and east. Something similar is happening on the city's northwest. The fence built to protect the settlement of Givat Ze'ev and highway 443, and to link them to Jerusalem, cuts thousands of Palestinians in this area off from Jerusalem and Ramallah. The system of fences that Israel has planned will create Palestinian "pockets" in Sheikh Sa'ad, and in the area of Bir Naballah and Beit Hanina in the west. In densely populated areas, in which there is no possibility of building a large system of fences and barriers, Israel has built a concrete wall 8 meters (26 feet) high. Such a wall already cuts across the central street in Abu-Dis along the 1967 annexation border. A similar wall has been built along the main road to Ramallah, near Beit Hanina and northern Neve Ya'akov, and by Rachel's tomb in the south.

Beyond enlarging the annexed area, Israel wants first and foremost to downgrade and control Arab Jerusalem and its metropolitan area. Its method is to surround the eastern city with a ring of Jewish neighborhoods, beyond which lie a fence and wall. Both cut East Jerusalem off from the West Bank. Israel is building two large border crossings—in the south near Beit Sahour and in the north next to the abandoned Qalandiya airport. Originally, there were no plans for any other openings. But, in 2004, the threat of Supreme Court action and international pressure prompted the authorities to plan a dozen more gates. At the beginning of 2005, Israeli officials declared unofficially that when the wall was completed, Palestinians from East Jerusalem would no longer be allowed to pass through the wall without a permit that would have to be obtained in advance. (As of this writing, the Jerusalem section of the wall has not been completed and enforcement of this provision has been sporadic.) In addition, Israeli police sporadically prevent residents of East Jerusalem from crossing into the West Bank, except at the Qalandiya roadblock, which Israel sees as the future international border checkpoint (*Ha'aretz*, June 30, 2006). The planned entry and exit points will have to serve some 130,000 people a day. This number includes workers and school children, but not West Bank residents with entry permits to Jerusalem, diplomats, and the press, who will also have to cross at these points. At this writing, procedures have not yet been established for how these gates will operate and to what extent they will provide for the needs of Jerusalem's Palestinians. The Israeli leadership is less concerned about the Palestinians' needs; it is focused on cutting the city off from its hinterland in the West Bank. To the extent it is taking the Palestinian population's requirements into consideration, it is as a result of international pressure and Supreme Court rulings.

When the fence and wall are completed, about 50,000 East Jerusalem Palestinians will find themselves in the West Bank and about 60,000 to 70,000 West Bank Palestinians will find themselves in Jerusalem, although they will not have permanent resident status in the city. Those who are left outside will be cut off from East Jerusalem. They will find it extremely difficult to reach their work places, schools, hospitals, holy sites, shopping centers, and business centers. Neither will they be able to exercise their legal rights as residents of Jerusalem. Even now, before the barrier's completion, these people are not receiving municipal services. For example, most mail sent to these areas is returned to sender with the stamp "closed area" (*Ha'aretz*, July 3, 2005). Neither will those West Bank residents who end up on the Israeli side of the fence be able to enjoy these services, since they are not legally residents of Jerusalem. Two surveys, conducted by the Jerusalem Institute for Israel Studies among residents of neighborhoods in which the wall has been completed, found that 52 percent complained of difficulties in reaching their places of employment, 44 percent said they no longer went to pray at al-Haram al-Sharif, 37 percent complained that their family and social contacts had been adversely affected, and 33 percent had difficulty reaching educational institutions. The surveys showed that commercial areas on the margins of the city were in dire straits and that the traditional business center in downtown East Jerusalem was in decline (*Ha'aretz*, October 9, 2005).

In addition to the implications for Palestinian neighborhoods, there will be major changes at the metropolitan level. Some quarter of a million Palestinian Arab residents of East Jerusalem, who constitute approximately 10 percent of the Palestinian population of the West Bank, will be cut off from their social, political economic, cultural, and linguistic hinterland. As noted above, East Jerusalem's metropolitan connections were severely damaged by Israeli actions at the beginning of the 1990s, and now they will be destroyed entirely. On the other side, it has not been easy for these Palestinians, who are permanent residents of Jerusalem, to access West Jerusalem since 2000. A mobile line of low-technology roadblocks and checkpoints has been deployed intermittently along the former international border or the demographic line. When soldiers and policemen check the papers and bags of Palestinians for security reasons, it inevitably underlines the isolation of the city's Arab population and their status as "others."

The Sharon and Olmert governments have tried to establish two political facts. First, they have sought to change the reality that the Oslo agreements created on the ground in Jerusalem, and to expunge the change in consciousness that was created by the permanent status talks on Jerusalem that took place in 2000. The wall and fence are meant to accomplish what the construction of new Jewish neighborhoods around the Palestinian neighborhoods in East Jerusalem failed to achieve. Those neighborhoods, built after 1967, imposed on the Palestinians a Jewish-Arab demographic balance in the territory that Israel annexed. The Israeli government wants to assert exclusive control over the Arab metropolitan space by weakening it, cutting it off from its natural hinterland in the West Bank, and dividing it into small units. The Israeli hope is that living conditions in the surrounded areas will be so harsh that most of their residents will abandon their national aspirations or move away. Israel will contain the territory and the population and will develop means of control, instead of sharing them with the Palestinians, as was proposed by the Barak government in 2000. In order to achieve exclusive Israeli control of the territory annexed in 1967, Israel must undermine the East Jerusalem metropolitan area both by striking at its periphery and by weakening the center.

The "Jerusalem envelope," as the line of wall and fences that chokes Jerusalem is called in security argot, is an attractive line for Israel. In keeping with the Zionist ethos of "taking our fate in our hands," it is a unilateral move to establish a fact on the ground in accordance with Israel's exclusive interest. This ethos has great drawing power in Israel, strengthened by the mistaken assumption that there is no partner for a peace treaty. This has been the common wisdom in Israel since the summer of 2000, and it is very tempting to use it to trump the will and actions of other actors.

The Intifada, burgeoning unemployment, the militarization of life in the city, the lack of central government and a law-enforcement establishment in most areas of East Jerusalem have put some neighborhoods, such as al-Tur, Silwan, and Ras al-Amud on the road to becoming slums. As the process accelerates, there will be a growing Israeli interest in confining and containing the Palestinian "other" on the Israeli side of the Jerusalem wall, and to minimize the damage for the dominant majority. As Bayat (2000) shows, in poor cities in which there is a severe social and economic gap, the weak side does not remain passive. The poor quietly encroach beyond the border drawn by the dominant side, and spread into the areas of the dominant side, at its expense. In certain cases, urban poor steal electricity from the municipal network, construct illegal structures, conduct a black- and gray-market economy and so evade tax payments, trespass into public spaces, and engage in other such actions that defy the order established by the stronger side. These actions, aimed at survival, challenge the state's authority. The state's harsh reaction to this bears the intruders into the political arena. They organize collectively in order to redistribute assets and social opportunities and achieve cultural and political autonomy. The state is not prepared to lose its authority or means of controlling those who are perceived as dangerous. These opposing interests lead to conflict.

The first signs of quiet encroachment appeared in Jerusalem long ago. In the long run, when the Palestinians who suffer as a result of the wall carry out their own Intifada—whether for purely economic reasons or for national-religious ones—Israel will find that it cannot effectively control these areas and they will become focal points of friction. Jerusalem's Jewish neighborhoods will be the first to pay the price of this confrontation and the quality of life in the city will decline.

From the start, Israel has seen the Palestinians in Jerusalem as a demographic problem and as a threat. Israel's inability to restrict the number of Palestinians in the city ended up breaking the taboo against dividing sovereignty in Jerusalem and increased Israeli anxiety about the "other." Israel is not prepared and not able to offer East Jerusalem the kind of affirmative action that would create full equality under Israeli sovereignty. Israel does not have the financial resources to do so, nor does it wish to see East Jerusalem's Arabs flourish. That would turn East Jerusalem into a magnet and a power center, exacerbate Israel's demographic problem, and cast a shadow over Jerusalem's claim to be a Jewish city. For the same reasons, Israel cannot agree to turn Jerusalem as a whole into a binational, open, and egalitarian city, shared equally by Jews and Palestinians. That would run counter to Israeli policy since 1967, but even more so to the definition of Israel and the Zionist movement, which defines Israel's capital as a Jewish city that belongs exclusively to Israel. Nor can Israel agree to the creation of a neutral city, blind to nationality, oriented to supplying the needs—some of them religious—of its inhabitants. Neither Israel nor the Palestinians want that. The Palestinians also want a capital that is exclusively theirs. They, like the Israelis, seek self-government with full sovereign powers over the members of their ethnic-national group.

The development of borders in Jerusalem has been characterized by an increasing level of politicization. There is no reason to believe that the political systems in Israel and the Palestinian Authority will retreat from their direct and deep involvement in Jerusalem. Each of them sees the city as its capital. As the diplomatic process advances, the city thus becomes more politicized. Any solution that seeks to neutralize politics in Jerusalem is therefore utopian. Moreover, border lines that were, in the past, largely flexible and permeable, are now toughening, as a result of the Intifada and permanent status talks. What were once bridgeable fissures become unbridgeable ones if the political system is unable to neutralize them. Both sides lose from the current situation, and Jerusalem is declining.

Rather than imposing on the city arrangements that clash with its natural development, the Geneva initiative proposes to take these realities into account and to institutionalize them. The agreement continues in the direction that Israel began at the Camp David summit and brings it to fruition, taking into account the circumstances created by the current Intifada. It should be recalled that the Israeli proposals on Jerusalem at Camp David did not come out of thin air, and that the taboo was not broken overnight. Their origin lay in the Israeli establishment's discourse in the 1990s on the need to "strengthen Jerusalem." The discourse tacitly acknowledged that the annexation of Jerusalem had left the city in a weak position. The discourse took place in the conceptual framework created in 1967, but did not produce a comprehensive policy. Here and there, Israel took measures to enforce its rule in East Jerusalem, but these were only marginally effective and did not produce a fundamental change. In 2000, the Barak administration realized that force and unilateral actions could not achieve what Israel had not succeeded in achieving in the past, before the first Intifada and the Oslo agreements. Israel would, they understood, have to further its objectives through diplomacy. The Barak government can take credit for an important and unprecedented breakthrough, but it was unable to take its analysis to its logical conclusion and reach the finish line.

IMAGINED JERUSALEM

Its inhabitants perceive Jerusalem first and foremost as a real place, as the place where they live. Their houses, streets, and neighborhoods are an urban space, a concrete place that the individual touches, walks and drives through, and smells each day. This personal, intimate space spreads into the public space.

But those who are not its inhabitants perceive Jerusalem as a symbol, as an impersonal space and as an abstract one. For them, Jerusalem symbolizes a space of collective entities, whose focus lies far from the physical space. Jerusalem thus turns from a reality into a symbol. The city's inhabitants are often also swept up by this perception.

Jerusalem's transformation into a symbol takes place simultaneously on several levels. As a national capital, it symbolizes the nation and national unity. As a historical city, it is a collective memory and symbol of a nation's past. As a holy city, it is a site of pilgrimage for both secular and religious pilgrims, whether Jewish, Christian, or Muslim. As a disputed and frontier city, Jerusalem is the largest outpost of both Israel and Palestine, a symbol of their hold on the land as a whole. Jerusalem's mystique, and the close connection among all these symbolic meanings—to the point where they become congruent—turn Jerusalem into an image, a place that is not a place, a place that is above place (Eran and Gurevitch 1991). This results in the "deterritorialization" of Jerusalem. The transformation into a symbol increases the number of people who live in the city virtually; Jews, Christians, and Muslims make a pilgrimage to it each time they pray. Jerusalem thus "exports" itself, and becomes a city-place beyond its physical being. This is significant for the struggle for control. Jerusalem grants a sublime, spiritual dimension to the political, mundane struggle for sovereignty. Its symbolic, as well as its physical, inhabitants enlist in the battle. These symbols and points of view are expressed in pictures, ceremonies, words, sculptures, songs, and sacred architecture. Jews, Christians, and Muslims living in Asia, Europe, or the United States are liable to view the Holy Land through these works. For all of them, Jerusalem is its essence.

Actual and imagined Jerusalem are connected in one more way. Both symbolically and physically, Jerusalem is a city of stones and of a holy mountain. It is the city of the Temple Mount, the Western Wall, the Holy Sepulcher, the cemetery on the Mount of Olives, David's Tomb, and the Old City walls. The public space is also made of stones—Sir Ronald Storrs, the British military governor of Jerusalem (1917–1920), ordered that all new structures be built of stone. The order was, for the most part, observed and reaffirmed by the regimes that subsequently ruled the city. Consequently, Jerusalem's hard and holy symbols have been reproduced throughout its public spaces, and they expand from the core of the Old City to all of its public spheres.

SHLOMO BEN-AMI PROPOSES

In the winter of 1996, a friend recommended me as a speaker on the Jerusalem issue for a young leadership seminar hosted by Professor Shlomo Ben-Ami, who was seeking a place on the Labor party's slate for the Knesset; the seminar was a platform for his primary campaign (this section includes passages from Klein 2003b). I met Ben-Ami a few more times before the general elections of May 1996, and the meetings became more frequent in the months that followed, as the new member of the Knesset put together a brainstorming team. The team served as a forum for discussion of parliamentary initiatives and of diplomatic, social, and educational issues that he sought to bring to the top of the public agenda. In mid-1997, after Shimon Peres resigned from the post of party leader, Ben-Ami was one of four candidates who sought to replace him. Ehud Barak won (followed by Yossi Beilin), but Ben-Ami made a good third-place showing. He enjoyed broad support from intellectuals and the disadvantaged, Jews and Arabs, religious and secular Jews, who believed that he could give the party a badly needed face lift and appeal to sectors of the public to which Barak, a former army chief of staff, had no connection. This set the stage for Ben-Ami's first-place finish in the next round of primaries for Labor's Knesset slate in 1999. I did not take part in the internal Labor contest, and Ben-Ami did not ask me to join the party, or to campaign for him. I had no interest or expertise in party politics. Ben-Ami, who had shown himself to be an adept politician, certainly needed no advice from me.

Ben-Ami spent 1998 writing his book *A Place for Everyone* (1998). In collaboration with his colleague, Professor Eli Bar-Navi, Ben-Ami presented his social and political philosophy. During his work on the book, Ben-Ami asked me to prepare him a working paper on Jerusalem. On the basis of data and recommendations produced by the team from the Jerusalem Institute for Israel Studies that examined this issue, and my own book, *Jerusalem: The Contested City* (Klein 2001), which I was then in the advanced stages of writing. I gave the paper the title "Jerusalem: A Mutual Israeli–Palestinian Embrace."

In 1998, it was impossible for any Israeli politician in the Labor Party or Meretz to propose drawing a border between Jerusalem's Jewish and Arab neighborhoods in the sharp and unambiguous way proposed by President Clinton in 2000, and as proposed in the Geneva agreement. I myself could not conceive of such a possibility.

My paper suggested dividing the Jerusalem region into three rings. The outer ring would include the more distant East Jerusalem suburbs, such as Abu-Dis, al-Za'im, Anata Hizma, al-Ram, Dahiat al-Barid, and Qalandiya. The Palestinian state would enjoy full sovereignty in this area, and a new Arab municipality of al-Quds would be established and wield full municipal authority. The outer border of the Arab city, within the territory of the Palestinian state, would be determined by Palestinian institutions.

The middle ring would be a narrow one. It would encompass those Arab neighborhoods that are part of the territory Israel annexed in 1967 but that lie outside the inner ring of Jewish neighborhoods and include the area between the inner ring and Israel's annexation border—among them Um Tuba, Sur Baher, Isawiyya, Sho'afat, and Beit Hanina. In this ring, the supreme sovereignty would be Israeli, but the Arab municipality would supply all services, control construction and planning, and be responsible for physical infrastructure and taxation.

The inner ring would encompass the area of Jewish population, and form an arch from Gilo and Ramat Rachel in the south, via the Mount of Olives, to Neveh Ya'akov and Ramot in the north and west. This ring, created by Israeli construction, would encircle the religious and historical heart of East Jerusalem and the Old City. The Palestinian community in this ring would remain under Israeli sovereignty, but the Palestinian municipality of al-Quds would supply municipal services and have certain powers, among these in the areas of education and culture, communications, street cleaning, preservation of ancient buildings, and archaeology. The Palestinian Waqf would manage al-Haram al-Sharif. These arrangements would express Palestinian national and religious attachment to these areas. If Israel opposed having these services supplied directly by the Arab municipality, consideration could be given to privatizing the services and contracting them to a private Arab body. Inhabitants of the Arab quarters would vote in the Palestinian national elections for Palestinian elective bodies, and on the municipal level they would have the right to decide whether to vote in the municipal elections of Jerusalem or of the Arab municipality.

The Arab neighborhoods in all three rings would be contiguous in territory, connected by roads under Palestinian control. If necessary to provide contiguity, these roads would run through tunnels under Jewish neighborhoods. Within the Jerusalem metropolitan area, there would be freedom of movement and employment for inhabitants and guests. An umbrella Jerusalem regional municipality would be set up to coordinate and resolve disputes between the Jewish and Arab cities. The regional administration would be divided into two branches, Israeli and Palestinian. Each of these branches would consist of the municipality and of independent settlements in the region and coordinate between them. On the Israeli side, these settlements would include Ma'aleh Adumim, Adam, Givat Ze'ev, Beitar, Kiryat Sefer, the Gush Etzion settlements, and settlements to Jerusalem's west. Above these two branches would be a Jerusalem regional council composed of equal numbers of Israeli and Palestinian representatives.

The pages (126–30) devoted to Jerusalem in Ben-Ami's book clearly reflect my paper. He challenged the concept of united Jerusalem. Unlike many other politicians, he had no hesitations about stating that the city was divided nationally and ethnically. Israel must acknowledge the constraints that the reality of Jerusalem placed on the dream that many

Israelis had held since 1967, and reach an arrangement that would take into account and institutionalize that reality. Ben-Ami proposed that, under Israeli sovereignty, the Palestinian quarters would enjoy functional sovereignty and would be linked administratively and politically to the Palestinian state and its capital. Coordination between the two municipalities and the neighborhoods would be accomplished in a metropolitan framework. The status quo regarding Jewish prayer would be preserved at holy sites. He also suggested granting the Temple Mount and the Church of the Holy Sepulcher extraterritorial status, like that of the Vatican. However, Ben-Ami did not in his book provide a detailed proposal for the administrative structure of Jerusalem and for the division of powers between the two municipalities on the metropolitan level.

Ben-Ami's book was an Israeli bestseller for several weeks, and his analysis of the Jerusalem dilemma attracted considerable attention. It was precisely what Ehud Barak needed on his way to the prime minister's office, which he won in May 1999. During his campaign, Barak cited A Place for Everyone's social policy proposals, but avoided addressing the section on Jerusalem. Constrained by his political need to avoid angering public opinion, his lack of knowledge, and his profound faith in the concept of "united Jerusalem under Israeli sovereignty forever" that had become part of the consciousness of more than a generation of Israelis, Barak promised to preserve a united Jerusalem as Israel's capital. He maintained this position until the Camp David summit.

The future of Jerusalem had, however, been under discussion in a number of the track-two negotiations discussed in chapter 1. The ideas and proposals that emerged from these discussions shared many common features. All accepted that Jerusalem must be addressed as a metropolitan area and not simply as a city. They also took as given that West Jerusalem is inalienably Israeli and that the subject of negotiation is the part of the city lying beyond the pre-1967 border. All the proposals also granted Israeli superiority in the administration of and sovereignty over the metropolitan area. Palestinian superiority was never considered. Most of the proposals call for a metropolitan coordinating committee but not an umbrella municipality. The exceptions in this regard are the Madrid document, which provides a model along the lines of a city-state and an egalitarian metropolitan administrative structure; and the Beilin–Abu-Mazen understandings, in which the umbrella municipality is the source of authority and resources for the two submunicipalities. It should be emphasized, however, that the Beilin–Abu-Mazen document specifies that the umbrella municipality's governing council will have an Israeli majority. All the proposals agree that the Jerusalem region will contain two national capitals, each of which will be in the sovereign territory of its state. Furthermore, all the models reject the physical division of Jerusalem and the construction of a physical barrier between the Israeli and Palestinian cities. Such a barrier was inconceivable before the Intifada of 2000. Everyone assumed that the metropolitan area would have two borders. The international border would be the outer line of the city, while within the city there would be an administrative border that was open and permeable. These approaches saw no difficulty in creating a barrier between the two cities and the interiors of their countries. In other words, there would be a barrier between each capital and the country to which it belonged. The principle was an entirely open Jerusalem, alongside a recognition that both Jerusalems, Israeli and Palestinian, had an urban character different from the cities of each country's interior. However, only some of the proposals took this idea further. They proposed to institutionalize this difference and enhance the status of each city. In this view, both the Israeli and Palestinian capitals would receive powers that, in the case of other cities, were held by the central government.

Most of these proposals specified that Israel would retain sovereignty over most of the Palestinian area, with the Palestinians receiving functional powers on the neighborhood level. A minority offered other models: joint sovereignty via the umbrella municipality, divided sovereignty, blurred sovereignty, deferment of the decision on sovereignty as part of an agreement on administrative procedures, or acknowledgement by both sides that sovereignty was contested while agreeing to divide administration between them. Dividing sovereignty along ethnic-national lines was proposed as only one alternative, and even then the Old City was not to be included under Palestinian sovereignty. None proposed partition in the Old City and Temple Mount, but most called for changing the status quo that had prevailed in these areas since 1967. It is important to emphasize that no proposed change in the status quo included permitting Jewish prayer on the Temple Mount or any other change in Israel's favor. On the contrary, the various proposals for the status of the Temple Mount stipulated granting administrative status to state representatives, as opposed to the Muslim Waqf administration that runs the site today. They also spoke of extraterritorial status as opposed to the sovereignty that Israel claims today, of religious administration based on Palestinian law, and of permitting a Palestinian flag to fly over the site. At the same time, it should be noted that none of the proposals suggested full Palestinian sovereignty on the Temple Mount.

The different proposals regarding the Temple Mount were seen as appropriate also for the area around it. Some of the proposals enlarge the special status of the Temple Mount to include the entire "Holy Basin." The concept of the Holy Basin was developed by the ECF (Centro Italiano Per La Pace in Medio Oriento 2001).

The Temple Mount is the symbolic and geographic center of the Holy Basin, which encompasses the historical and religious heart of Jerusalem: the Old City, Mt. Zion and its adjacent Christian cemetery, the archaeological excavations in the City of David and along the Old City walls, the Muslim cemetery outside the Golden Gate, and the Mount of Olives. The ECF offered four alternatives regarding sovereignty in the Holy Basin: divided sovereignty, with each side, or an agent for it, responsible for administering its art; indefinite sovereignty, unspecified in the agreement; postponement of a decision on sovereignty; and joint sovereignty, in which there would be specific arrangements allowing for the common administration of the entire area as a single unit, or in which the basin would be divided into smaller areas, each one to be administered by one of the sides. Joint management was also proposed in the case of the two alternatives in which the question of sovereignty was left undecided. The ECF alternatives also presented three options for how administrative powers would be divided. In the first, they would be divided on an ethnic-national basis, leaving only the Old City's Jewish Quarter under Israeli administration. The Christian, Armenian, and Muslim quarters would be run by the Palestinians, and sites in the Holy Basin would be managed by the community for which they were holy. In the second, the entire Holy Basin would be administered as a unit, with no partition. In this case, the administrative body would be the metropolitan coordinating committee or an agent for it. In the third, the general administration of the second option would be limited to infrastructure, planning and construction, architecture, preservation, and archaeology. Educational and religious services would be provided by the two submunicipalities. Water, electricity, telephones, gas, and garbage disposal would be provided by subcontractors chosen by the inhabitants. In each case, overarching security powers for the Holy Basin would be retained by Israel. In places where there is contact between Israelis and Palestinians and in cases of contention between members of the two communities, a joint police force would take action.

According to the ECF proposals, the Temple Mount does not include the Western Wall, only the inner compound. The Western Wall appears as a holy site within the Old City, of equal status to, for example, the Church of the Holy Sepulcher. There is no question of sovereignty for these sites if the parties decide that only the Temple Mount remains in dispute. In such a case, the Western Wall would be under Israeli sovereignty and the Church of the Holy Sepulcher under Palestinian sovereignty. The ECF's options for sovereignty on the Temple Mount were: no decision, with the question of sovereignty remaining open; postponement of a decision; joint sovereignty over the entire area; a declaration by both sides that they view God as the sovereign; and Palestinian sovereignty over the area of al-Aqsa only, granting Israel the status of a claimant to sovereignty on the area of the Dome of the Rock. Regarding administration, the proposal was that the Temple Mount continue to be run by the Waqf, whether directly or at the behest of the joint metropolitan council, which would allow each religion to manage its own holy sites. Construction, archaeological excavations, and physical changes would require the council's approval. Nonreligious activity, such as political rallies and nationalist incitement, would be forbidden. Free access to the site would be guaranteed, but Jewish prayer would be forbidden on the site. A second possibility was to hand the management of the Temple Mount over to an international commission. This would include representatives of Israel, or representatives of Israeli and Diaspora Jewry. Alternatively, the commission would be composed of representatives of the Arab countries and perhaps also the United States and Europe, but without Israelis. Like the provisions for the Holy Basin mentioned above, overarching security powers for the Temple Mount would remain in Israeli hands. An Israeli force would be responsible for perimeter security of the Temple Mount from the outside. In the case of a serious security danger, an Israeli or a joint Israeli–Palestinian force would enter the compound. In normal periods, however, public order on the

Temple Mount would be in the hands of a unit under the auspices of the Islamic body that runs the site.

THE ISRAELI GOVERNMENT PROPOSES

The Barak government can take the credit for a breakthrough on the Jerusalem issue during the official permanent status talks. It was preceded by a broad public debate that took place, first and foremost, in the local and international press. The issue was also discussed in public and closed conferences and gatherings. The first to change their positions on Jerusalem were members of various elites with whom politicians converse. The change in these elites radiated out into the broader public, and from there back into the elites. The affect on the public seems not to have been direct, but rather through mediators. These were intellectuals, professionals, and members of the middle class, who were the first to revise their positions. The effect spread out from this core. The more the issue became current and central to the national agenda, the more the public turned its gaze to knowledgeable experts. Nonestablishment experts were at the service of the public and had the good fortune not to have competition from the establishment. The establishment was silent because the issue was a taboo. As always, the last to realize that they needed to change their previous positions were the politicians. But they would not have changed had there not been a change in the environment they acted in.

Paradoxically, the right-wing political parties, those most vocally committed to the concept of united, indivisible Jerusalem, made a key contribution to opening the public's eyes to the deficiencies of the position they so ardently advocated. Figures from this side of the political map had accused all Israeli governments since 1994, including the Likud government of Binyamin Netanyahu, of allowing PLO institutions and agents to function in Jerusalem, of the lack of Israeli governing institutions on the east side of the city, and on the failure to enforce Israeli law there. But the effect of these right-wing tirades was to inform the Israeli public that, in fact, Israel was losing control of East Jerusalem and that there was a significant disparity between the rhetoric of a united city and the reality in the field.

This is not the place to provide a detailed account of the official talks and the crystallization of Israel's position on Jerusalem during their progress. It will suffice to sum up Israel's position at the end of the Camp David summit in July 2000 and the Taba talks of January 2001, according to the parameters noted above with regard to the preparatory documents and the understandings reached in track-two talks (Arieli and Pundak 2004; Ben-Ami 2004; Klein 2003b; Matz 2003; Pressman 2003; Pundak 2001; Ross 2004; Rubinstein et al. 2003; Shamir and Maddy-Weitzman 2005; Sher 2001; Swisher 2004).

In general, Israel proposed, under the influence of the preparatory documents from track two, a graduated system of forms of sovereignty over various parcels of territory lying beyond the June 4, 1967, lines. At no time was West Jerusalem on the negotiating table. Israel demanded full sovereignty over its territories in West Jerusalem, as well as over areas in East Jerusalem that were inhabited by Israeli Jews. In areas of Palestinian population, Israel proposed various models of sovereignty. The Palestinian rationale and starting point were different. The Palestinians demanded full sovereignty over those territories inhabited by Palestinians or not inhabited by Israeli Jews. The Palestinians refused to budge from this position. The Israelis, for their part, had more room for maneuver and could display more flexibility. Their positions were modular, as opposed to the one-dimensional and firm Palestinian position. Within a certain framework, to be detailed below, Israel could switch types of sovereignty and parcels of territory. Furthermore, Israel set the agenda for the negotiations, and its delegation had working procedures much superior to those of the Palestinians. The members of the Israeli delegation had fewer differences of opinion, a clear and accepted hierarchy, and procedures for resolving internal disputes. The Palestinians were dysfunctional on all these counts. Further difficulty was added by the American mediator.

A detailed examination of the negotiations reveals that, at the Camp David summit, Israel treated Jerusalem not just as a municipal issue. Israel viewed Jerusalem as a metropolitan area, but this served as a way for Israel to demand the annexation of settlements on the city's far periphery—Gush Etzion, Givat Ze'ev, and Ma'aleh Adumim. There was no discussion of the powers and structure of the components of the city's umbrella municipality. Israel was prepared to accept a Palestinian capital only in that part of Jerusalem in which the Palestinians would enjoy full sovereignty. The idea presented in the Madrid non-paper, that both municipalities would be empowered by their countries to create unique entities, did not enter the discussion. Most of the discussion was about what areas would be under Palestinian sovereignty, and about the Temple Mount.

Israel's position at Camp David was reminiscent of Ben-Ami's concept of the three circles. Israel was prepared to come to terms with Palestinian sovereignty in outer East Jerusalem neighborhoods like Sho'afat, Beit Hanina, Azariya, Abu-Dis, and Sur Baher. For the inner neighborhoods, Israel proposed municipal autonomy, limited to the neighborhood level. Overarching responsibility for the security of the inner arc of neighborhoods, including the Old City, would remain in Israeli hands. The Palestinians, for their part, demanded that all the Arab neighborhoods come under their sovereignty. The Jewish neighborhoods built in formerly Jordanian territory would remain Israeli, but Israel would provide equal territorial compensation for them.

The two sides were also divided over the Old City. Israel wanted the entire area within the city walls to remain under its sovereignty, with the Christian, Muslim, and Armenian quarters receiving municipal autonomy. Alternatively, it proposed that the decision on sovereignty be deferred, or that the two sides agree that both claimed sovereignty and that in the meantime the Old City would be under an autonomous administration. The American compromise offered at the end of the Camp David summit was that the Old City be divided between Israeli and Palestinian sovereignty. The Muslim and Christian quarters would be Palestinian, while the Jewish and Armenian quarters would be Israeli. Israel was prepared to accept this as part of a package deal in which the Palestinians accepted Israel's other positions on the Old City and Temple Mount. The PLO firmly rejected the compromise.

Israel's proposals about the Old City were part of its concept of the Holy Basin. As a first possibility, Israel proposed that the Holy Basin be under Israeli supreme sovereignty, with the Palestinians there enjoying municipal autonomy. Christian and Muslim holy sites would be administered by their religious bodies, and the Palestinians would receive full sovereignty over several compounds of homes in the Muslim Quarter, through which would run a road linking al-Haram al-Sharif to Palestinian sovereign territory. The Palestinian state could locate its president's office in these homes.

A second possibility that Israel suggested was that both sides declare that the issue of sovereignty over al-Haram al-Sharif/the Temple Mount was unresolved, and that resolution of the issue would be deferred to an unknown date. A third Israeli alternative was that Israel retain supreme sovereignty over the Temple Mount, but that Palestine would have religious custodianship of the site under the aegis of an international body to be established by the Islamic states and the UN. This arrangement would permit the use of national flags and symbols on the Temple Mount. To balance the picture, Israel insisted at Camp David that a Jewish prayer compound be set aside on the site.

The Palestinians rejected all these proposals. They demanded full and exclusive sovereignty over al-Haram al-Sharif, while agreeing to Israeli sovereignty over the Western Wall and the Jewish Quarter. The American compromise proposed toward the end of the summit was that Palestine would have sovereignty over the al-Haram al-Sharif plaza, while Israel would enjoy sovereignty under the surface, where Israel claimed the ruins of the Temple lay. Israel accepted this proposal, but it was rejected by the Palestinians.

In the negotiations conducted at the end of the summit, Israel withdrew its demand for a Jewish prayer compound on the Temple Mount. On the other issues, its position remained the same. It proposed a special regime for the Old City and Holy Basin, in which administrative powers would be divided between the two sides, with the question of sovereignty to be deferred. Alternatively, an agreement could state that both sides maintained mutually exclusive claims to sovereignty. According to the Israeli proposal, these incompatible claims would not prevent the two sides from agreeing to an end to their state of conflict and to end their claims against each other. The Palestinians rejected this idea because an end to claims would prevent them from seeking to change a fundamental state of affairs that they opposed—the lack of Palestinian sovereignty over al-Haram al-Sharif and the Old City's Arab quarters.

Israel suggested another possibility—agreeing that God would have sovereignty over the area. But, from an administrative point of view, Israel proposed institutionalizing the status quo, which granted the Palestinians limited powers while Israel retained supreme authority. The Palestinians perceived this as a trick that sought to enlist God to justify their limited authority on al-Haram al-Sharif, and to give Israel preferred status. It seemed to them unfair and inequitable. Israel also reiterated its proposal from Camp David that the Temple Mount be placed under the sovereignty of an international body that would in turn grant the Palestinians custodianship of the site. But under this proposal Palestinian authority would also be limited.

The two sides made progress during the Taba talks, and the areas of agreement expanded. As in the Camp David talks, Israel proposed viewing Jerusalem as a metropolitan area only to justify the annexation of settlements. There was no discussion of the possibility that both municipalities, Israeli and Palestinian, upgrade the status of their respective parts of Jerusalem. Both sides agreed on the establishment of a committee that would coordinate between the two municipalities, rather than an umbrella municipality. For the first time, Israel proposed a "soft" physical partition between the two cities—a barrier containing several crossing points. Only Israeli inhabitants of Jerusalem and Palestinian inhabitants of al-Quds would be allowed free passage between the two cities. Everyone else would require visas. The Old City would be open, and people could enter it freely. Control would take place at the exits. The Palestinians did not accept the Israeli proposal—they wanted to maintain a completely open city. In keeping with this, they proposed that the check points be placed outside both municipalities. In other words, they suggested that Jerusalem have only an external physical border, while the administrative boundary within the city be totally permeable. Alternatively, they demanded a "hard" border that would completely separate the Palestinian and Israeli municipal areas, with no free passage for the residents of al-Quds and Jerusalem between the two sides.

The discussion of the sovereignty issue at the Taba talks was based on President Clinton's proposal—all Jewish neighborhoods would be Israeli, and all Arab neighborhoods Palestinian. Israel accepted this idea in principle. Its argument with the Palestinians focused, first, on the Har Homa neighborhood. Israel considered this neighborhood an established fact and claimed that, according to the Clinton parameters, the neighborhood should fall under Israeli sovereignty. The Palestinians refused to apply the Clinton parameters to the small existing part of the neighborhood, on the grounds that it had been built subsequent to and in violation of the Oslo agreements. For its part, Israel was unenthusiastic, to put it mildly, about applying the Clinton parameters to the Holy Basin and the Old City. President Clinton's proposal about the Temple Mount recognized that each side felt a connection to the site, which was central to their religion. Hence the proposal to grant Palestine sovereignty over the compound and Israel sovereignty underneath. Alternatively, Clinton proposed that Israel receive functional sovereignty in the issue of excavations under the al-Haram al-Sharif compound.

The Palestinians were extremely indisposed to these proposals and demanded full sovereignty over the site—which Israel was utterly unwilling to accept. Because of these diametrically opposed positions, the issue of the Temple Mount was not discussed at Taba. As an alternative, Israel proposed the establishment of a special regime, in accordance with its proposal at Camp David, or division of sovereignty in the Old City. According to this proposal, Palestine would be sovereign in the Muslim and Christian quarters, whereas Israeli would be sovereign in the Armenian and Jewish quarters, the archaeological parks in the City of David and along the Temple Mount wall, as well as the Mount of Olives and its access road. Israel also offered options familiar from the previous stage of negotiations—suspension of the sovereignty issue and joint administration of the Old City, in accordance with the parameters Israel presented at Camp David; or giving sovereignty to an international body that would grant the Palestinians co-administrative powers, so that the source of authority would not be Israeli. The Palestinians, however, stuck tenaciously to the Clinton parameters.

In general, during the official negotiations Israel conducted on the Temple Mount during 2000, it sought to change the status quo by establishing a Jewish prayer compound and/or creating an official division of sovereignty, so that Israel would have sovereignty-expressing powers. Israel did not treat the Temple Mount/al-Haram al-Sharif as a single unit that included the Western Wall/al-Buraq, as was accepted practice in Judaism and Islam. It claimed the Western Wall entirely for itself, and a part of the Temple Mount. In addition, Israel was not prepared to give full recognition to sole Palestinian sovereignty over the site.

TIME TO CHANGE DIRECTIONS

I began to rethink my position in September 2000, even before the outbreak of the second Intifada. I told Ben-Ami that Israel's insistence on receiving subterranean sovereignty on the Temple Mount, on the grounds that the ruins of the Temple were there, was a problematic position. The belief in the existence of the ruins was characteristic of Christian and Jewish fundamentalists, but was not accepted by mainstream Judaism. This the seminal exegete of the Talmud, Rashi (Rabbi Shlomo Yitzhaki), wrote in his commentary on the Talmud's Sukkah Tractate (41a; also in Tractate Rosh Hashanah 30a): "The future Temple we await, built and perfect, will be revealed and will come from heaven." The commentators, known as the Tosefot, state (Tractate Shavu'ot 15b) that the Third Temple "is made by itself, by heaven." For generations, these two glosses have appeared on the same page as the Talmudic text. Furthermore, for a believer, whether Muslim or Jewish, sanctity and perfection are congruous. Sanctity cannot be physically divided. Even before the Camp David summit convened, I believed that Israel's central interest was gaining Palestinian and Islamic recognition of our historical and religious ties to the Temple Mount. Such recognition would be no less significant than the PLO's recognition of Israel in 1993. It would constitute recognition of the Jewish people's organic connection to the land of Israel and of the legitimacy of the Jewish return to Zion. This is far more important than a theoretical right to conduct archaeological excavations on the Temple Mount. My conviction grew even stronger after the brusque Palestinian rejection, at Camp David, of any Jewish rights on the site. That rejection came in response to the Israeli demand for a Jewish prayer compound that would operate under Israeli authority. The Palestinian response boomeranged—it burned into the consciousness of many secular Israelis that the Palestinians did not recognize a Jewish claim to Jerusalem. That had to be corrected.

I further revised my position in November that same year, this time with regard to the concept of the Holy Basin. In the face of the Intifada and the vast fissure that had opened between the two peoples, it had become problematic. The Holy Basin had originally been meant to remove the area from political dispute and to grant it a special status. In light of the Israeli–Palestinian dispute after Camp David, and the violent confrontations of the Intifada, I doubted whether such a removal was possible. The segregation of an area under a special regime, in which there would have to be close cooperation in a large number of functions, required a great deal of good will and mutual trust. Such was lacking in Jerusalem after the uprising began. In a situation of mutual distrust on the municipal level, between religious establishments, and between the populations, it would be difficult to maintain a special regime—at best because of misunderstanding and, more likely, because of malice. It would be difficult to achieve a high level of cooperation, at least at the first stage of the special regime. Furthermore, it was necessary to respond to a justified Palestinian question: would the lives of the special area's inhabitants be intolerable? How would the inhabitants find their bearings in the tangle of special arrangements? Operational simplicity is an important criterion for judging whether an arrangement can endure. It would have been a consideration even if there had been no Intifada.

I therefore advised Ben-Ami to restrict the application of such special arrangements. Instead of applying them to units of territory, I maintained, they should apply to specific areas of life. They would apply only in locations in which there is intensive and frequent contact between Israelis and Palestinians. In practice, this meant a few streets in the Old City (the *shuk* or bazaar, the road to the Western Wall and the Temple Mount, the Mount of Olives, and the Nablus Gate plaza) and a small number of areas of life. Territorially, these regimes would apply both to places under Israeli sovereignty and to places under Palestinian sovereignty. They would not apply to the entire Holy Basin, nor to the entire arch of internal neighborhoods. In areas in which there was not contact between the two populations, there would be a clear division of sovereignty and powers, according to the parameter that Arab neighborhoods would be under Arab control, while the Jewish Quarter and Western Wall would be under Israeli sovereignty. Since this would give the Palestinians three of the Old City's four quarters, leaving one to Israel, it was also called the 3:1 proposal.

The Camp David summit and subsequent events demonstrated that the religious issue in Jerusalem had not been addressed properly. Barak blocked two observant members of his party, Avraham Burg and Rabbi Michael Melchior, from being involved in the religious issue, even though both men were keen to contribute. Barak and his associates assumed that the involvement of religious people in the negotiations, and opening a religious discourse, would necessarily dictate a fundamentalist line that would restrict political room for maneuver and Barak's control over the negotiations. This was a typically "yuppie," elitist view of religion. They assumed that all religious people were fundamentalists, and that only extremists were authentic Jews. Unaware of the variety of Jewish religious discourse, they failed to encourage moderate religious voices. Paradoxically, Barak and his advisers wanted to gain the favor of Jewish fundamentalists by changing the status quo on the Temple Mount and providing a Jewish prayer site there. This misconceived notion contributed no little to the failure of the Camp David talks. It was an error to assume that the establishment of a synagogue on the Temple Mount would help achieve an agreement, guarantee that the agreement be observed, and produce mass support for it. The opposite was true. The demand stymied an agreement, and the Palestinian delegation rudely rejected the Israeli proposal. This poured more fuel on the fire. Even if there had been a Palestinian leadership that would sign such an agreement, it could not have been sold to Palestinian Muslims. Furthermore, a synagogue on the Temple Mount would not make the agreement more durable. Since the minority opinion that Jews are allowed to tread on the Temple Mount is held largely by Jewish extremists, they would be the worshippers in the synagogue. During their prayers, they would see hundreds of thousands of Palestinian and other Muslims walking undisturbed on the Temple Mount, headed by a Palestinian president who would host foreign heads of state there. The contrast between the small compound where the Jews were permitted to pray and the much larger area open to Muslims, like the gap between the Jews' vision of rebuilding the Temple and the reality of their small synagogue, would lead to profound frustration. That, in turn, would lead to attempts to eliminate the dissonance. The proximity to the holy site would not dampen their messianic fervor. Rather, it would fan the fires to heights not ever seen before.

No less problematic was the link the Israeli delegation at Camp David made between the demand for Israeli superior sovereignty on the Temple Mount, or for subterranean sovereignty, and the justification it cited: the existence of the Temple's ruins underground. This claim roused Palestinian fears dating back to the 1920s, when their leadership declared that Zionism's ultimate goal was to build Judaism's Third Temple on the ruins of the existing Muslim shrines (Porath 1995, chapter 7). The Israelis thus transferred the link between political sovereignty and the Temple from the past into the future, and this without preparation or consultation on the religious issue.

It was also politically motivated—Barak wanted to market his agreement with the Palestinians to religious and hawkish-nationalist camps by a dramatic change in the status of Jewish prayer on the Temple Mount. A year before the Intifada, in October 1999, I published an article in the newspaper *Ha'aretz* arguing that Palestinian recognition of

Israel's historical, religious, and national rights on the Temple Mount does not require translating that into a Jewish right to pray on the site. I had good reason to believe that such would be Israel's position. But I was unable to get my message across.

In December 2000, I reached the conclusion that, in light of the way negotiations had been conducted, and in the wake of the al-Aqsa Intifada, there was no choice but to respond to the Palestinian demand for full sovereignty on the Temple Mount. In parallel, the position held by the vast majority of the Israeli public, which viewed the Temple Mount as an expression of the Jewish people's religious and historical connection to the Land of Israel and Jerusalem, would be acknowledged. Most of the Israeli public does not want a Third Temple built and does not see the renewal of the sacrificial service as an ideal way of worshipping God. Israelis have a hard time accepting modern religious Judaism, which is a relatively democratic and open replacement for the cult of the Temple and its sacrifices. They certainly do not seek a return to ancient practices that are foreign to modern sensibilities. The Temple Mount is sacred to Jews because it is the place that God chose to establish his presence, not because of Israeli sovereignty. Sanctity does not require sovereignty. The state of Israel has no right to concede the Temple Mount's religious sanctity, because it is religion and not the state that determines sanctity. But the state can impose or concede sovereignty, just as it can make arrangements for the observance of religious rituals on the site (Klein 2003b). Furthermore, there is a distinction between, on the one hand, practical powers and a future demand to actualize the Jewish connection to the site, and, on the other hand, the Jewish people's historical and religious roots there. The latter are historical facts accepted in the Jewish and Christian worlds, and the Palestinians can recognize them if Israel does not demand, in their name, sovereign or administrative powers. In exchange for giving up its claim for symbolic sovereignty, Israel can demand that Palestine offer a concession of equal value—recognition of the Jewish people's religious and historical connection to the Temple Mount. It would be an extension of the mutual recognition that Israel and the PLO declared in 1993. Barak tried to reach this result by negotiation from Camp David onward. Paradoxically, he achieved the opposite—the Palestinians refused to accept any Jewish tie to the site.

On November 10, 2000, a declaration signed by 150 Palestinian intellectuals stated that they did not accept the Palestinian Authority administration's position that the Jews and Israel have no link to the Temple Mount. The declaration stated that "Both sides must recognize the spiritual and historical affinities of each other to sites and locations within their own borders and they must affirm and guarantee the access and protection of the other people to these places within their own borders. But in neither case should the existence of such sites be used to advance extra-territorial claims to locations within each other's borders." Some of the signatories would later support the Geneva initiative and some would become part in the Palestinian negotiating team. The declaration sought to preserve the principle of reciprocity. Recognition of the Jewish spiritual and historical tie to the Temple Mount must be accompanied by a parallel recognition by Israel of the Muslim stake in the site. The signatories were concerned that Israel would use Palestinian recognition to support its demand to political sovereignty over the site, or to deny sovereignty to the Palestinians, as in the proposals submitted at Camp David. A similar formulation about mutual recognition of religious and historical ties to all of Jerusalem, and not just to holy sites, was discussed in several track-two meetings. The goal was for the Israeli side to recognize the historical fact that neighborhoods in West Jerusalem—Baka, Katamon, Malha, Lifta, and Ein Karem—were until 1948 partly or entirely Palestinian Arab neighborhoods. In turn the Palestinian side would recognize the Jewish link to East Jerusalem and to the historical and religious heart of the city, and not just to the new, western side of the city.

President Clinton hinted at this direction when, on December 23, 2000, he presented to both official delegations his ideas for resolving the conflict. He said: "I know you have been discussing a number of formulations, and you can agree one of these. I add to these two additional formulations guaranteeing Palestinian effective control over the Haram while respecting the conviction of the Jewish people." The Geneva initiative continues in this direction.

ONE CITY OR TWO OPEN CAPITALS?

February 2003. An English winter night. A Japanese driver in a Mercedes picked me up at Heathrow Airport. He took me to Woking, in south London, for a meeting funded by Japan in the framework of what would later become the Geneva initiative. I was headed for a night session devoted to Jerusalem, the city I had left a few hours previously, deep in thought. The question was whether the Old City should be open or closed. The concept of the open city had for long been a fixation when Israelis approached the subject of Jerusalem, but it now seemed to belong to a distant time and place. An Israeli-dominated city, in which the Palestinian "other" was either partly or completely ignored, had been the cognitive model for thinking about the city since June 1967. In the meantime, the "other" became ever more visible, concrete, and active; East Jerusalem took on flesh and blood. As talks with the Palestinians progressed, East Jerusalem grew more distant from Israel. It became al-Quds, part of the Palestinian territory, designated as Palestine's future capital. In its bloody way, the Intifada contributed to raising walls between the two parts of Jerusalem (Klein 2004a, 2005).

At the Taba talks, the debate over sovereignty narrowed to the city's historical and religious center. Continuing from there, the Geneva negotiators agreed on a complete vertical partition between Israeli and Palestinian Jerusalem. The goal was to allow both cities to develop in their natural space. Separate cities meant that the Israeli side would not control and oppress the Palestinian side, even through the fiction of an umbrella municipality with an Israeli majority. Roads would link Arab neighborhoods to each other, just as roads would link all the Jewish neighborhoods together. Israeli and Palestinian citizens would be able to travel freely through the territory of their sovereign states without encountering controls or check points. A committee made up of equal numbers of members from both municipalities would coordinate issues relating to the common space of the two cities. The Old City would remain open, but sovereignty there would be divided. Israel would enjoy full sovereignty over the Jewish Quarter and the Western Wall, while Palestine would be sovereign in the Armenian, Christian, and Muslim quarters, and on the Temple Mount. The Old City would be a weapons-free zone, and special permission would be required for those bearing arms because of their responsibilities—police and security personnel—and for special occasions, such as a swearing-in ceremony for soldiers. The Old City would be policed by a multinational force, in addition to Israeli and Palestinian police.

Why did we retain the idea of an open city for the Old City, after we had discarded it for Jerusalem as a whole? Once we agreed that a Palestinian state would be established alongside Israel, and that Palestine would have a sovereign stake in Jerusalem, the consequence was that an international border would run somewhere through Jerusalem, and there would be border crossings between Israel and Palestine. Israel can not permit every Palestinian or tourist visiting the city to enter Israel without any border checks. Similarly, Palestine will not want Israelis to enter its territory without permission. The dilemma was whether it was best to establish border checkpoints outside Jerusalem and al-Quds, and in so doing separate the two capitals from their hinterlands in each country, or to separate the two halves of Jerusalem. In other words, is the idea of an open city preferable to the idea of two open capitals? Even if the preference is for an open city, it might still be necessary first to create a separation. Israel must cease to treat the Palestinian side as inferior, and the Palestinians must construct their own municipality and institutions to empower their population, and establish the norms of a political community after four decades spent on the margins of the Israeli governing apparatus.

Opinions on this cut across both delegations. Nabil Qassis and 'Abd-Rabbu favored complete partition. I also leaned in that direction, after long years in which I had thought in terms of an open city. Like most of the other experts that took part in track-two talks, I had, while advising Barak and Ben-Ami, maintained that check points would be positioned around the two cities, equipped with an electronic identification system that would allow quick and easy passage across that line for Israelis. That was also the preference of the Palestinian delegation at the Taba talks, in response to the Israeli proposal to establish a "soft" physical border between East and West Jerusalem. Now, in London, I had doubts about the necessity and usefulness of maintaining Jerusalem and al-Quds as a single area, in which the two cities would be open to each other. More important, I felt, was freedom of movement in an Israeli Jerusalem that would be open toward and undivided from Israel. Furthermore, it was essential to allow the Arabs of East Jerusalem to establish an independent municipal system, free of Israeli dominance. Partition also makes it possible to maintain the status quo in which there is continuous Israeli sovereignty from West Jerusalem to the Western Wall, without crossing any check points at the Old City gates. Every Israeli will thus feel that the Jewish Quarter and the Western Wall are part of the state of Israel, while every Palestinian will feel the same on his way to al-Haram al-Sharif. Finally, the inhabitants of the Jewish Quarter have a psychological need to have a fence that defends them against the Palestinian majority in the Old City. They will be especially sensitive on Islamic holidays and pilgrimage days to al-Haram al-Sharif. On such days they will be able to close the gates in the wall that will remain open for commerce and tourism on other days. (To make passage through the fence expeditious and easy, I suggested that it have a large number of gates.) Closing the gates will give the Jewish Quarter's residents a sense of security. The Geneva agreement contains concessions that will be very difficult for both sides to assimilate. Success in marketing them to the public depends on our ability to create the least possible change in current living conditions, and to maintain the sense of security of those who are liable to suffer from the change. A drastic change, a sense of reduced security, and mutual distrust, especially after the long and bloody current Intifada, is liable to abort the agreement.

Nazmi Jubeh disagreed, arguing that a rigid division of the Old City would ruin Jerusalem as a living and functioning entity. Every barrier imposes on daily life, and this is especially the case in the Old City, which under conditions of peace can attract millions of tourists. Most of the tourist spots will be in the Palestinian area, and any peace agreement should provide free access to these sites. The check points should thus be placed some distance from the Old City walls. Furthermore, he maintained, a rigid physical barrier is impossible; in some cases Jewish houses share walls with Palestinian walls, and in a few places Jews and Palestinians live on different floors in the same buildings. In other places, you can jump from a roof in one quarter to a roof in another quarter, as he himself had done as a boy. Jubeh's position was that the Old City must remain open, because of its power to fire the imagination of so many in the world. The development of tourism and auxiliary services will help ameliorate the high housing density of the Muslim Quarter and the huge burden now born by the quarter's shoddy infrastructure. Many residents will prefer to move into more spacious apartments outside the Old City and to turn the structures they vacate into stores, restaurants, galleries, and cafes. Jubeh's ultimate vision was of an Old City without residents. It would be a living museum preserving its rich architectural and archaeological treasures, alongside holy sites and the colorful *shuk*. He was supported by Samih al-'Abd, who favored expanding the Old City district to outside the walls. Such a zone would be bounded on one side by the eastern ring road and on the west by the Begin highway. But such a scheme would have required the erection of check points between different Jewish neighborhoods in West Jerusalem, and was thus not realistic. For his part, Yossi Beilin wanted to soften the division, both by establishing a joint municipality that would administer an open Old City, and by registering the two-state ownership of the site some place in the world.

The debate was not about the division of sovereignty, because everyone agreed on partition according to the Clinton parameters, and that the division be marked so that residents and visitors would know in which sovereign territory they were in. The debate was over the regime that would prevail in an Old City divided into two sovereign areas. What was the best way to limit the impairment of municipal operations, to preserve the flow of life, and to create a flexible system that could adjust to future needs? What was the best regime to ensure close coordination between the organs of two countries functioning in an open city, in a situation where, at least in the initial years, there would not be a great deal of mutual trust between them?

The Palestinian delegation had to maneuver among a range of constraints—Israeli interests and the pressures exerted by the Israeli delegation, Palestinian interests and expectations, and the specific expectations of the Arabs of Jerusalem. The latter expectations were less known than the expectations of Palestinians throughout the country. To remedy that, in September 2003 the Palestinian delegation sponsored a survey of East Jerusalem Arabs. The survey included 650 individuals eighteen years of age and older, interviewed in person on a large range of subjects.

Here are some of the results. Of those interviewed, 72 percent felt threatened by Israel, and 71.1 percent named public order and security as the most important things for the al-Quds municipality to ensure after an Israeli withdrawal. A full 56 percent were dissatisfied with the services provided by the Jerusalem municipality, and 89 percent were dissatisfied with the current state of East Jerusalem. In other words, East Jerusalem's inhabitants do not feel that the Israeli regime provides them with security, nor are they satisfied with the way their own institutions and leadership function in East Jerusalem. They are more satisfied with Israel's social security and health insurance systems, which cover the Arab inhabitants of East Jerusalem. Of these, 20.9 percent expressed complete satisfaction, and 55.1 percent partial satisfaction. Only a small number of the respondents frequently cross the invisible line that divides Jewish and Arab Jerusalem. Just 11.2 percent visit West Jerusalem each day, 16.6 percent do so several times a week, 42.8 percent less than that, and 23.5 percent never cross the line. East Jerusalem's Palestinians are highly ambivalent about the future of their city. Only 22 percent think that life will be much better when there is Palestinian sovereignty in East Jerusalem; 40 percent think it will be somewhat better, and 16 percent think it will remain the same. This may link up with the fact that 78 percent of those surveyed estimate that, if Israel withdraws from East Jerusalem it will stop making social security payments there. For that reason, only a narrow majority expects a better standard of living after Israel is gone. It is thus not surprising that only 41.5 percent said that it is vital to assert full Palestinian sovereignty in East Jerusalem. A similar proportion, 40.9 percent, favored only partial Palestinian sovereignty. In other words, the public is divided and there is ambivalence about Palestinian rule. Israel should not, however, be overly pleased with these figures, since they show that it does not enjoy a great deal of support.

The picture is a bit clearer regarding the need for cooperation between the Jerusalem municipality and that of the future al-Quds. A total of 47.7 percent support partial cooperation, while 35.4 percent reject any cooperation between the two. Despite their doubts about whether either an Israeli or Palestinian regime could provide for the needs of the Palestinian population, 69.8 percent stated that they would continue to live in their current location if East Jerusalem were freed from Israeli control, and only 21.1 percent would move elsewhere in Palestine. Only 4.8 percent would consider emigration.

The same ambivalence is evident in other areas. According to 22.3 percent, it is vital to agree on the division of Jerusalem into two capitals. Another 35.5 percent agreed to partition on condition that the border be a "soft line." A further 35 percent favor no division at all. Similarly, when asked about the future relations between Arab East Jerusalem and Jewish West Jerusalem, 48 percent said they support an entirely open city, while 35.4 percent favored a partially open city. Only 9.4 percent supported an absolute partition. Paradoxically, the desire to preserve complete or controlled accessibility characterizes a society in which a majority seldom crosses into West Jerusalem. One possible explanation for this seeming contradiction may be found in the expectations of East Jerusalem's Palestinians. They were asked to rank the areas in which, they believe, there should be unimpeded relations between the two cities after an Israeli withdrawal. The labor market came in first, with 35.5 percent, health insurance and social security scored 26 percent, barrier-free tourism 13.4 percent, and barrier free commerce 11.8 percent. The need to create closer relations between Jews and Arabs scored only 6.2 percent, while the exchange of knowledge and technology scored but 4.9 percent. In other words, the major concern of the Palestinians in East Jerusalem is to continue to benefit from instrumental contact with the Israeli side in areas of daily life, and to have high accessibility to these benefits. Only a few percent want to become closer to the Israeli side.

The findings were unambiguous with regard to the Israeli neighborhoods in Jerusalem. For the Palestinians these are settlements, and the attitude toward them is sharply negative. For 22.5 percent, the solution is to evacuate and destroy the neighborhoods, while another 37.7 percent wants them emptied of Israelis and handed over to Palestinians. Only 8.3 percent advocated letting the Jews remain in the neighborhoods under Palestinian sovereignty.

On the matter of Jews and holy sites, only 6.3 percent of East Jerusalem Palestinians thought it very important to allow Jews to visit their holy sites. Another 57.2 percent supported such access, on the condition of reciprocity—that is, that the Palestinians would be able to visit their own holy site. A full 34.2 percent would not grant the Jews any access at all to holy sites.

Al-Haram al-Sharif arouses very strong feelings, and positions on it contradict the pragmatic approach reflected in the positions on daily life cited above. A full 46.5 percent stated that al-Buraq (the Arabic name of the Western Wall, seen as part of the al-Haram al-Sharif compound) is very important for them and should not be ceded even if that prevented conclusion of a peace agreement. A further 35.8 percent said that no negotiations should be conducted on this issue; only 11.5 percent said that the site could be given up. In other words, potent feelings of absolute and eternal ownership of the Jewish neighborhoods/settlements in East Jerusalem and of the Western Wall gainsay the pragmatic positions the interviewees expressed on their particular interests in the area of daily life. Any agreement will have to balance these two factors, as well as take into account national, Palestine-wide considerations and the need to achieve agreements in other sectors. Gains in other areas may require concessions in Jerusalem. It is therefore reasonable to assume that no Palestinian negotiator could accept anything less than full sovereignty on al-Haram al-Sharif but could recognize Israeli sovereignty over the prayer compound in front of the Western Wall. Furthermore, the unequivocal positions on the East Jerusalem Jewish neighborhoods/settlements and the Temple Mount are inconsistent with the doubt that the survey sample expressed regarding a future Palestinian administration. Neither is it consistent with the hesitant support for some sort of Israeli rule in East Jerusalem. For the Palestinians, Jerusalem is a religious, political, economic, municipal, and social center lying in the center of the West Bank, on the road linking Hebron and Nablus. In the eyes of the Palestinians who negotiated in the Geneva framework, the Jewish people have a religious and historical connection to Old Jerusalem and nearby sites, but the Arabs' ties to the place are stronger in their daily lives, and should trump the Jews' religious and historical claims. The Palestinian delegation wanted to defend every Arab house inhabited by Palestinians and include it in the borders of their state. The Israeli side, for its part, was not prepared to evacuate a single Jewish neighborhood in East Jerusalem, even though, as far as the Palestinians are concerned, these are settlements just like any other. If there is a need to give up sovereignty, or some components of Palestinian sovereignty in East Jerusalem, the Palestinian strategy was that the same should apply to the Jewish side. A special regime could not limit only one side. Amos Oz put the problem succinctly late one night at the final round of negotiations at the Dead Sea, while the Israeli delegation waited to hear the results of another Palestinian consultation. The Palestinians, he said, view Israelis as arrogant occupiers, not as people who are insecure and plagued by nightmares of destruction. The Israelis, for their part, view the Palestinians as cheats, not as people who desire honor, who seek to be treated with respect rather than disdain, and who want to be recognized as human beings and equals.

The dilemmas were quite real throughout the negotiations on Jerusalem. Neither side had a sole claim to all the truth. As always, Jerusalem offers more questions than answers. The choice, then, is not between solutions but between which problems will remain after decisions are made. The Geneva initiative's preferences took form through teamwork. The approach was pragmatic, and we were focused on problem-solving and on how to improve the way the city functions. Open dialogue, and the ability of the participants to work together and respond to their counterparts' needs and fears, paved the way to reaching agreements.

We decided that only the Old City would be completely open. The gates in the city wall that serve primarily those arriving from Israel—the Zion Gate and the Dung Gate—would continue to function, under Israeli sovereignty, as they do today. The gates to the east and north—the Lion's Gate, Herod's Gate, the Nablus Gate, and the New Gate—primarily serve the Palestinian population, and would thus be under Palestinian sovereignty. People could enter the gates freely, and would be monitored on their way out. Israelis and Palestinians would be able to exit freely from the same gate they entered. To exit from a gate under the sovereignty of the neighboring state, an Israeli or Palestinian would have to produce an entry permit to that state. Recognizing that there would be situations and times that require it, each side would be able to seal off its portion of the Old City, for security reasons, for up to a week at a time. A longer closure would require consultations with the other side and with the international force that would be responsible for keeping order in the Old City. This force would help resolve disputes and would, alongside Palestinian and Israeli personnel, police the Old City, and in particular places where the two populations come into contact. Following an initial three-year period, the parties would review these arrangements, which could be revised with the consent of both sides. Among the possibilities will be that of extending this regime beyond the Old City. One option must be to extend it to Mt. Zion, the adjacent Christian cemetery, the City of David archaeological park, and the Mount of Olives. Doing so would require very detailed planning that provides an answer to a range of questions. But the sine qua non is a Palestinian partner in Jerusalem that operates reasonably, and that can serve as an equal partner to the Israeli side. This is important not only to ensure fulfillment of the Palestinian side's commitments, but also to create a situation in which the arrangement is one between two equivalent parties, rather than one between a strong side and one that does not, in fact, exist as an active force in the field.

As the details of the Old City understanding were being put together at the London talks, it became apparent that the two sides could not resolve the disposition of the Jaffa Gate. They had wrangled over the issue at the Taba talks, and it remained in dispute up until the signing of the Geneva agreement. The question was who would have sovereignty at this gate and over the road that follows the inside perimeter of the Old City wall from the Jaffa to the Zion Gates, via the Armenian Quarter. Specifically, this meant the power to order the gate and road closed for security reasons. The Israeli delegation argued that, since the gate faces west, serves those who reach the Old City from the Jewish side of Jerusalem, and constitutes the principal entrance for vehicles headed for the Jewish Quarter, it clearly should be under Israeli sovereignty. Furthermore, the Tower of David, a powerful and important Zionist-Jewish symbol whose symbolic importance equals that of the Western Wall and Rachel's Tomb, lies adjacent to the gate inside the city walls. It could even be said that, in national secular Zionist consciousness, the Tower of David is a more potent symbol than the Temple and Temple Mount. Israel operates an amphitheater, archaeological park, and municipal museum on its grounds. The Palestinian delegation countered by saying that Israeli sovereignty over these sites contradicts the Clinton parameters—no Jews, only Palestinians, live in the area of the Jaffa Gate and Tower of David. The Armenian Patriarchate is situated along the Jaffa-Zion Gate road, and the square inside the Jaffa Gate is a center of Palestinian life for those who come from the Armenian and Christian Quarters to the *shuk* and the Muslim Quarter. If Israel were to close the area, it would infringe on the freedom of movement of the Palestinians who live and work there.

The Palestinians agreed to give Israel the right to undisturbed use of the gate and the road, in accordance with a special protocol to be implemented by the international force. Israel would not, however, be sovereign. In consideration of Israeli sensitivities, the Palestinians were prepared to promise not to fly a Palestinian flag over the Tower of David.

The Israeli side bolstered its claim by arguing that, at the Taba talks, the Palestinian delegation had agreed to Israeli sovereignty over the gate and road. But the Palestinians denied that there had been any such consent to Israeli sovereignty over this section of the Armenian Quarter. The only agreement had been that Jewish-owned homes in the Armenian Quarter would be considered part of the Jewish Quarter if they were contiguous with it. The Palestinians proposed that Israelis could drive to the Jewish Quarter through the Zion Gate (by way of what is called the Pope's Road) and through the Dung Gate. The Israelis countered that the road in question is much too narrow. The Jewish Quarter requires two one-way roads, just as traffic is currently routed in the area. Furthermore, in peacetime tourism will increase and a single road will not be sufficient. True, ideally motor vehicles would not enter the Old City, but the elderly, handicapped, children, and pregnant women require closer access. Furthermore, the Jewish Quarter's population needs to have the use of private vehicles. Banning vehicles could be considered only if the Old City ceases to be a place of residence.

During the discussions in Jordan, I proposed a compromise—that Israel have sovereign powers in defined areas of the administration of the Jaffa Gate, of the road, and of the Tower. The idea was to anchor Israel's authority in the form of sovereign-functional powers. Every function noted in the agreement would be under Israel's sovereign power, and whatever was not specified would be retained by the sovereign—the state of Palestine. This would ensure that, practically, as far as Israeli citizens were concerned, the status quo would continue. If the Palestinian side would not agree to the term "functional sovereignty," the phrasing could be "sovereignty for the purpose of"—for the administration of the Jaffa Gate, security, and policing of those entering and leaving from Israel (including police patrols on the western part of the city wall, which we requested because of Israeli distrust of the Palestinian police). This would also include a right of free passage through the Jaffa Gate and along the road for those entering from the Israeli side, responsibility for developing and maintaining the road (out of fear that the al-Quds municipality would use this as an excuse for repairs that would block Israeli access), the power to close the road in emergencies, and the sovereign operation of the Tower of David compound.

The Palestinians were not prepared to accept this. The term "functional sovereignty" was unfamiliar to them. "Sovereignty," as far as they were concerned, was sovereignty in the classic sense—either it's all mine or it's all yours. The disappointments of the Oslo years and the unsuccessful negotiations for a permanent status agreement, along with their weariness of the long discussions on the Dead Sea shore, took their toll.

If we give you functional sovereignty, what does that leave us? Kadura Fares grumbled. Everything that is not explicitly cited, Shaul Arieli replied—thirty-eight territorial powers, including tax collection, planning, and construction. But the Palestinians were unable to assimilate this. A lack of diplomatic experience and legal knowledge seems to have played a role, as did a fundamental lack of faith in the sincerity of Israeli intentions. The Palestinian side viewed the proposal as a trick aimed at depriving them of sovereignty over the area. "You gave me sovereignty and then took it back with these details," Yassir 'Abd-Rabbu fumed, and added: "here you want precise details because it's important to you, but on the subject of refugees, which is important to us, you want to leave everything vague and noncommittal about the number of refugees you are willing to take in to Israel."

Lack of trust, anxieties, and the disappointments of the Oslo period reared their heads. "We have bad and bitter experience with the presence of Israeli forces in our territory," Zuhir Manasra said. The Palestinians feared that these powers would enable Israel to exert control over a much larger area. They also worried that they would lose freedom of movement and the ability to carry on routine life when Israel closed the area for security reasons. "If you want to close the gate, you can do so from the outside, in the area under your sovereignty," they said."Just don't interfere with our current of life, said other members of the Palestinian delegation. Finally, the Palestinian negotiators wanted the municipal museum in the Tower of David to be under joint management.

I had prepared my compromise proposal before leaving for the talks at the Dead Sea. But I was permitted to offer it only when we were on the verge of a final agreement. At this point, the Swiss mediators went into action. It was the first point during the entire negotiations that we required their intervention, and it came at the most critical time. After hearing in the corridor from 'Abd-Rabbu what he was willing to do on the Jaffa Gate issue, the Swiss inquired of the Israelis what the limits of their concessions could be. They then drafted a compromise proposal. The Swiss proposal addressed, for the most part, the problem of the Jaffa Gate, but the Israelis conditioned a positive answer on achieving agreement on the other questions that remained open—the run of the border at points that still remained in dispute (see below), the neutral zone near Latrun (see chapter 1), Givat Ze'ev and Ma'aleh Adumim, and the area of Wadi Fukin, southwest of Bethlehem. The dispute regarding Wadi Fukin was whether the road linking the settlement of Beitar Elit to Tzur Hadassah and Jerusalem would be in Israeli hands, or be used by the Palestinians to link the small village on the far side of Wadi

Fukin to Bethlehem. The Israelis proposed that the Palestinian link be through a tunnel under the road, and this was the final disposition of the issue. Regarding Ma'aleh Adumim, there was an Israeli consensus that it could not be conceded (see chapter 1). The question was whether there could be an exchange in which the Israelis would give up Givat Ze'ev and the Palestinians would give up the Jaffa Gate. Mitzna had checked out this possibility in a face-to-face meeting with Mohammad Hourani, along with the remaining points of territorial dispute. But 'Abd-Rabbu and Manasra said that Hourani did not have the authority to reach any sort of territorial package deal with Mitzna.

At this point, when we had almost reached the signing stage and were making an effort to resolve the final issues, not all went as planned. Already-settled issues about the border in Jerusalem were reopened by the Palestinians—for example, the Pisgat Ze'ev road and the Police Academy compound (see below). This may have happened because of lack of internal coordination within the Palestinian delegation, jockeying for status among its members, a lack of organizational memory, a fear of closing a deal and facing the Palestinian public with the results, or as a negotiating tactic. At this hour of turmoil, Haim Oron estimated that the Palestinians could not concede sovereignty over the Jaffa Gate, but would agree to withdraw its demand for Givat Ze'ev. The negotiations would focus on the road to Givat Ze'ev, on which we would display flexibility, while the Palestinians would show flexibility regarding special arrangements for the Jaffa Gate area. This is indeed what happened, after Beilin and Mitzna met with 'Abd-Rabbu and Manasra.

It was agreed that the Jaffa Gate, the Tower of David compound, and the road to the Zion Gate would be under Palestinian sovereignty. But at Jaffa Gate there would be entrance and exit paths administered by Israel, just like the ones it would administer at the gates that fell under its sovereignty. The gate would serve those coming from the west on foot or in private vehicles, and Israeli law would apply to Israelis entering and exiting this way. Where the Old City wall also marked the international border, the outside of the wall would be under Israeli sovereignty and the inside under Palestinian sovereignty. The international force that would oversee the agreement's implementation would determine whether maintenance work on the Jaffa Gate-Zion Gate road were being carried out in reasonable time frames or were aimed at blocked free passage. The security of those coming from Israel would be in the hands of an Israeli security team. The international force would be responsible for the implementation and supervision of the agreement. The Kishla compound, located at the Jaffa Gate, across from the Tower, would serve as the headquarters of the international force and would house the liaison staff between the two sides. This would ensure a high presence of Israeli and foreign police and security personnel in the area. The Tower of David and its museum would continue to function in their current format, and would be exclusively Israeli. In other words, Israel's functional interests and powers would be guaranteed without making use of the term "sovereignty."

Besides the Jaffa Gate question, the negotiators had to resolve a list of disputes regarding the run of the border through Jerusalem, all of which required "microsurgery." The two delegations had spent many long hours in these issues since the London talks the previous February. They determined the distance from the last house in each neighborhood to the border by using computerized maps and aerial photographs. A joint tour along the seam between Jewish and Arab Jerusalem in May 2003 allowed them to begin to solve other problems. While the tour made the solutions to some questions clear, decisions were postponed until the entire package was put together at the Dead Sea.

Nevertheless, problems remained. There was no ideal way to resolve them, but they had to be decided for the agreement to be concluded. From north to south, the disputes were as follows. First, there was the question of how to link Pisgat Ze'ev and Neve Ya'akov to West Jerusalem. Would this be done with a single road, as the Palestinians demanded, or with both of the existing roads, as the Israelis insisted? One of the roads the Israelis wanted passed between a few Palestinian houses, but the Israelis pointed out that the Palestinians would have at their disposal two other roads, the one connecting Sho'afat, Beit Hanina, and al-Ram, and the northern branch of the Begin highway. But the Palestinians wanted to use one of the roads the Israelis claimed to link Ras Hamis with the intersection under the French Hill bridge that goes to Pisgat Ze'ev, where the handful of Palestinian houses lie close to the same road that the Israeli delegation wanted. On the tour, the most likely solution seemed to be construction of an elevated route for the use of transportation to the Jewish neighborhoods. From the French Hill intersection, it would pass over the Palestinian houses. That was indeed the agreement reached at the Dead Sea. In the future, so it seemed to the Israeli team, it would be possible to dig two crossing tunnels, one that would link Neve Ya'akov and Pisgat Ze'ev to the western part of Ramot and to the main highway to Tel Aviv, and another that would connect Beit Hanina and Sho'afat with the area to the east. Were this plan implemented, the two sides would have to agree that the roads used by one side, that pass underneath the sovereign territory of the other side, would be under the sovereignty of the side using them. The same principle was applied in the Geneva agreement to the Mt. Scopus tunnel, which links Jerusalem to Ma'aleh Adumim.

A second problem was the division of traffic and lanes at the French Hill intersection. Here, too, a technical solution easily presented itself during the tour. An additional elevated road would link the inhabitants of Pisgat Ze'ev to the Yadin and Ramot roads, while a sunken lane or short tunnel under the intersection would link Givat HaMivtar to French Hill. Today, the French Hill intersection and the bridges leading to it divide traffic along ethnic and national lines. Jewish traffic turns one way and Palestinian traffic another, in accordance with their respective neighborhoods.

A third problem was the tangle of Palestinian and Jewish homes around the Hyatt Hotel on Mt. Scopus. The Jewish homes include Hebrew University dormitories. It was necessary to mark on the map and aerial photograph a convoluted border that allowed the Palestinians to link up with municipal Route 1 on its Palestinian side. The principle was established on the tour, but the line was drawn at the Dead Sea conference.

UNRWA, the United Nations Relief and Works Agency for Palestine refugees in the Middle East, runs a school situated on municipal route 1. The road runs along the seam between East and West Jerusalem; the school, located in a building that had been a police academy under Jordanian rule, lies on the west side. So the negotiators agreed that the school would be moved to the eastern, Palestinian, side of the road. The cluster of Israeli government buildings, including the national police headquarters, which also lies to the east of the road just before the intersection that connects Ramot Eshkol with Mt. Scopus and Ma'aleh Adumim, would be handed over to the Palestinians. This road would remain Israeli. The Israeli team agreed to this settlement only during the final talks at the Dead Sea. Up to that point, they had demanded that the government complex remain in Israeli hands. But most of the Israelis understood that this was a bargaining chip and not a matter of principle.

During the tour and thereafter, Samih al-'Abd demanded that Palestinians be allowed to use the road running south from Jaffa Gate, below the Old City wall, linking up with Hebron road, the major north-south axis in southern Jerusalem. This road, which connects the Old City with Bethlehem and Hebron, is used regularly by Palestinians today. His objective was to divert the traffic crossing East Jerusalem from Sultan Suleiman Street in East Jerusalem's business center. The Israeli negotiators refused; in their view, a road used by both Israelis and Palestinians invited trouble. Furthermore, it contradicted one of the cornerstones of the Geneva agreement—a sharp and simple partition of territory, and the traffic therein, between Israel and Palestine.

Al-'Abd offered an alternative: only the section of the road from Jaffa Gate down to the Sultan's Pool would be binational. From that point, Palestinians would descend the Gai Ben Hinnom Valley to Silwan, along an existing road that would be improved. But in addition to violating the partition principle, this was not practical. The road in question is very narrow. It cannot be widened and it cannot bear more traffic. The problem of routing Palestinian traffic was a real one, not just an excuse for demanding rights to an Israeli road, but its solution was the construction of the eastern ring road that Israel already had planned. Until that road's completion, Palestinian traffic would have to be routed past the Nablus Gate, the Lion's Gate, and Ras al-Amud.

Another issue examined during the tour was the possibility of building a bridge from the Ophel Road, which runs on the outer perimeter of the Old City wall at its southeastern corner, to the Mount of Olives. The purpose would be to provide Israeli access to the Jewish cemetery on the Mount of Olives without requiring Israeli traffic to use a Palestinian road. A bridge turned out to be impossible, because its pillars would have to stand on the cemetery and would therefore violate graves. Furthermore, such a bridge would ruin the historic landscape. On the other hand, designating the road to the Mount of Olives as an exclusively Israeli one was inequitable. It would privilege a relatively small number of visitors to the cemetery over the daily needs of thousands of Palestinians living in Ras al-Amud and Abu-Dis, who would be left without direct access to East Jerusalem's commercial center and to the Old City. In light of this, the two sides agreed on special arrangements that would allow Israeli use of the road when needed. In parallel, there would be special arrangements for Palestinian access via the Israeli-held Mt. Zion road to the Christian cemetery on Mt. Zion. Use of the roads to reach the cemeteries is much less intensive than is their use for daily needs, so the problem presented by joint use would be minimal. Amos Oz again displayed his talent for summarizing the situation by noting that this was a divorce in which both parties had to continue living in the same building. Instead of sharing an apartment and making each other's lives miserable, the couple decides to divide the apartment in two. But the stairwell outside can't be divided and must be shared by both apartments. The couple has no choice but to reach an agreement about the stairwell that allows them to live as neighbors.

Another very problematic point on the map was to the city's south, where Beit Safafa and Givat HaMatos are situated. The cease-fire agreement of 1949 between Israel and Jordan divided the Arab village of Beit Safafa between the two countries. In 1967, the two sides were reunited under Israeli rule; the Jordanian side was incorporated into the larger Jerusalem that Israel created by annexing former Jordanian territory. The residents of the Israeli side were Israeli citizens and those on the former Jordanian side, like the residents of East Jerusalem, retained Jordanian citizenship but received Israeli resident status. But by the time of the Geneva talks the population of the two sides had intermingled and most of the former Jordanian sector's five thousand residents were Arab citizens of Israel. Beit Safafa is contiguous with a Jewish neighborhood, Pat, and runs very close to the Teddy Kollek sports stadium, the Jerusalem Mall in Malha, the Biblical Zoo, and the Jerusalem-Tel Aviv train route. The main access road to the Jewish neighborhood of Gilo, runs past the margins of Beit Safafa and another Arab village, Sharafat, leaving the Palestinian Musa 'Alami compound isolated on its western side.

The Israeli negotiators maintained that geographic logic dictated that the entire village be Israeli. In exchange, the Palestinians would receive the Jewish neighborhood of Har Homa, under construction on the east side of the Jerusalem-Bethlehem road. Under this arrangement, neither Israelis nor Palestinians would impinge on the other party's side of the road, and the border would be simple. But the Palestinians adhered to the Clinton principle, according to which an area in which Palestinians resided would come under Palestinian sovereignty.

The field trip and aerial photographs, which showed just how large the Palestinian-inhabited territory was, reinforced their conviction, even though Beit Safafa would be connected to Bethlehem only by a narrow road. Perhaps this was their way of getting back at the Israelis for annexing Ma'aleh Adumim and Givat Ze'ev, each of which would be connected to West Jerusalem by a narrow road. Moreover, the Palestinians would not agree to an exchange between Beit Safafa and Har Homa, which they claimed was not open for negotiation. It had been built during the period of the Oslo agreements and in violation of them, so it had to be turned over to the Palestinians without any exchange.

At one point, the members of the Palestinian delegation entertained the idea of asking the residents of formerly Jordanian Beit Safafa if they would consent to living under Israeli sovereignty. Those who refused would be able to receive alternative housing in Palestine. But they rejected the idea, because it could constitute a precedent for other neighborhoods. Furthermore, the fact that a difficult decision had to be made with regard to Beit Safafa did not justify placing the problem on the doorsteps of the village's Palestinian inhabitants, so as to save the negotiators the problem of making a decision. The only solution the Israeli and Palestinian delegations to the Palestinian talks could find was to repartition Beit Safafa, and reestablish the 1949 border. Clearly, this was far from ideal.

On the tour, we realized that the Musa al-'Alami compound could be linked to Sharafat via the existing tunnel under the Gilo road. Gilo's 30,000 inhabitants could not be compelled to use only a single route, Hebron Road, into the city, merely to provide an above-ground link to a small Palestinian enclave. Here, as in other cases in which the Palestinian case was weak, it was clear to us that they were keeping it as a bargaining chip and taking a tactical position.

For a time, the Palestinians also demanded that Israel cede, in the framework of a territorial exchange, a small area around Malha in south Jerusalem and another one near Lifta, in the city's northwest. We expected this demand—it had come up in the Palestinian preparatory talks before the official negotiations in 2000. At that time, the East Jerusalem leadership and the experts who aided them argued that the negotiators should require that an area in West Jerusalem be handed over in compensation for some of the territory of the Jewish neighborhoods in East Jerusalem that would be annexed to Israel. They wanted to make this claim in order to establish that West Jerusalem was also on the table, and also to include the East Jerusalem Jewish neighborhoods among the settlements for which the Palestinians were to receive territorial compensation. Furthermore, it was important for them to accomplish a territorial exchange in the Jerusalem area for symbolic reasons—they wanted to establish symmetry by changing the status of an area in West Jerusalem just as was being done in East Jerusalem. But, in the end, the official Palestinian negotiating team did not make this demand, whether because of a short circuit in the communications between the experts and the preparatory discussions, or because of lack of coordination, or perhaps because the negotiators judged that Israel would reject such a demand out of hand. The latter was, in fact, precisely the reaction of the Israeli delegation at the Geneva talks. Palestine could not, the Israelis maintained, be brought so close to the entry point of the main Tel Aviv-Jerusalem highway into the capital city, nor to the Jerusalem Mall in Malha and the Teddy Kollek stadium—close to which a new road to Jerusalem from the south was to be constructed. Neither did the Israeli team want to impinge on the symbolism of any border changes in Jerusalem being in Israel's favor. This would make the agreement easier to sell to the Israeli public. In the end, the Geneva negotiators agreed that the territory of the annexed East Jerusalem be included in the computation of the amount of territory for which the Palestinians would be compensated. But the Palestinians would not receive this compensation in West Jerusalem, but rather from the cultivated fields of the kibbutzim adjacent to the Gaza Strip, and in the Beit Jubrin area.

The border was drawn in accordance with the following principles: people should not be evacuated from their homes in places where there is a homogeneous continuity of built-up area. However, isolated enclaves of one population within a larger area populated by the other population would be evacuated. To the greatest extent possible, the two populations should not be in direct contact. The border should be as smooth as possible, without tentacles of one side's territory extending into the other side's territory. And the border should allow both the Jerusalem and al-Quds municipalities to function well.

In the translation of these principles into the reality of Jerusalem, there were some places in which a contradiction arose between the aspiration not to remove people from their homes and the aspiration to create a simple, smooth border and avoid intrusions of one side's territory into the other side's. Not all these objectives could be achieved near the Hyatt hotel on Mt. Scopus, in the area of Beit Safafa, and in the Old City. In some places in the Old City, the Jewish Quarter intrudes into the Muslim and Armenian quarters, and the border traced on the Geneva agreement map is a convoluted one. In some homes near the *shuk* in the Old City, the ground floor serves as a Palestinian store and the upper floor is a Jewish residence. In these places, it will apparently be necessary in the future to straighten out the line proposed by the Geneva agreement. In any case, the Old City's dense population, the twists and turns of the sovereignty border, and the fact that homes at the edge of the Jewish Quarter physically touch homes at the edge of the Palestinian quarters, all require close coordination between the two municipalities to enable them to provide services to their citizens. The two municipalities may decide on ad hoc and special arrangements for the provision of vital services to the residents of the seam, such as road cleaning and maintenance, garbage collection, and maintenance of physical infrastructure. The division of sovereignty can actually help achieve and institutionalize these arrangements, because they will keep the two sides from competing for sovereignty via special arrangements and the provision of services, and will neutralize hostile suspicion by state apparatuses of special arrangements that blur sovereignty.

BACK TO BACK WITH FRIENDLY OPENINGS

The question is not whether Jerusalem will be divided but how. The Geneva initiative is built on an examination of current municipal function and the interests of both sides, with the intention of preserving these to the greatest extent possible in the framework of a vertical partition. There will be a physical barrier along the sovereign borders between the two cities, but it will be environmentally and user friendly, the opposite of the brutal wall being built today. However, there should be no illusions. A Geneva-style settlement in Jerusalem will only work in an environment of peace, under a permanent status agreement. There must be government and municipal agencies on both sides that work to implement the agreement, alongside strong incentives to ensure that the complex agreement will hold over time. For this reason, the Geneva initiative's calendar states that the arrangements in Jerusalem will be made at the end of the process, after change has been effected in the West Bank and Gaza Strip. The delicate fabric of life in the city cannot bear a hostile border where distances are so intimate as to sometimes be an arm's reach.

The physical division of Jerusalem requires creating, in addition to a border, a border regime. The interest of both sides is that people be able to cross the border regularly, but in a controlled way. The two cities will not be entirely open to each other, because West Jerusalem and East Jerusalem do not turn their faces to each other. Rather, each faces its ethnic hinterland, its own interior.

After so many years of Israeli dominance, it is difficult to expect Israel's municipal or national governing institutions to treat the Palestinian side as a partner of equal status from the moment the agreement is signed. Therefore, arrangements based on large-scale cooperation between equals and joint administration are doomed to failure. Beyond the problem of the relatively low level of Palestinian institutionalization and professionalism, an Israeli sense of superiority has crystallized since 1967. This consciousness has an internal contradiction. On the one hand, there is a sense of failure in coping with the "demographic threat," existential anxiety, and a feeling that Jewish-Israeli identity is in danger. Added to this is a perception of the Palestinian other as a military threat, a potential or active terrorist. On the other hand, there is an Israeli-Jewish sense of security backed up with military power, technological superiority, and control mechanisms. The combination of this sense of security with fear of the "threatening other" prevents equality in Jerusalem. Institutions such as an umbrella municipality, joint administration of a metropolitan area, of the two sides of the city or only of the Old City, may be theoretically attractive but impractical at least for the foreseeable future. Furthermore, there is a large economic gap between the developed Israeli economy and a Palestinian economy in which development is a challenge. Accommodation requires that the threat be excised and distanced by partition. Jewish and Palestinian ethnic and symbolic foundations must be enhanced separately.

Palestinian consciousness also contains internal contradictions. The Palestinians are aware of their political, military, organizational, and institutional weakness in East Jerusalem. On the other hand, their numerical presence gives them potential power. They want to escape

Israel's grip, but they are dependent on Israel's institutions, gain material benefit from some of them, and have developed an ability to make the best of life on the neglected margins on both the Israeli and Palestinian governing systems.

The challenge in Jerusalem does not end with an agreement. It requires the coexistence of two separate entities that have gates for controlled and friendly passage to the other side. Here the Geneva initiative left a number of questions open to be settled in annexes to the agreement. On some, the Geneva group, led by the architect Ayala Ronal, has original ideas. One is to create a border strip in which the sovereign territory of one side is higher than that of the other side, thus preventing the need to construct a brutal barrier that would ruin the landscape. Another is to build the physical barrier from different materials, with a width and height that varies in accordance with the terrain. The border strip will change in accordance with topographic data and the functioning of the border area. A border running between the homes of Abu Tor, for example, must be different than one running through an open area. A border running between the city's two parts close to the 1967 line will not look like one that will separate the Jewish neighborhoods built after 1967 from the Palestinian state to their east. In these places, the border will have to be sturdier, thicker, and run relatively far from the last house in the Jewish neighborhood. The border must also take into account the character of the area it passes through—a wadi, a wood, or a major traffic artery. Particular thought must be given to planning the border that will run along municipal Route 1, the road running along the seam between the Old City and French Hill. It will continue to bear considerable traffic, and a few crossing points will be stationed along it. Architectural students from Tel Aviv University and the Technion proposed some original ideas along these lines, submitted as their honors project. The border seam has architectural potential and is important to all humankind. When it comes time to plan the border structure along the road, the planners must think with great clarity about the landscape. The border should not be a physical barrier that blocks the view of the Old City from those in the west. Therefore, in places that have a view of the Holy Basin, the physical barrier must be transparent, or take advantage of a natural or artificial difference in elevation, in order to prevent uncontrolled passage. In other places, massive use of trees and hedges should be considered, as a dressing for the physical wound of the border.

The physical planning of the border in Jerusalem should be opened to an international architectural competition. The assignment would include the aesthetic design of the border crossings and check points at the exits from the Old City in a way that would not be detrimental to Jerusalem's singular landscape. The planning, construction, and administration of the border strip must be uniform on both sides, even though each side is a separate sovereign entity. The physical structure and land uses must be identical on both sides, so as to prevent damage to the landscape and to create an impression of unity and continuity. The planning of the large border crossings must take into account vital functions (parking, crossing terminal, offices, cafeteria, toilets, store rooms) and not allow other functions (peddlers, commerce, and hotels). The planners must also consider the marking of the border, and the question of how to maintain security and police supervision along it in a way that will not create anxiety and aversion, but will rather be as friendly and inviting as possible. Upkeep of the border strip will be carried out jointly on both sides of the line. This will require the establishment of a joint management and coordination body. In establishing and maintaining the border regime, it will be necessary to forbid functions such as refuse dumping, damage to the landscape, air pollution, massive construction, unacceptable noise, sewage flow, uses that would be provocative and offensive to the other side, high supporting walls, and open parking lots that ruin the landscape. The plan must also determine what institutions will be allowed to operate close to the border, with the purpose of preventing it from becoming an area of friction or an area of neglect, as happens with urban borders in many places in the world. Both countries can together ask international organizations to locate their offices and delegations along the seam. But there should not be too many of these, since international institutions do not attract large numbers of people and are not open to all. The border strip must be accessible and welcoming.

The Geneva negotiators initially thought to separate large from small border crossings. The larger ones would be for trucks and busses. These would serve as international border terminals and would lie outside city centers and near major, broad traffic arteries—the north Begin Highway, on the southern ring road between Bethlehem and Jerusalem, near Ras Hamis at the northeast, and next to Sur Baher in the southeast. Small border crossings would serve pedestrians and smaller vehicles and would be located near Neve Ya'akov/Beit Hanina, next to the university on Mt. Scopus, at the Sheikh Jarah-French Hill intersection, near the Olive Tree Hotel along Municipal Route 1, near Musrara and Nevi'im Streets, on the two central street of Abu Tor, near East Talpiot, and on the Begin Highway. Each of these crossings would have a quick lane for Jerusalem residents, in order to encourage ties of work, business, and tourism. There will also be a procedure for allowing the rapid passage of emergency vehicles. No crossing will be allowed over small streets or the yards of houses—for example, in Beit Safafa and Pat, and in Abu-Tor—and such places will be blocked. There will also be a check point near each of the Old City gates.

Holy sites will receive special attention. There will be arrangements to allow one side to visit holy sites that lay within the sovereign territory of the other side, using special transport. The sites in question are Rachel's tomb, Nabi Samuel, Mt. Zion, the tomb of Simon the Just, the Ramban (Nachmanides) Cave, and the Monastery of the Cross. The arrangements must prevent extremist religious elements from taking advantage of them in order to stymie the agreement.

The operational rules of the border region also require joint Israeli–Palestinian elucidation, with the participation of an international party. How will decisions be made about the border regime and its administration? Can the decisions be changed, and what sanctions and what coercion can be imposed if one side violates the regime?

No permanent agreement can be reached in Jerusalem without a transition period. Neither can an agreement be implemented immediately, because the new arrangements will require the construction of facilities and changes in infrastructure. If the two sides wish it, the physical infrastructure (electricity, water, sewage, gas, telephone) shared by East and West Jerusalem will not be separated immediately and sharply. First, management and maintenance will be separated. The physical separation will be accomplished afterwards, gradually, as part of the need to build new infrastructure for East Jerusalem.

This transition period can be divided into three stages, in keeping with the Road Map. The two sides need to decide whether these stages will be carried out before, or in parallel, to the implementation of the permanent status agreement in Jerusalem. The stages, detailed below, were formulated in April 2003, at the Israeli–Palestinian meeting sponsored by the Israel-Palestine Center for Research and Information

(IPCRI). In the first stage, there will be a freeze on the penetration of Israeli settlers into Palestinian neighborhoods in Jerusalem, and they will be forbidden to enter housing compounds they have already purchased on the private market. Israel will cease to demolish houses in East Jerusalem, and it will also freeze the sections addressing East Jerusalem in the zoning plan it is preparing. Israel will halt construction of the unilateral fence and wall, and will dismantle those sections that run through Palestinian neighborhoods. The fight against terror will be carried out in cooperation with Palestinian security agencies, whose representatives will resume functioning in Jerusalem, on the basis of the unofficial arrangements that prevailed in the city until summer 2000. In addition, both sides will be aided by a special international force that will operate along the Jewish-Arab seam, alongside military forces from both sides. Private and public security will be returned to East Jerusalem through community involvement. Identification cards that Israel confiscated from residents of East Jerusalem from 1996 onward will be returned. All unilateral archaeological excavations in areas of high sensitivity, such as the Temple Mount and its surroundings, will be halted immediately. They will be able to continue only under international supervision and with the participation of all parties with historical and religious ties to the sites. Services that Israeli agencies provide to East Jerusalem Palestinians, such as consular services and social security, will be improved drastically. Palestinian institutions closed by Israel will be reopened, and they will be able to operate without interference. Both sides will encourage the development of the private sector and of Palestinian civil society institutions, with the goal of transferring to them administrative powers, representation of the Palestinian collective, and budgets, whether by neighborhood or on a functional basis. The right of association and political activity will be guaranteed in East Jerusalem. East Jerusalem will take part in Palestinian national elections to parliament and the presidency, along the same lines used since 1996. Both sides will declare their intention of reaching a solution based on two states in the former Palestine Mandate, both with capitals in Jerusalem. There will be free access for all to the Temple Mount, just as there was before the outbreak of the Intifada, and there will be international oversight of the fulfillment of this section.

In the second stage, empowerment and construction of Palestinian capabilities will continue with redoubled force. Palestinian actors will receive not only further municipal powers, including planning and construction, but also the possibility of raising financial resources and managing budgets. The Palestinian public municipal administration will be enlarged, with the intent of laying the foundations for the establishment of a municipality. A special effort will be made to encourage and attract foreign investors and donors, in order to improve physical infrastructure and develop projects in East Jerusalem. Palestinian parliamentarians will be allowed to operate without restriction throughout East Jerusalem. Cooperation between the two police forces and security services will be tightened, in order to solve local problems likely to arise on special occasions, such as mass pilgrimages to holy sites.

In the third stage, the legal and political framework for the permanent agreement in Jerusalem will be designed, and this will end all mutual claims. The organs of the Palestinian state will officially replace Israeli institutions in East Jerusalem. The Palestinian al-Quds municipality will begin to function officially and with full powers, and elections will be held to its governing bodies. A liaison and coordinating body will be established to prevent mutual damage and to advance subjects of importance to both sides, such as preservation and reconstruction, high construction, and environmental quality.

FROM A BINARY CITY TO TWO MULTIDIMENSIONAL CITIES

Territory and borders shape national norms, patterns of power, and daily life. But they also shape social identity and the symbols that express it. The territory and border symbolize the national collective and, as symbols, they influence the actions and construction of state institutions. The process of symbolization is not one-dimensional, and it does not end with the definition of "we." As the territory and borders define who is within, so they also define who is alien. A border defines collective identity. The border is created by a system of symbols and physical barriers, as well as by verbal and visual symbols: texts, rhetoric, posters, and ceremonies that create a defined narrative of the collective I, and of the I as opposed to the other. The border constructs a social reality, and it is also the product of social forces and political institutions, which have written a kind of text and identity narrative while conducting a campaign of power relations with the other. The other plays a key role in shaping the border, personifying the antithesis of the group. The other is perceived as an entity that wishes to penetrate, without consent, for the purposes of immigration, economic exploitation, or in order to take control, sabotage, and destroy. At the border, characterized by hostility, the other is converted into a stereotype, a label—he is generalized, made alien, excluded. A hostile border is characterized by the use of massive force, imposed on one of the sides. In many cases, a border of this type creates resistance on the weak side, which rejects the legitimacy of the border imposed on it and seeks to change it. But a border can also be established by agreement and as part of peace-making processes. Such processes can construct new borders, change previous borders, or grant new meaning to existing borders and ratify them. In the context of peace agreements, hostile borders open up and become permeable, sometimes even friendly. Blocked borders open and invite the other side to look beyond them, to visit the other's land. Unmediated, non-hostile acquaintance with the other changes how he is represented in the national narrative (Ackleson 2000:155–79; Bollens 1998:729–50; Bollens 1999:267–98; Falah and Newman 1995:689–706; Newman and Passi 1998:186–207; Passi 1999:69–88; Pratt and Brown 2000:275–95).

Open borders create a complex and dynamic system of mutual relations between territory and identity. A hostile border is static. An open border is dynamic and creates changes in collective consciousness. It enables encounters between the identities on either side of the border. The encounter creates changing patterns of exclusion and inclusion, which in turn produces border communities, frontier societies, and frontier regions. A frontier is a region of confrontation if the two sides are hostile and in combat, but when peace prevails it is an area of continual interaction. In the latter case, diplomatic agreements provide for neighborly relations and interaction. In addition to excluding and including, the border also filters. This is especially the case when the borders are flexible, soft, and easy to cross. In these cases, border-crossing cultural influences coexist with the creation of firmer ethnic and national lines, which preserve the collectives on either side and their authority to approve or prevent entry into their territories.

As long as there is no consensual Israeli–Palestinian border as part of a permanent status agreement, Jerusalem remains a binary city. The strong Israeli side conducts a zero-sum game in which it wins and the

Palestinians lose their assets. The Geneva initiative seeks to change this and to reach a situation in which both sides win. However, Jerusalem will never be Geneva. For the reasons enumerated above, Jerusalem will always be a holy city, a frontier city, and a terminal city. But implementation of the Geneva agreement can transform Jerusalem from a polarized, conflicted city into a multidimensional space in which there is friendly passage between urban areas and between symbolic territories. Tensions will not disappear from the lives of Jerusalem and al-Quds. The symbolic city will continue to constrict and compete with the material city. Almost certainly, the two capitals will compete with each other. Evocations of Palestinian independence and of its liberation of al-Quds from Israeli occupation will pierce the hearts of some Israelis like knives. Jerusalem will continue to be a city of stone, but when a political settlement is effected, it will cease to be a place of gunfire. A political agreement will not eliminate Jerusalem's problems, but the city will cease to dance a deadly pas de deux with itself. Instead, there will be two cities, back to back, that divide, and share, the dimensions of Jerusalem's space—political, symbolic, sacred, and governmental.

3

GENEVA IN PERSPECTIVE

FROM THE PERSPECTIVE OF THE OFFICIAL NEGOTIATIONS

According to Omar Dajani (2005), a former adviser to the PLO's Negotiations Department, Palestinian negotiating style was fundamentally shaped by two, mutually reinforcing factors: a lack of a state establishment and high expectations. Dajani's analysis of these talks between a strong Israeli occupier and a weak Palestinian side is, however, incomplete. Another factor can be discerned, deriving from the gap on the Palestinian side between improper function and structure, and expectations and legitimacy. The lack of organs of statehood precluded the adoption of working procedures typical of governments, encouraged competition between negotiators and office-holders, and kept institutionalization and organization at low levels—longstanding characteristics of the PLO's dysfunctional operation (Sayigh 1997). As a result, decision-making was carried out on a personal rather than an institutional basis, allowing Arafat to intervene directly down to low levels of the PLO bureaucracy. As long as Arafat retained a high level of charisma and patron-client relations with most Palestinian officials, the PLO functioned smoothly—charisma and patronage to a large extent made up for the institutional defects. The organization produced positive outcomes.

But when Arafat became head of the Palestinian Authority, serious flaws soon became evident. Chaos overwhelmed centralism in decision-making. Corruption metastasized, the Palestinian Authority proved itself ineffective, and internal rivalries between people and institutions intensified. The lack of political planning, characteristic of the PLO from its earliest days, was inherited by the Authority, together with low levels of coordination between its different branches. The establishment's legitimacy eroded while personal and political competition for resources, power, and information increased. Israel was no help. The Palestinian Authority was unable to prevent the expansion of Israeli settlements in the territories, nor could it achieve independence through diplomacy.

The Palestinians had high hopes—expecting they could achieve their entire agenda in the negotiations. It therefore became politically untenable to make too many of the concessions that Israel required. Each issue became a matter of principle, with symbolic, and not just practical, importance. The Palestinian side was thus extremely sensitive to any formulation that infringed on its sovereignty or implied that the permanent status agreement might perpetuate aspects of occupation. This sensitivity was evident during the period of the Oslo agreements. The PLO's room for maneuver was limited, so the Palestinians created frequent crises and threatened to walk out of talks.

Another problem was the Palestinian leadership's and negotiating team's flawed preparation and working procedures. The leadership tended to remain passive during negotiations and pursued no politically costly initiatives. The PLO hoped to bridge the gap between its high expectations and its limited ability to realize them via the "international legitimacy" of United Nations decisions, and through international mediation that would achieve the best possible agreement for the Palestinians. In keeping with this, the Palestinians sought American involvement in the talks. Yet, as Dajani has written, when the Americans took an active role in 2000, the Palestinians did not know how to communicate with them properly.

When permanent status negotiations commenced, the consequences of the lack of a state establishment became more acute. The occupation intensified, reducing the legitimacy of the Palestinian negotiators and restricting their room for maneuver, which sent the negotiations into crisis. Furthermore, because of its flawed working procedures, the Palestinians did not prepare its public. Members of the negotiating team did not dare to publicly criticize the conduct of the talks, or offer suggestions for rectifying them. They feared that doing so would harm them politically.

The Palestinian leadership's view was that the permanent status treaty had to be something entirely different than the Oslo documents, which were interim agreements. By atoning in the permanent agreement for concessions and errors it made in its conduct of the interim arrangements, it sought to prevent further erosion of its legitimacy. The Palestinians based their position on the international legitimacy of UN Security Council Resolution 242, along with their consent to a solution creating a Palestinian state in the 1967 territories that would comprise only some 23 percent of the area of Mandatory Palestine. Unlike Israel, the Palestinian leadership sought to begin the talks from these principles, and not from the details. This point was important substantively, but all the more so in light of the structural constraints of Palestinian working procedures. Yet the Palestinian claims were not accepted by Israel and the United States. Both refused to make international law the framework for an agreement.

Arafat put together his negotiating teams in consultation with a small number of close advisers. The principal criteria were political loyalty and the patron-client relationship he had with the appointees. He placed much less weight on experience in previous negotiations and professional expertise. Attempts by the PLO's negotiations department to place their experts in the delegations either failed or were only partially successful. The Palestinian negotiating teams were large, with little coordination among their members. The teams did not hold preparatory sessions to establish their agenda, their priorities, to discuss ideas, or to establish negotiating tactics. When the leadership met to discuss the negotiations, they made speeches and issued political declarations, but they conducted no operative discussion about strategic goals and the tactics for achieving them. No criteria were set for possible concessions. They did not define clear roles and authorities. The result was that every member of the Palestinian negotiating team was involved in the discussions on every issue.

Arafat involved himself in the details of the negotiations, and did not give his representatives much freedom of action—in particular in matters of security and finance. His office frequently reversed decisions made by the negotiators, or replaced the head of the team. Arafat also conducted, in parallel, several other negotiating channels, without giving any of those involved clear instructions. This management style made the Palestinian negotiators passive—they sought Arafat's approval for every little step. It also created suspicion and uncertainty among the negotiators, and the consequence was competition between the senior negotiator and those who were potential replacements, and between him and those who conducted parallel negotiations. Each of them wanted to be the one who would close the deal and enter the history books, but at the same time each feared being accused of being weak and of surrendering to Israeli dictates. The fear of losing legitimacy at home and of being fired by Arafat explains a discrepancy that many Israelis and Americans who took part in the negotiations complained about in their memoirs (Ben-Ami 2004; Ross 2004; Sher 2001; Shamir 2005). Some Palestinian negotiators displayed considerable flexibility in private talks, where they sought to promote an agreement, but took a hard line in public. In practice, the Israelis and Americans received contradictory messages that made them doubt whether the Palestinians were serious and sincere.

Since the PLO did not work with its planning bodies, there were not, after the Camp David summit, any intensive discussions between the professional experts who had been enlisted for the negotiations and the team of negotiators that had faced Israel across the table. As Dajani wrote from his own experience, the technical and professional assistance teams, led by lawyers from the PLO's negotiations department, fumbled in the dark. Sometimes Palestinian Authority and PLO agencies did not provide them with information, because conveying it was perceived as giving up prestige and bureaucratic power.

The Palestinian delegation was also confronted by Israel's refusal to grant the Palestinians access to its data bases, such as aerial photographs of settlements, for the purposes of the territorial negotiations. In many cases, the technical staff did not know in advance what issue was to be discussed at a given session and what possibilities the leadership was prepared to entertain, approve, and turn into a legitimate position. Concessions and compromises were achieved without advance planning, solely in response to negotiating pressures.

Israel's working procedures were, in contrast, efficient and professional—that is, characteristic of an established state. Invariably, it was the Israelis who tabled proposals, thus setting the agenda. Their red lines, and the low price they were prepared to pay, became the starting points. The asymmetric relations of the Oslo period were thus reproduced in the negotiations, instead of being replaced by an exchange between equals and joint decision-making. Israel's attitude put the Palestinians on the defensive, so at Camp David they adopted a strategy of survival in the face of Israel and the United States, and in the face of their own public opinion at home. The Palestinian public was profoundly disappointed with the implementation of the Oslo agreements and Israel's behavior. It concluded that the PLO had conceded too much too soon in the interim agreements. Palestinians were concerned that the strategic concessions that the PLO made in the Oslo agreements (recognition of Israel, acceptance of UN resolution 242, acceptance of a Palestinian state in the 1967 territories, renunciation of the armed struggle) had not been met by equal concessions by Israel in the permanent status talks. Instead, Israel cited, at Camp David, the Palestinian concessions at Oslo as a precedent and as an opening position.

The Palestinian team's advance work improved after the failure of the Camp David talks of July 2000. Most of the improvement after Camp David was in the much greater involvement of professional experts in the negotiations, and the establishment of goals and red lines by the Palestinian leadership. Professional input became vital as the discussions became focused on more pragmatic issues. The summit had already broken the taboo of dividing Jerusalem, so discussions about the city could get beyond the symbolic issues. Similarly, at the Taba talks the following January, the two sides began discussions about the 1948 refugees, and officially exchanged maps marking which settlements would be annexed to Israel (Klein 2003b). But it was too little, too late.

Ψ   Ψ   Ψ

In his analysis of Israel's negotiating practices, Professor Aharon Kleiman of Tel Aviv University found that statesmen and statecraft were trumped by military personnel and the security ethic (Kleiman 2005). Military officers held key political and negotiating positions in politics and in the negotiating teams, and also imposed styles and patterns of thinking. The military accepts the formal superiority of the political leadership. But when the politicians go beyond what the military sees as its red line, the army applies pressure to the political leadership, high-ranking civil service officials, and the Knesset. It mobilizes the media and public opinion, exploits political differences in the governing coalition, exploits rivalries between ministries, and takes advantage of the ministers' personal and political interests. It also uses information that

the security system possesses to circumvent government oversight and
to compel the political leadership to take steps such as the suspension
of negotiations or stiffening of negotiating positions (see also Ben-Ami
2004; Drucker and Shelah 2005; Kaspit 2000).

The superiority of Israel's military over its diplomats is rooted in the
pre-state period. The defense establishment has always taken a lead over
the foreign ministry in formulating Israeli foreign policy. An aggressive
military culture has created a subculture of groupthink that views the
country's foreign relations through rifle sights, and uses worst-case sce-
narios as the basis for diplomacy. The military subculture's fundamental distrust of the intentions of the gentiles—of the world as a whole and
of the Arabs in particular—has led it to the conclusion that Israel must
depend only on itself. The Arabs, and most of all the Palestinians, are
permanently suspect, and no third-party guarantees should be trusted.
Israel must secure itself against every threat and may not take any significant risks. It must play tough in negotiations, and give preference to
short-term goals over long-term ones. This perspective governed both
Israel's positions and its negotiating style with the Palestinians. Israeli
negotiators were blunt and condescending, impatient and unwilling to
listen. The Palestinians felt humiliated. The military ethos makes the
Israeli side goal-oriented, interested in practical details rather than abstract principles or legal and formal questions. Territory is conceived of
in practical military terms, such as topography and what areas must be
demilitarized, rather than in symbolic and emotional terms. The typical
Israeli negotiator equips himself with maps, charts, quantitative data,
and presentations. He expresses himself with great self-confidence and
eschews sentiment. Israel tends to solve diplomatic problems by military means, and it prefers the defeat of a rival to compromise. If necessary, Israel will mislead its rivals, make large numbers of demands,
and exert heavy and ongoing pressure. Israel's diplomats use ideas and
proposals the way its army uses exploratory fire—to probe, expose, and
exploit the enemy's weaknesses. It uses divide-and-rule tactics to dominate the opposing negotiating team. The goal is to obtain the maximum
gains in exchange for minimal concessions. Each concession is perceived as a sign of weakness and capitulation, rather than as a consen-
sus-building act and a means of creating mutual gain.

For the Israelis, Palestinian weakness is an opportunity to be exploited, and a fact to be perpetuated in the agreement. This attitude was dia-

metrically opposed to Palestinian expectations. Israel's goal was to push the Palestinians into a corner so that they would make the concessions that Israel sought. Israel had suspicions about how serious Palestinian intentions were, about the professionalism of the Palestinian partner to negotiations, and about the Palestinian negotiators' ability to display flexibility and to stand behind the commitments they made. Israel had no hesitation about maneuvering between the personal interests of the Palestinian negotiators and manipulating them in accordance with their rivalries, the organizations they represented, and the internal rifts that divided them.

During the course of Israel's history, a few military leaders—such as Yitzhak Rabin and Moshe Dayan—have internalized some diplomatic qualities. But they are the exceptions. Furthermore, their learning processes were lengthy and took place during the course of negotiations. Most Israeli statesmen and women have stood in the shadow of the security forces, or have internalized the military subculture. Among them was Ehud Barak, who failed to divest himself of the military ethos. In any case, the Israeli negotiators did not intend to apply the lessons they learned to the Palestinians, except in small measures and slowly. The permanent status negotiations failed not only because of the objective gap between the two sides' positions, but also because of the profound contrast between their patterns of action and their negotiating cultures. According to Kleiman, Camp David was doomed to fail.

The case of South Africa shows that the success of peace talks depends much on each side's ability to achieve majority support and maintain leadership credibility within its constituency. Without these, they cannot sell their publics controversial compromises. Both sides' deficient implementation of the Oslo Accords eroded the support of each public's middle ground for the process, as well as the commitment to peace by the opposing side's leadership. Based on their study of the South African case, Heribert Adam, Kanya Adam and Kogila Moodley suggest (Adam et al. 2004) the following steps to salvage peace talks that are hindered, or are likely to be halted, by violent attacks.

First, unconditional negotiation should resume even in the absence of trust between the parties. The end of hostilities is the intended result of, not a prerequisite for, negotiations. All too often, the official Israeli–Palestinian talks were broken off or delayed following Palestinian terrorist attacks.

Second, external pressure on both sides, and the offer of incentives to be awarded after agreement is achieved, can be helpful. If the third party takes one side, as in the case where the United States leans toward Israel, no breakthrough is achievable.

Third, when a breakdown in the talks is likely, moderate leaders must create popular expectations of gains and evoke the perception of that the talks will produce positive outcomes. Otherwise, they will not have public support for necessary concessions. In the context of violent operations, carried out for the most part by Palestinian peace opponents, and unilateral Israeli settlement expansion, each side demonized the other instead of creating a win-win atmosphere. "One day it may well be necessary for Israel to negotiate in good faith with Palestinian activists who are jailed as terrorists. Most independent leaders in Africa took this route. More often than is realized, activists aim at bombing their way to the negotiating table" (Adam et al. 2004:239).

Fourth, negotiations must include leaders of all factions willing to participate, rather than "waiting for the outcome of the necessary Palestinian civil war" between Fatah and Hamas, as many in and outside the region think.

Points of similarity also exist between the negotiations between Israel and the Palestinians and those between France and the Algerian independence movement. In both cases, the negotiations began when the ruling country recognized the subject party's right to self-determination. Israel did this in the Oslo agreement of 1993, while Charles de Gaulle and his regime did so in 1960. In both cases, the strong, ruling party did not intend to cede full control over the territory that the subject side demanded for itself. During the permanent status negotiations in 2000, Israel wanted to annex Palestinian territories and to reserve for itself a number of military and security oversight powers. This followed Israel's peace negotiations with Egypt (1977–1979), in which Israel recognized the existence of the Palestinian nation but offered only personal autonomy under Israeli sovereignty. During most stages of the contacts over the Algeria question, de Gaulle refused to sever the "special relations" between France and Algeria. He also refused to allow the United Nations to play a role in administering Algeria—in his view, it was an internal French problem and not an international conflict. The fundamental difference between the two cases was the plebiscite of 1961, in which 75 percent of French voters awarded their president a mandate to end the war on the best terms he could achieve. The plebiscite caused a rupture between France and the French settlers in Algeria. Of those settlers eligible to vote, 42 percent boycotted the vote, as their local leaders called on them to do. Another 39 percent voted "yes," while 18 percent voted "no" (Adam et al. 2004:234).

Israel has not yet held a plebiscite on the peace process with the Palestinians, or general elections in which this is the only issue. The leaderships on both sides have only gone so far as to promise that when a permanent agreement is reached, it will be put before the two publics for a vote. While the peace process and the Intifada have, since 1993, been the central issue in Israeli and Palestinian elections, they have not been the only major issue. Furthermore, these election campaigns were not deliberately focused on the future and were not framed as a request for authority to negotiate, as de Gaulle's plebiscite was. Instead, the peace process was projected backward; the questions before the public were whether the existing agreements had been observed by the other side, and whether the other side's leaders could be trusted in the wake of the existing agreements. Voters were asked to reach conclusions about the future based on the answers to these questions.

Throughout their negotiations, the French sought to guarantee the settlers special status within the Algerian civil system. For example, they demanded separate schools, a distinct legal status, fixed representation in the government and economic institutions, and the preservation of the settlers' French citizenship. Of course, France could not avoid expressing its putative cultural superiority, in the name of which it demanded that Algeria guarantee the status of French culture in the new country's educational system, and the continued employment of the school system's French teachers. On security grounds, France demanded control of its nuclear testing ground in the Sahara, while recognizing the Algerian citizenship of the indigenous population. France also demanded control of the port of Mars al-Kabir. At an advanced stage of the talks, France was prepared to grant joint sovereignty over the Sahara region, as Israel offered the Palestinians at Camp David in 2000 regarding Jerusalem, its Old City, and the Temple Mount.

The parallel in the Israel-Palestinian negotiations is Israel's security demands at the expense of Palestinian sovereignty, and the response of the Palestinians. In both cases, the subject side demanded full independence over the entire territory in dispute. The Algerian delegation claimed that Algeria had its own identity, that its people were a single entity, and that the French were foreigners. They rejected the French demand to grant the settlers status as a collective, but were prepared to allow those settlers who wished to do so to become assimilated into the Algerian state as individuals.

On this point, the Israeli and French cases differ. Since the Israeli conquest of the West Bank and Gaza Strip in 1967, except in East Jerusalem, where there is limited interaction between Israeli Jews and Palestinians, there has been no integration at all. In the 1967 territories, the ethnic-national divide is sharp and deep despite the geographical proximity between the settlers and the Palestinians. Israel has not demanded collective rights for its settlers in the framework of a Palestinian state. Rather, it has demanded to annex land on which settlements stand. Of course, the Mediterranean Sea did not separate Israel proper from the occupied territories, as it did France from Algeria. The geographical difference, however, is not the salient distinction between the two cases—the ethnic and legal differences are far more important. With the exception of East Jerusalem, Israel has not annexed, de jure, the Palestinian territories. France claimed that Algeria was a department of France, an integral part of the national territory, whose inhabitants were French citizens with the same rights as those living in European France.

The turning point in the talks with the Algerian independence movement came in 1961. In parallel talks it was conducting with the Tunisian national movement, France withdrew its demand to maintain control of the port of Bizerta. France's grant of full independence to Tunisia, which followed its grant of full independence to Morocco, weakened the French demand for special powers and status in Algeria. Similarly, Israel's position that it did not recognize the June 4, 1967, lines as the basis for a territorial agreement with the PLO was weakened when it signed peace treaties with Egypt and Jordan that included Israeli withdrawal to precisely these lines.

A second turning point in the French-Algerian talks came when France changed its position and ceased to battle over points of principle. It felt out what the Algerian position was on a list of technical questions, such as compensation for the property of French settlers who left the country; how long Algeria would permit French army bases in the Sahara to remain in place; and how many bases could be included if the area were under Algerian sovereignty; and whether Algeria would allow French access to Mars al-Kabir if it fell entirely under Algerian sovereignty. At this point the negotiations turned to practical issues, and to the task of reaching an interim arrangement with a clear ending point. During the negotiations with France, the Algerians were allowed to dismantle the colonial establishment and to assume a maximum number of positions and powers. The break between the mother country, France, and its settlers, and the uprising by the latter, helped. The French agreed to transfer to the Algerians many powers during the interim period, and to send a special force from mainland France to fight the French settler rebellion. Unlike the Algerian case, the Oslo agreements left the future vague. Furthermore, there was no break between the state and the settlers. On the contrary, Israel doubled the settler population of the territories during the Oslo period.

Recognizing the superiority of the French culture in which they had been educated, the Algerians agreed during the negotiations to grant cultural autonomy to the French people who would remain in their country after it achieved independence. They also agreed to teach French language and culture in the country's Arab schools. But they refused to grant the French a representation quota in government institutions, except in peripheral cities in which a minority of the French settlers lived. The French had difficulty accepting the Algerian demand that the settlers choose between French or Algerian citizenship, without receiving any special civil-legal status in the new country. The compromise was that, for three years after independence, the settlers could integrate into independent Algeria without deciding which citizenship to accept. At the end of this period, those who chose to become citizens of Algeria, with equal rights and obligations, could maintain dual citizenship. Those who preferred exclusive French citizenship would become residents of Algeria. In the end, the French continued to operate the Mars al-Kabir port for fifteen years, and the Saharan nuclear testing site for five years. The rest of France's soldiers retreated in stages over a three-year period. France, which had fought politically and militarily to preserve the preferential rights of the settlers, expected only 20,000 to 30,000 settlers to leave, but in the end 800,000 did so—this despite the sense of the negotiators in Paris that they had achieved provisions that would allow the settlers to remain.

In a similar way, the breakthrough in Israeli–Palestinian relations came when the discussion moved from points of principle to practical questions. It is interesting to note that in both the Algerian and Palestinian cases, the strong, ruling side set the negotiating agenda. In both cases, the subject party suffered from a lack of experts and needed to use external experts. Nevertheless, the Algerians neglected the question of their refugees and the demand to compensate them. Some two million Algerians had become refugees during the war with France. This is notably different from the PLO's position, which stressed the refugee issue again and again. The issue most important for the Algerian delegation was sovereignty over the entire territory. The principle of full sovereignty over the entire territory was critical for the PLO as well, but the refugees, the Temple Mount, and Arab Jerusalem were of equal importance (Connelly 2002:215–75).

Ψ   Ψ   Ψ

The reader of the previous chapters will have identified in the Geneva talks the footprints of the flaws that Dajani and Kleiman noted. Why was the Geneva framework able to succeed where the official negotiations failed? There are a number of reasons. In general, they can be divided into two groups—factors that minimized the structural, cultural, and functional flaws pointed out by Dajani and Kleiman, and differences between official negotiations and the citizens' diplomacy of the Geneva initiative (see below).

In the Geneva process, Israel and the Palestinians constructed heterogeneous teams. The leading criterion in choosing participants was the individual's ability to contribute to reaching an agreement. Political loyalty was secondary. Professionals and experts on civilian issues were included, alongside people with military background and politicians. Political considerations were not alien to the Geneva initiative, but they were not the only criteria for participation.

First, the teams were run democratically. The method was to reach agreement within the team, so as to avoid a situation in which one element, such as the military representatives, dictated its perspective. The effort to reach agreement was implicit in the voluntary nature of the initiative. The goal was to create the greatest possible commitment to the initiative and to prevent resignations from the teams because of fundamental disagreements.

Second, communication between the two sides was open and free. The disputes were intense, but good communication between the sides kept the talks going.

Third, a large part of the preliminary work was accomplished in the official negotiations that preceded the Geneva initiative. The Geneva negotiators began from the point where the official negotiators concluded, studying the reasons for the failure and seeking to avoid the same mistakes.

Fourth, involved and supportive coalitions were built on both sides. While they did not extend far beyond the peace camp, they did create a critical mass that prevented others from dismissing it as the work of the eccentric fringe. Having a coalition involved in the negotiations and supportive of its results neutralized political and personal objections within the peace camp on each side. The coalitions were also broad enough and of sufficient quality that local opinion, and supportive governments in the Arab region, and the world, could not ignore them when the agreement was brought to their attention in a major campaign.

Fifth, a process that is voluntary has, by nature, an escape hatch—concessions do not obligate each side's governments. However, the hatch is a small one. It exists in the consciousness of the negotiators until a document is signed. Once that happens, and the agreement is placed before the public, the hatch shrinks or even closes.

Sixth, the strategy of the Geneva initiative negotiators was fundamentally different from that of the official negotiations. Instead of Israeli dictates and a strategy of "red lines," the Geneva team decided on a strategy of mutual gain. In keeping with this, they agreed with the Palestinians on organizing principles and the document's foundations, and then went on to discuss details. The tactics and style were also largely different from those that characterized the official talks. The Israeli side did not seek to "divide and rule," and provided the Palestinian team with all the information and tools it needed for the negotiations. This minimized the consequences of the Palestinians' lack of a state apparatus, and did much to close the gap between Palestinian expectations and the limits of their ability to realize them. The Palestinian side could see that the Israelis were not aiming to reproduce, in the permanent agreement, the existing relationship of conqueror and subject people.

The most important difference between the Geneva initiative and the official negotiations was Arafat's choosing not to intervene in the Geneva process. He kept his distance, so his defective leadership was not a factor in the talks, which allowed the members of the Palestinian team to negotiate as they saw fit, without constantly looking over their shoulders at their leader. Also of critical importance was the fact that the Israeli side was not permeated by a security subculture. Furthermore, the power mechanisms of both sides remained outside the game, and their organizational interests and outlooks did not interfere. The Israeli security establishment did not impede the Geneva negotiations—either because it disregarded them, or because the negotiations took place outside the establishment, as a citizens' initiative.

Because it was a citizens' initiative, violence and terror did not impact the talks negatively. Neither party to the talks controlled the apparatuses that carried out these actions. Violent incidents severely hampered, and sometimes even led to a suspension of, the official talks. In sum, the Geneva negotiators had far fewer constraints to deal with than do negotiators sent at the behest of ruling apparatuses and governments.

These points are relevant in the comparison of the Geneva initiative to other citizens' diplomatic initiatives.

FROM THE PERSPECTIVE OF CITIZENS' DIPLOMACY

The Geneva initiative was what the professional academic literature calls track-two or citizens' diplomacy—in other words, unofficial talks between elements in the elites of two societies, acting as citizens and not as government representatives (Adwan and Bar-On 2004; Agha et al. 2003; Chigas 1997; Chufrin and Saunders 1993; Davis and Kaufman 2002; Fisher 1997a, 1997b, 2002; Gidron et al. 2002; Gurr and Davis 2002; Kaufman 2002; Kaufman and Salem 2006; Kelman 1992, 1994, 1996, 1998, 2002; McDonald 1991, 2002; Montville 1987; Rouhana 1995, 2000; Saunders 1995; Susskind et al. 1996). A large spectrum of subjects and participants falls under this rubric, from meetings between citizens on each side—such as bereaved parents or mothers—to meetings between professionals such as urban planners, psychologists, economists, educators, and clergymen, to self-appointed negotiators.

Evaluations of hundreds of people-to-people projects during the Oslo years (1993–2000), which included different kinds of civil society cooperation and dialogue groups, show that they suffered from inadequacies similar to those that characterized the official track. Civil society contacts were ultimately subject to the asymmetry between the Israelis and Palestinians. The Israelis were more capable and experienced diplomats, were privileged with knowledge, coordination and management skills, and bureaucratic experience, so they almost always took the lead. From the Palestinian side, this looked like more Israeli paternalism and dominance. People-to-People contacts lacked a defined agenda, and the different NGOs competed with each other over the donors' financing. Thus funding conditions and donor agendas were more crucial in forming those meetings than the need to address the reality of Israeli–Palestinian relations on the ground.

On the Palestinian side, more than on the Israeli side, political considerations determined the selection of the participants by their coordinator and shaped the meetings' goals. Furthermore, each side had quite different objectives. While the Palestinians considered dialogue to be a part of its liberation campaign against the Israeli occupation, the Israelis sought to establish peaceful cooperation, as if all problems had been solved. The Palestinians put forward their national political agenda, whereas the Israelis were motivated by social and cultural considerations and tried to avoid political topics. The frustration was mutual. Israelis could not find peace partners, and the Palestinians, facing Israel's imperfect implementation of Oslo agreements, felt that People-to-People activities were not bringing about the change they were seeking. People-to-People activities reproduced the differences and misunderstandings between the sides, rather than bridging over them or creating meetings between equals (Hanssen-Bauer 2005/6; Nassar-Najjab 2005/6).

Track two is one of the areas in which civil society can enter the vacuum that governments have created, deliberately or by lack of initiative. Citizens' diplomacy prepared the ground for conciliation between France and Germany after World War II, led to agreements between the United States and the Soviet Union during the Cold War, promoted contacts between the black community and the apartheid government of South Africa, and paved the way for the Oslo agreements and progress towards a permanent status agreement between Israel and the Palestinians.

The Geneva initiative is no exception, and like these other projects it was accused of being illegitimate. Despite the temptation to avoid responsibility and to leave hard questions to the national leaderships and future negotiations, the Geneva agreement contains not a few tough decisions. These could easily have been avoided by preferring a theoretical or ideal model that would not have had to face the test of public and political approval. Participants in track-two talks have in the past often taken just this tack. They have limited themselves to professional and technical questions and evaded the need to integrate these details into political decisions. But the convergence of the political, the public, and the professional is absolutely necessary when two countries negotiate a peace treaty. In this and other respects, the Geneva initiative is the track-two channel that has come closest to reality. True, there have been other track-two efforts involving substantive talks, but in those cases the national leaderships directed the talks by remote control. This was not true of the Geneva initiative. On the Palestinian side, the national leadership was passive, or supported the effort in no more than a general way behind the scenes. The Israeli national leadership—when it woke up and realized the importance of the initiative—was hostile and sought to delegitimize the agreement and the team that achieved it.

The Palestinian negotiators received a general authorization from their top political leadership. It was given with the clear knowledge that the channel was an unofficial and nonbinding channel, a way of talking with Israeli opposition figures who could influence public opinion, and through it the Sharon government. The authorizers, like some of the participants and their supporters, had three tactical goals: to pressure the Sharon government, to help the Israeli left reorganize as a political force, and to renew diplomatic activity, not necessarily according to the model proposed by the Geneva initiative.

The Israeli negotiators had no authorization from their government. On the contrary, they actually sought to discomfit their government by offering an alternative to its policy of annexation and repression. They also sought to provoke a debate on the Palestinian side and accelerate political and social processes there in the direction of coexistence and accommodation. This was not manipulation of the other side but rather common agreement on these goals, and mutual assistance in achieving them. At the foundation of this consensus was the joint assumption that both societies would never be ready to accept an agreement and make concessions if there were not public discussion of a concrete model for a permanent status agreement, and without the existence of public bodies that would argue for the agreement and push its adoption as official policy.

As civilian diplomats, the initiators of the Geneva process were unaffected by some characteristic problems of official negotiations, such as the need to keep a governing coalition intact and the need to obtain the cooperation of ministries and defense personnel and harness them to making the talks a success. These are not inconsequential matters. The governments of Yitzhak Rabin and Ehud Barak failed at this, and this contributed much to the collapse of the Oslo accords. The fact that the Geneva talks were conducted at a time when no official negotiating channel was open to discuss the same questions also prevented tensions between the two tracks. Such tension arose at the time of the secret negotiations over the Oslo agreement in 1993, which were conducted in parallel with the official talks in Washington. Track-two negotiations can be affected by the positions taken in, and development of, official negotiations; the official talks can hold back or push forward unofficial ones. In the absence of official talks, that did not happen. For the same reason, the Geneva talks had no effect on official talks.

Nevertheless, the Geneva track did not take place in an absolute vacuum. The Road Map was on the diplomatic agenda, and the Geneva teams navigated their way in the context it created. As one of their marketing tactics, the Geneva teams said that their initiative fit in with the Road Map and could serve as its third stage. Furthermore, Sharon and his political advisor, Dov Weisglass, emphasized that the Geneva initiative, and support for it in the world and in Israel, was the principal motivation for their proposal of the unilateral disengagement plan from the Gaza Strip and northern Samaria (Shavit 2004).

While the Geneva initiative was a project of citizens' diplomacy, it was not devoid of politics. Every act of citizens' diplomacy has political goals. In some cases, the purpose is to influence decisionmakers and public opinion, and through them to shape a different political reality. In other cases, the political-personal agendas and interests of the participants take the front seat, as was the case with the Geneva track. The aspiration to use a citizens' diplomatic project to achieve or enhance political power can motivate participants no less than their desire to change the relations between two clashing nations. Active politicians, both Israeli and Palestinian, were involved in the Geneva initiative, and this amplified the political input. In general, the governmental status of the members of the Palestinian team kept them cautious, compared with the greater freedom enjoyed by the Israeli negotiators, who were members of the opposition. Political considerations were also taken seriously in marketing the Geneva initiative, and in the response of all those involved to the Sharon government's unilateral disengagement program and its construction of the wall/fence in the West Bank. The Palestinian side fell into line with public opinion in its community, which virulently opposed Sharon's policies. The Israeli side, for its part, refrained from vociferous opposition to these same policies, because they had the overwhelming support of the Israeli public. The result was a blow to Israel-Palestinian common action. It made the Geneva initiative irrelevant as long as the Israeli unilateral withdrawal from Gaza Strip and parts of the West Bank and the Road Map were the only games in town. Getting it back on the public agenda depends, consequently, on the failure of these policies, and on the public and political pressure that its participants exert.

Some civilian diplomacy is conducted with the sanction of governments and is used by them to convey messages. In the Geneva talks, however, the messages were conveyed from the peace camp on one side to the peace camp on the other. As a result, the messages were much less complex than those exchanged by national leaderships. The latter act under much tighter constraints, both internal and international. The same applies with regard to acquiring knowledge about the other side and testing its intentions. In the case of the Geneva process, these were accomplished as a joint activity of the two peace camps, rather than in the framework of negotiations between two national leaderships. Opposition groups have an easier time cooperating and being open with each other than do governments.

The relations between the Palestinian delegation and its national leadership were complicated. Central members of the Palestinian delegation were members of the national leadership, in the cabinet or the parliament. But they were in competition with their colleagues in these governing bodies over symbolic and material resources as well as political status and esteem. The fact that the Palestinian delegation was led by the leader of a small party, Yassir 'Abd-Rabbu of FIDA, and that his associates were independents and professionals like Nabil Qassis and deputy minister Samih al-'Abd, made it difficult to bring in members of the largest political faction, Fatah. This happened only at a late stage and created tensions within the Palestinian delegation, as well as between its members and those who remained outside it. The Palestinian delegation's relations with the Palestinian Authority's president were also far from simple. Arafat consented to the talks in principle, but as always he remained extremely suspicious as he maneuvered between the interests of 'Abd-Rabbu's doves and those of Palestinian hawks. The Palestinian Geneva team had no way of knowing clearly in advance what the Palestinians leadership's red lines were, precisely because these were not official negotiations. Even during the official permanent status talks that ended in January 2001, these red lines were not clarified completely. All they had available were the red lines stated in the leadership's rhetoric, and the various positions taken during the official negotiations. The Palestinian Geneva team's members knew their own red lines, and those of their Israeli colleagues, better than they knew those of Arafat and the Palestinian government. The Israeli team had its internal tensions and differences of approach and opinion, but all its members belonged to the opposition. In the opposition such interests and tensions are weaker and simpler than those that rulers must cope with.

The participants on both sides did not construct delegations representative of the entire spectrum of opinions in their societies. Their common goal was to reach an agreement, not to open a dialogue between the two societies and all their ideological and political components. The main criterion was the ability to contribute to an agreement, as well as political, personal, and marketing considerations. Representation of all strata of the two societies, under conditions of escalating, bloody conflict, would have seriously impaired the operation of the delegations. Most of the participants had long been active in the peace camp. The Israeli delegation included some centrists and members of the "soft" right, but only a small number. The Palestinian delegation did not contain any representatives of the refugee camps, Hamas, the Popular Front, or Fatah hawks. Sociologically, decisive majorities of both delegations had Western academic educations, were of the upper-middle class, secular or traditional rather than devout patriots in their national cause, and people of public standing. Their common backgrounds and previous acquaintance facilitated interaction between the delegations, encouraged openness and dialogue, and made it possible to build bridges between the two groups. The result was a positive and educational group dynamic that encouraged participants to revise their positions, as opposed to a negative dynamic that causes negotiators to barricade themselves behind "our" positions, facing off against "their" positions.

Although neither delegation included hardliners and most of the positions expressed by the negotiators during the Geneva initiative ran counter to the consensus in their respective societies at this stage of the violent conflict between them, the negotiations proceeded neither easily nor rapidly. Clearly, the negotiators on both sides belonged to their respective peace camps, which did not ensure a successful outcome. The Geneva negotiators sought an agreement that could gain the broadest possible support, so they gave weight to opinions that lay somewhat to their right. In other words, the central stream of public opinion was present at the negotiating table even though the composition of the delegations did not reflect this. While both Israeli and Palestinian critics of the initiative claimed that their side's delegation went farther beyond the national consensus than the opposing delegation did, that is hardly the case. Any agreement between the sides would meet opposition, and opponents would label any agreement as a surrender made by the lunatic fringe. But, as noted above, public opinion polls show that between a quarter and a half of the Israeli and Palestinian publics support the Geneva initiative. This is a respectable level considering that these were not official negotiations. It is also respectable considering that the Israeli government's internal and international campaign against it, and that Palestinian Authority leaders did not support it explicitly and unambiguously.

Most stages of the negotiations were conducted without the help of mediators. The Swiss, preceded by the Japanese, Swedes, and British, served for the most part as hosts and sources of funding for meetings and marketing campaigns. Other than encouragement, financial support, emotional involvement, concern, and prodding, the Swiss did not involve themselves in the substance of the negotiations. Only at the very last stage, in the dispute over the Jaffa Gate and the road leading from there to the Zion Gate, did Swiss diplomats intervene to formulate a compromise proposal that allowed the agreement to be signed (see chapter 2). In this, the Geneva process differed structurally from a summit meeting convened by a mediator (such as the Camp David summits of 1979 and 2000, called by presidents of the United States). By nature, a summit meeting can last for only a limited time. It is a dramatic event that creates high expectations. A summit meeting generally convenes in the final stage of negotiations, after long preparation and after differences have been reduced to a few points that require the decisions of national leaders. The Geneva process clearly did not fit this model. Decisions on questions that remained in dispute after extended work by small teams were not made at summits but rather in the broader forums that convened in London and at the Dead Sea.

Furthermore, the existence of an active third party, one who mediates throughout the negotiating process and who organizes the summit, turns the mediator into an arbitrator and judge of the complaints each side has of the other. The Geneva initiative had no such mediator. This does not mean that the Swiss mediators did not hear complaints from each side about the other. The Swiss also at times expressed their disappointment at the behavior of both sides. But they did not serve as mediators or arbitrators of these complaints—there was no need. The Israeli and Palestinian teams had open and excellent lines of communication between them, and the complaints were conveyed directly. Furthermore, there was not a single third party from the project's inception to its successful end. The sponsor changed several times. All of them were involved in only a limited way, principally offering generous and warm hospitality and financial assistance. The third party's low profile channeled the energies of both sides into negotiations with each other. In the official negotiations of 2000, in contrast, the two sides invested considerable energy in seeking to influence the Americans' position, in the hopes that it would support them and dictate its terms to the other side. As the experience of that year shows, Israel was more adept at this than the Palestinians were (Rubinstein et al. 2003).

Years of acquaintance were a good foundation for a dialogue between equals. The resulting atmosphere was open and free and allowed us to seek our mutual interests. Each side was aware of internal differences and disputes on the other side, and of the differing interests of the members of the opposite delegation. This created an intimate atmosphere that made discussion easier. Neither side exploited the other's internal differences to manipulate or split the other side. This intimacy, familiarity, and sense of partnership were expressed in the jokes participants told to cut through moments of tension and dissension. Such moments were in large supply. At the worst moments of crisis, it seemed that the entire enterprise would come to an end, but the cost of failure was high. It would mean that even the peace camps could not find partners to talk to on the other side. So the negotiating door was never slammed shut. The two sides dispersed only to return and make another effort. At the final meeting at the Dead Sea, when there were disagreements, Yossi Beilin and Yassir 'Abd-Rabbu met privately between one round of talks and another, or together with Mitzna and a senior Palestinian member of the delegation, to talk through the issue at hand and how it might be resolved. These meetings were able to address matters that could not be elucidated in a broader forum, because of personal or political sensitivities. Such small tête-à-têtes prepared bridging proposals that were later presented to the negotiating teams for approval. Daniel Levy and Ra'ith al-'Omari conducted similar meetings. These aided, but were not meant to replace, the negotiating forums. They contributed to an atmosphere of trust and open discussion, and helped prevent each side from receiving false impressions of the other. Contacts between the team members on both sides were not restricted to the formal talks. They extended beyond the official negotiating table—to coffee and cigarette breaks, and to the dining room, where members exchanged ideas, impressions, and complaints. Communication was excellent at all levels—personal, professional, and political. This had a positive effect on the identification of mutual interests and on the formulation of the text, as well as on establishing the goals of the common effort made after the document was signed.

Since the Geneva channel was a track-two channel in which the participants do not represent the establishment and bureaucratic interests, there was no formal hierarchy within the delegations, and the contacts were open and very democratic. The assistants' voices were heard as much as those of the members of the Knesset, and experts in one area expressed themselves freely about all issues. Negotiators in the small teams were given authority and authorization to discuss all methods and issues, and on the Israeli side there was a high level of discussion and confidence among the members of the small teams and the larger team that led the project. The leader of the initiative and the broad team clearly defined what achievement was in Israel's national interest, and its range of flexibility. When it was necessary to go beyond that initial flexibility, the definition of the Israeli interest was reexamined, and the possibility of achieving an alternative interest was also examined.

A track-two channel does not have the benefit of a large staff and professional bureaucracy, as official negotiations do. The staff work in unofficial talks is hardly comparable to that of official negotiations. The state apparatus has financial resources and trained personnel that track-two and civilian diplomacy lack. This structural difference is especially palpable when the discussion is over a model agreement like the Geneva document. It is hardly a simple matter for a civilian apparatus to construct a detailed permanent agreement. That is one of the reasons why past negotiating efforts outside the establishment concentrated on drafting statements of principles rather than detailed treaties. The exceptions have been channels run by institutions that employed research teams, such as the Jerusalem Institute for Israel Studies, Orient House, and the ECF. These organizations did preparatory work for negotiating sessions, and maintained lines of professional communication with colleagues on the other side over the course of many months. Track-two talks benefited from this. Nevertheless, none of these channels aspired to achieve a detailed model permanent status agreement. At most, they sought to resolve individual issues, such as Jerusalem or the 1948 refugees.

The Geneva initiative was exceptional in this regard. Those who directed it bridged the gap by bringing in people who had acquired knowledge during their government service, and who had participated in official talks. The Geneva talks also brought in academic experts. Furthermore, they benefited from the expertise of the ECF, the think tank that Yossi Beilin founded, with Yair Hirschfeld, in 1990. This organization had exceptional professional human capital.

Track-two talks benefit when they make up for their lack of a supporting bureaucracy by enlisting professionals and experts, academic scholars, or former senior government officials. These people provide the unofficial talks both with knowledge and with contacts within the bureaucracy. But former government officials must overcome the work habits of government service—formal approaches, adherence to the official line, conformism, and an aversion to large risks. In government service, there is a tendency to focus on immediate rather than long-range issues, to engage in crisis management and the search for short-range solutions rather than engaging in a long-term effort to resolve large problems and to engage in innovative and original approaches (Agha et al. 2003:173–81). They also need to overcome biases that have their source in previous negative experiences. The former officials must use the rest of their government experience to gauge the limits of the establishment's ability to digest the results of the track-two process. In short, they must limit the influence of their official experience and realize that they do not represent the establishment.

The Palestinians had no governing establishment behind them. The number of local experts in the West Bank and Gaza Strip is small. They have insufficient knowledge and do not have access to information that Israel possesses. For that reason, the Palestinians have, since the mid-1990s, made use of overseas experts, particularly those at the Adam Smith Institute in Britain. These specialists attended various meetings and participated in the work of the PLO's negotiations department, which prepared the professional foundation on permanent status issues. They were not, however, participants in the Geneva track meetings, and their contribution, if they made any, remained in the background. The lack of a supporting government service was made up on the Palestinian side by the participants' own professional knowledge and their previous experience in official negotiations. This enabled them to carry on from the official talks and bring them to a conclusion. However the relation to the official talks had a cost. Geneva Initiative negotiators who were graduates of the failed official track carried with them some of the frustration and disappointment they had experienced during Camp David and Taba talks (see chapter 1). Unlike most track-two initiatives, the Geneva negotiations were characterized by its leaders' determination and their public support for the project.

Such support cannot be taken for granted. Many track-two contacts remain secret because their participants are afraid to be associated with the enterprise and with its results. In some cases, this fear is accompanied by the participants' preference for influencing official policy in quiet ways. A smart government can co-opt track-two negotiators by displaying openness and a willingness to listen, thus giving the negotiators the illusion that they are affecting policy. In this way, the official system avoids conflict and exposure. In many cases, the Israeli government has indeed functioned this way, even when the government has been headed by individuals of great discernment. If the bureaucracy expresses discomfort with official policy, the leadership can silence it by allowing the protestors to attend track-two talks as auditors and write reports about what they hear. Usually, such reports are filed away and have no affect. The leadership succeeds in silencing dissent, while the track-two negotiators are led to believe that they have influence. The Israeli government did just this in many cases after 1993.

Public exposure of track-two talks, and negotiations without government sanction, require the leaders of the initiative to be determined and free of dependence on state funding. The leaders of the Geneva initiative could stand firm because they were financially independent and because their starting point was a recognition on both sides that an agreement could be reached. During the two years of negotiations, there were times when that assumption seemed to be in doubt. But the talks quickly got back on track, and with more effort and more time an agreement again seemed to be in reach. This assumption kept the participants in the Geneva process from preparing a fallback position for the eventuality that the talks might end without an agreement.

During the talks a draft agreement was prepared, in which a number of points remained in dispute. On each of these points, the document included two wordings, one Israeli and one Palestinian. But some alternatives—for example, agreeing only on a statement of principles or an interim arrangement—were not on the agenda. Two alternative wordings on a given point mean that the document has not been finalized and that full agreement is not possible. Such a document would have much less public impact than would one in which all points of dispute had been resolved. During the talks, various options other than a comprehensive final agreement were proposed, but all were tactical moves deriving from the parameters of the sole common strategy that shaped the Geneva understandings—reaching a complete model permanent status agreement. In these respects, the Geneva negotiators did not work according to the book—the academic literature on track-two talks recommends that participants not adhere to a single strategic alternative (Agha et al. 2003:181–82).

In other respects, however, the Geneva process worked according to the book. First, the two sides developed a pragmatic approach, in which they sought to solve problems. If solutions were not possible, they sought to minimize the points of dispute and to isolate them from other issues, rather than to insist that their positions be accepted by the other side. The talks did not address controversial subjects immediately. Such issues were postponed to a more advanced stage of the talks, but were not taken off the agenda. There was progress on these tough questions, as the easier ones were addressed. Furthermore, not all the talks focused on technical matters or issues that could be resolved easily. From time to time there were talks about principles, in order to clarify the roots of each side's views and how they were expressed in various proposals. This helped release tensions and clarify common goals at times when differences were sharp. This approach is also "by the book"—the goal of the talks was clear and agreed on by both sides. They also agreed on the role of a third, mediating party, the status of the product, the public relations policy, the entry of new participants, and the need to consult with figures outside the circle of negotiators on each side. The inclusion of technical efforts in the negotiating teams can be a hindrance if they manufacture obstacles in their fields of expertise and are unable to see beyond them to the package as a whole. Guidebooks for track-two talks (Kaufman 2002; Agha et al. 2003:181–96) recommend against including experts of this type in negotiating groups. Instead, they favor the inclusion of experts with wide professional, social, and intellectual perspectives, problem-solving approaches, and readiness to take considerable risks in order to achieve peace gains, as the Geneva process did. Finally, in keeping with the recommendations of the academic literature, the Geneva track refrained from addressing day-to-day issues and to offer solutions for immediate problems. Such issues come under the authority and expertise of the participants in official talks. Furthermore, attempting to resolve immediate problems can bog down track-two negotiators, and prevent them from engaging in strategic thinking.

LEGITIMACY: WHO GAVE THE ORDER?

By definition, track-two talks are unofficial and do not represent governments or have any formal sanction. Even when a regime gives track-two initiators oral or tacit permission, it retains the option of denying any connection. An administration can disavow any agreement that it has not reached, because the negotiators were not its representatives or employees. Such a disavowal is not like one meant to preserve the confidentiality of talks, as sometimes happens when secret talks are sanctioned and authorized, but denied when they become public. In that case, the denial is not fundamental and comes after there has been at least one negotiating session between government representatives. In contrast, disavowal of track two is fundamental, because the talks are not conducted by the government and do not obligate it. Furthermore, track-two talks can create political facts that are inconvenient for the government, and over which it has no control.

Civilian diplomacy that seeks influence needs legitimacy. This is all the more the case for the Geneva initiative, which produced a complete model permanent status agreement, with the same form as a legal document drawn up by two governments. Furthermore, it is led by political figures from the opposition who offer an alternative to the government's policy. When the leaders of the Geneva project put the agreement before the media, they hoped that exposure would help gain the initiative legitimacy.

In general, track two can gain legitimacy in several ways (Agha et al. 2003:146–57; Klein 2003:23–32). It can receive informal sanction and legitimacy. Its organizers can report to the government before or after meeting the other side's representatives. Beyond listening to the report, the government does not participate in the talks. In this way, the organizers enjoy indirect legitimacy from above, while the government remains passive. This method of tacit sanction has been used for years, on both sides, by many track-two efforts between the Israelis and Palestinians. Furthermore, in some cases government representatives—for example, experts from the relative government ministries—may join a meeting. In such cases, they label their participation as private, but of course everyone understands that the label is only for the record. The government and the organizers of the track-two meeting benefit mutually from their cooperation. At such meetings, governments can obtain knowledge of the other side that they would find difficult to learn in any other way. In return, the body that organizes the talks receives access to the government. Such access may help the negotiating process by, for example, making it easier to gain exit permits for Palestinians so that they can attend other meetings. The negotiators can also benefit from data and information held by the government and that cannot be obtained in other ways. Track-two talks also enable government officials to contribute to other channels. This can lend weight to the negotiating team, both in the eyes of the public and in the eyes of the other side's delegation. Such participation also means that the track-two leaders can convey recommendations to the government and affect its policies.

A direct appeal to public opinion is an entirely different way of achieving legitimacy for a track-two effort. It provides legitimacy from below, and also creates partnerships that cross national lines (Kelman 1992, 1994, 1996, 1998, 2002). Such partnerships can come into being between two parties to a conflict that seek to resolve their dispute. But the appeal can also be broader, growing out of international cooperation centered on a third party who initiates the channel and mediates between its participants. Close contact with the peace camp on the other side, or with a third mediating party, can promote mutual recognition, demonstrate that a broad agreement is achievable, which in turn leads to international legitimacy. This can, in turn, sweep up the public and grant legitimacy that can serve as a bulwark against the government's attempts to delegitimize the track-two process by portraying it as subversive. Ami Ayalon and Sari Nusseibeh did just this when they called on Israelis and Palestinians to sign their statement of principles, and the Geneva initiative did the same, in its own way. This model is preferable when the leaders of the track-two initiative realize that the government will neither lend its support nor remain noncommittal, because the track-two project is not consistent with the government's principles. Public legitimacy is the answer that track-two leaders can offer to the government's portrayal of them as betrayers of their country's interests.

In practice, the Oklahoma track (named after the university that sponsored the meetings) was the first that appealed to public opinion. This track produced a statement of principles regarding a permanent settlement in Jerusalem, and submitted it to the heads of the participating countries: Israel, the Palestinian Authority, Jordan, and Egypt. The Oklahoma channel was an initiative of Prof. Yossi Ginat of the University of Haifa, and it produced cross-national cooperation among negotiators from Israel, the Palestinian territories, Egypt, and Jordan. It should be noted that the Oklahoma channel did not appeal to the public in order to make common cause against government policy. Rather than offer an alternative to official policy, it sought to encourage decision makers to go in certain directions, and to support them when they did so. In contrast, and like the signers of the Geneva document, Ami Ayalon and Sari Nusseibeh had lost their faith in the ability of the government to produce a fundamental change without heavy grassroots pressure. Their goal was to achieve direct legitimacy for their initiatives, outside the establishment, by getting large numbers of Israeli and Palestinian citizens to sign their principles. Furthermore, the Oklahoma channel sponsored a single event, where as Ayalon and Nusseibeh, like the Geneva team, conducted an extended campaign. It is important to note that the goal was not to take control of the state or change the government, but to exert public pressure so that the existing regimes would change their policies. The campaigns remained within the bounds of legitimate public expression in a democracy.

Track-two efforts can seek legitimacy for the process—for the talks themselves—or for their products. Gaining legitimacy for the process does not necessarily guarantee legitimacy for the document the process produces. The opposite is also true—a legitimate outcome does not necessarily indicate that the process was legitimate. The Geneva initiative had to achieve both kinds of legitimacy, without the aid of their governments' sanction for their work. Furthermore, Sharon and senior figures in his government sought to delegitimize the process and its participants in an effort to destroy the entire initiative. As shown above, Sharon came out against the Geneva initiative even before the two delegations left for what turned out to be the final stage of the negotiations. When the Israeli delegation returned from Jordan with the signed Geneva document, the government continued its negative campaign for a time. A few days later, Sharon had the cabinet decide to fight the Geneva initiative, and he attacked it vociferously at the opening of the Knesset's winter session. Ministers Olmert, Landau, Lapid, Joseph Paritzki, and Avraham Poraz also ladled on the epithets, Ehud Barak did his best to climb on the bandwagon. Instead of a public discussion of the contents of the document, the debate centered on how it was achieved. The leadership sought to negate the substance of the agreement by delegitimizing the process that produced it. The first step succeeded—the public as a whole did not accept the legitimacy of the process. But the second step did not. To a certain extent, the leadership's own policy initiatives contributed to the failure to delegitimize the Geneva document itself. The appearance of rival programs—such as Sharon and Olmert's unilateral disengagement plan; the alternative version of that plan proposed by the minister of education, Limor Livnat; the program offered by Avigdor Lieberman, head of the right-wing Yisrael Beiteinu party, which called for the transfer of some Israeli Arab villages to Palestinian sovereignty; and the canton program of the Yesha settlers' council—helped establish the Geneva plan as an alternative to policies that sought to continue settlement activity, lash out at the Palestinians, and prevent any diplomatic process. It was also helpful that the sponsors of each of these plans stated repeatedly that the only real choice was between their own initiatives and the Geneva document. Most of the public believed that the Geneva process had been flawed and even subversive, but took a great interest, as did the media, in the document itself. During the first week after the signing, public support for the document was relatively high—39 percent in an authoritative survey conducted by Dr. Mina Tzemach and published in *Yediot Aharonot*, and 32 percent in the survey published by *Ma'ariv*. The story remained in the headlines, partly thanks to the advertising and marketing experts who were an integral part of the Geneva team.

On the Palestinian side, there was at first little dispute about the process. Most of the very lively debate that took place during the initial weeks after the document was made public was on its contents and process. The counter-arguments made by the Palestinian establishment and other opponents focused on what they claimed were excessive concessions made too soon. Furthermore, said the critics, the concessions were made to Israeli negotiators who held no official positions and were therefore unable to provide any concrete return for the Palestinian concessions. The Palestinian Geneva team was only at a preliminary stage of creating legitimacy for the results it had achieved. By the end of 2004, interpersonal and interorganizational rivalries, flawed management, and a public whose central concern was Israel's actions in the field (expansion of settlements and outposts, offensive military operations, the construction of a fence, detrimental to the population, on Palestinian territory) rather than the more distant future had all marginalized the initiative. The Palestinian public perceived it as irrelevant. Also harmful to the effort to achieve legitimacy was the Palestinian team's inability to convince the Israeli team to oppose, categorically, the construction of the fence and the unilateral disengagement plan.

The dissemination of the agreement to all Israeli homes at the end of 2003, and its presentation to the public in Israel and the Palestinian territories in an unprecedented campaign, redirected the debate from the process to the agreement itself. As the public learned of the agreement's provisions, its support for the document grew. Opposition also increased. But according to the Shamir and Shiqaqi polls of December 2003 and December 2005, the rise in the level of support was greater than the rise in the level of opposition, among those who had not previously formed an opinion. The surveys also show that support for the provisions of the Geneva document was higher than was support for the program when it was presented as the initiative of 'Abd-Rabbu and Beilin, or labeled the "Geneva initiative" (Palestinian Center for Policy and Survey Research 2003, 2005; Truman Institute 2005). In other words, the process's delegitimization by the Israeli establishment, and the lack of official support from the Palestinian leadership, were detrimental to public support for the initiative's leaders and for its "brand name." But they did not lower support for the agreement's specific provisions—in fact, this grew when the provisions were explained to those who were uncertain about them. It is reasonable to assume that if achieving a permanent agreement again appears on the public agenda, the Geneva initiative will again be relevant as a detailed model for a Palestinian-Israeli peace agreement.

The attempt to achieve legitimacy was conducted on two axes. One was directed and internal Israeli and Palestinian public opinion. The second was meant to achieve the support of governments and important figures in the international community. This latter effort includes the international launching ceremony held on December 1, 2003, in Geneva, and the Geneva teams' meetings with the U.S. secretary of state, the secretary-general of the United Nations, the heads of European countries, the president of Egypt, and the kings of Jordan and Morocco. The two axes were mutually reinforcing. For the Palestinian side, international backing was important in its effort to gain support at home for the far-reaching concessions it had made. It was also a means of pressuring the Sharon government, which was at the time conducting a war against the Palestinian Authority. The Israeli team had a similar goal. Both Israelis and Palestinians criticized the Geneva teams' frequent trips overseas, which were interpreted as an attempt to avoid confronting the criticism of hawks at home. The question of balance between achieving legitimacy overseas and gaining support at home is a problem for both parties to the Geneva initiative. Both sides were concerned about this and were unable to reach an easy, unambiguous answer. It is, in fact, a marketing problem—how to market in Israel the legitimacy achieved outside the country, at a time when some of those granting the legitimacy are perceived by the Israeli public as either hostile or, in the case of Western Europe and the UN, as interfering in matters that should not be their concern. The United States, in contrast, is well-regarded by the Israeli public. Yet, for the Palestinian public, the situation is the reverse. Furthermore, as active politicians, the leaders of the Geneva initiative cannot refrain from meeting world leaders. This is especially true of members of the Israeli opposition, and of Yassir 'Abd-Rabbu, who no longer serves as a Palestinian cabinet minister, but rather only as a member of the PLO executive committee. Since the establishment of the Palestinian Authority, the latter body has been of secondary importance and its members have not had executive powers. The leaders of the Geneva initiative have had to maneuver between political necessities at home and their political imperative to go overseas.

It is rare for participants in a track-two process to appeal to public opinion. Such an appeal creates a process that is the opposite of a government initiative. When central governments discuss a treaty, each one appeals to its own public opinion, whether in parallel with the negotiation process or at its end, in order to obtain support and legitimacy. In contrast, a track-two process appeals to public opinion when its initiators reach the conclusion that official channels are blocked. The goal is not to change the regime, but rather to show that the government's claims and polices are unacceptable, to prove that there is an alternative, and to press the government to change its policies. The Geneva participants wanted to offer a detailed permanent agreement as a point of reference, both to show that an agreement was possible and to offer practical solutions to specific problems. The Geneva teams did not present their document to the public as a treaty that would soon be put into effect, nor did they seek public support to effect it. Neither were they asking the public to support their program over a rival one that their governments intended to present in talks they were conducting or would conduct. The battle for public opinion began at a much more fundamental point. The job was to convince the public that the diplomatic stalemate, in which each side was presenting the other as an obstacle to peace, should end and negotiations resumed. In this, the Geneva process succeeded. Sharon decided on a unilateral withdrawal from the Gaza Strip in order to block the Geneva program, as he himself acknowledged. But that did not have to be the end of the Geneva initiative's public campaign. After having achieved movement on the

Israel-Palestinian front, the process could continue into the following stages: adoption of parts or all of the Geneva document by the public, to be followed by their governments; and negotiations along the lines of the Geneva document, ending with an agreement fairly similar to it. Unlike a government-initiated diplomatic process, a track-two agreement cannot achieve formal or legal legitimacy if the regime opposes it. It must achieve legitimacy from below, from the public, and from the other side participating in the process. The participants in the Geneva process seek to conduct an ongoing and varied dialogue with different audiences. They aim to create pressure groups and lobbies, to receive legitimacy through talking to public figures, and to cooperate with a range of organizations and political figures.

THE CONSTRAINING CONTEXT

The context in which the Geneva track operated was not amenable to reaching an agreement. It presented any number of impediments: the personal and political status of some team members and their contention with rivals at home; the disparities in the formal status of central members of both delegations; political crises on both sides; the level of the Israeli–Palestinian conflict in which the process took place; and uncertainty about the possible effects of the American war in Iraq on Israeli–Palestinian relations.

Geneva was not a classic case of unofficial talks conducted when the violent conflict between two parties reaches a point where neither side is able to win (Agha et al. 2003:133 5). In such a case, the political leadership on each side is prepared to allow citizens to put out feelers to see if secret negotiations are possible, or to check out creative ideas in a nonbinding, deniable channel. The Sharon government did not see itself at such a point. Even if had reached such a point, it would not have offered tacit consent to the parliamentary opposition to engage in such contacts. In contrast with other instances of track two, such as the talks that produced the Oslo agreement of 1993, the Geneva process was not begun by the regime, nor was it adopted by decisionmakers in order to break a stalemate in official talks. It was what Hussein Agha, Shai Feldman, Ahmad Khalidi, and Ze'ev Schiff call a "hard" track-two process, one that did not avoid the conflict's toughest and most fundamental issues. A "soft" track two limits itself to purely personal or professional discussions and does not touch on political issues (Agha et al. 2003:133–36).

The Palestinian leadership's preference, in mid-2003, for talks with Sharon caused a suspension of the Geneva process, even if that was not stated explicitly. True, the delays resulted from disagreements and the failure to reach consensus on issues in dispute, as well as from the reopening of issues that had already been resolved. But they were also the product of the context—in this case, Sharon's willingness to accept the Road Map and to meet with Prime Minister Abbas and President Bush in Aqaba (Agha 2003:157–61, 191–93).

The war in Iraq also delayed the process. The London talks of February 2003 were conducted in atmosphere of uncertainty on the eve of the war. It was not clear whether the expected American victory would distract the United States from addressing the Israeli–Palestinian conflict or, alternatively, encourage it to push forward. This uncertainty contributed to the Palestinian delegation's reluctance to conclude and sign the document. Likewise, the Palestinian negotiators were unsure what effect the war would have on Palestinian and Arab attitudes toward the United States. 'Abd-Rabbu and his team thus considered that it might be worthwhile for them to broaden their ranks before an agreement was signed. Doing so would also gain them time and allow them to see which way the winds were blowing. They were not persuaded by the arguments made by Alexis Keller of Switzerland that there would be no ideal time to sign, nor by Beilin's argument that they should sign an agreement that both sides could live with and bring in new participants afterward. By the way, the issue of attitudes toward the United States also created a textual problem—should it be mentioned explicitly as the leading force in the international verification and oversight force provided for in the agreement, or only as one participant alongside other countries? What was the way to bridge between the Israeli public's positive attitude to the United States and the Palestinian public's, and Arab world's, negative feelings—especially after the American victory in Iraq?

A second problem of context was linked to the political standing of the initiative's leaders. Did 'Abd-Rabbu's colleagues in the Palestinian leadership support the process, or stridently oppose it? Did he believe that he would be able to enlist support or mollify his opponents when the time came? Problems of timing and personal status also played a role. During the process's second year, the Palestinian Authority experienced a number of political crises. Internal pressures for reform of the structure of the regime and of the operations of the president and ministries, alongside external pressure from Israel, the United States, and the European Union, led at the beginning of 2003 to the creation of the post of prime minister and the appointment of a new government headed by Mahmoud Abbas. That government lasted only six months, to be replaced by a small emergency government headed by Ahmed Qurei (Abu-'Ala). Two months later a broader coalition replaced it, with Qurei remaining prime minister. This political instability affected the process. Members of the Palestinian delegation did not know if they would continue to serve as ministers or deputy ministers, or what the designated prime minister would think of the process. As noted, in light of the Likud's overwhelming victory in the Israeli elections of 2002, and the close relationship Sharon developed with President Bush, the Palestinian leadership preferred to speak with the winning Israeli camp rather than the defeated left, and to advance the Road Map as a device for expediting an Israeli withdrawal. Alternatively, Abbas hoped, the United States would help him and pressure Israel to do its obligations under the Road Map. Sharon's pretense ended when he and his government failed to do anything—namely, withdraw from Palestinian territories and slow the construction of settlements—to help Abbas gain support among his people. Sharon believed that he could maneuver Abbas into a position in which he would have no option but to accept the map that Sharon would dictate to him.

The Palestinian public and establishment, for its part, expected Abbas to use his connections with Sharon and Bush to ease the occupation. Abbas was pushed into a corner and forced to resign. The Palestinian leadership realized that the Likud was not a partner. Change would begin, as it had in the past, from the left, after the Israeli left rebuilt itself. Erekat, Sha'ath, Abbas, and Qurei, who held the political and diplomatic portfolios, concluded that 'Abd-Rabbu's channel should be given a chance to make a breakthrough.

A third problem of context was the disparity in the formal status of the negotiators on each side. It presented difficulties throughout the process because it affected the structure of the talks. The Palestinian delegation included people who held government posts, while the Israeli team included no one higher ranking than opposition members of the Knesset. As a consequence, any Palestinian concession could be interpreted publicly as obligating the leadership, whereas Israeli concessions were made by people with no connection to their government. The Palestinian team feared that any concession it made would be filed away by Israel and serve as a starting point for official negotiations. But the Palestinians could not receive anything commensurable from the Israeli opposition. The Israeli delegation could offer support for, but not order, an Israeli withdrawal or a cessation of settlement expansion. This asymmetry seems to have played a role in the delaying the conclusion of the negotiations.

Signing the side letter was meant to solve some of these problems. The letter stresses that the document is only a model agreement and is in no way a binding document. It also states that the Geneva document supplements the Road Map and is not meant to replace it. Furthermore, according to the letter, the Geneva talks were a private initiative, in which even office-holders were not representing their governments. The agreement is an appeal to public opinion on both sides, to show that a permanent status agreement is achievable, and is in no way an agreement between governments. The original draft of the letter stated that the campaign to gain internal and international support would begin with the consent of both sides. But the media coverage of the final talks in Jordan made this provision irrelevant and it was removed from the final version.

Most of the Palestinian participants came from Ramallah, and thus needed permits from the Israeli army to cross the Qalandiya roadblock—a fourth context problem. The Israeli team always submitted the request for permits. Therefore, the meetings could take place only with Israeli sanction, in a situation of ruler-subject relations, which had a psychological effect but did not dictate the outcome of the discussions. The same is true of meetings that took place overseas and that required Beilin's office to obtain exit permits for the Palestinians.

Neither was the international context helpful for the Geneva channel. The Road Map had wall-to-wall international support, and had also been adopted formally by Israel and the Palestinian Authority. It was deliberately vague regarding permanent status questions because its drafters saw no hope of bridging the huge gap between the two sides. The international effort was aimed at a staged process, which would focus on short-range goals, cognizant that the positions of the Sharon and Arafat governments were polar opposites. In this, the Road Map was a continuation of the report produced in 2001 by a commission headed by former Senator George Mitchell, and another report prepared by then-CIA chief George Tenet. The Geneva negotiators, in contrast, decided to begin from the end. In other words, the Geneva negotiations were conducted with only one eye on the official track, and in large measure with considerable skepticism about the Road Map. The official track was not a positive reference point, and the intention was to offer an alternative. The Road Map was going nowhere, but that had no influence on the Geneva initiative. As noted, the Israeli team was prepared to sign the document months before it was—precisely when hopes for the Road Map skyrocketed. At most, it could be said that when the Road Map proved unproductive, that was an incentive for the Palestinian team to sign the Geneva agreement. Furthermore, the Road Map's lack of progress helped the Geneva initiative's international campaign for acceptance.

Because the Geneva negotiations were not conducted by governments, neither side could use violence to sabotage the agreement or to coerce the other side to accept it. Even though the Palestinian team included Palestinian Authority office holders, they had no control over the armed militias associated with Fatah, Hamas, and other organizations that perpetrated the Intifada's violence. There was no question that the Israeli team could control its country's use of force. Yet violence was part of the problematic context in which the Geneva channel operated. While the agreement's opponents did not use force to sabotage the process, they disregarded it and pursued a cycle of violence and terror that had its own pace, independent of the Geneva track.

GENEVA AND ITS CRITICS

The Geneva initiative was criticized from the start (earlier versions of these pages were published in Klein 2004c; 2004d; 2004e). The criticism is hardly surprising, since alongside its achievements, the agreement contains extremely tough concessions. Until it was signed on October 23, 2003, in Jordan, the public had never been presented with a detailed permanent status agreement, including a map. The official talks, as noted, had been inconclusive, and no other track-two talks produced a document of similar scope. Furthermore, the Geneva document was signed by more than twenty people on each side. This created a personal obligation on the part of a large and respected group of both Israelis and Palestinians. Furthermore, the Palestinian signatories included ministers, deputy ministers, legislators from the Fatah faction, senior officials, and scholars. While the officeholders declared that they had signed the document as private individuals, they could not have taken such a dramatic step, nor even have engaged in the negotiations, without unofficial sanction from the Palestinian leadership. The Israeli signatories were opposition legislators, peace activists, writers, reserve offices, businessmen, and scholars.

Whatever the context, criticism of the Geneva agreement is legitimate, and debate over its provisions is vital to the future, and to the democratic functioning, of both societies. The critics are not homogeneous. Some challenge the document's foundation principles, while others are critical of one or another provision. The latter are in large part much like the agreement's signers, most of whom, on both sides, had serious reservations about some provisions. Yet they decided to sign the document nonetheless, sometimes after considerable agonizing, because the attraction of the package as a whole was greater than their concerns about any individual detail.

Israeli critics of the Geneva agreement (Avineri 2004; Cristal 2004; Susser 2003) face a difficult problem. In similar situations in the past, they could point to Palestinians who had participated in the talks and been partners in the agreements, but had then recanted. Nothing of the sort has happened in the case of the Geneva initiative. The Palestinian team has adhered to the text and bravely conducted a public debate of a type that Palestinian society has not seen for many years. At times, the debate has slipped into verbal and physical violence, yet the signers have not retracted their signatures. It is interesting to note that the criticism on both sides focuses on the same issues. This can be seen in the MEMRI summary of Palestinian criticism of the Geneva initiative (MEMRI 2003), and in a more focused way in an internet petition organized by an organization that advocates the right of return, al-Awda (2003). The petition was signed by Palestinian intellectuals who claimed, as did dozens of articles in the Palestinian press, that the Geneva agreement negates the right of return, supports Israel's claim to be a Jewish state. Furthermore, they claimed, the agreement obliterates the national rights of the 1.2 million Palestinians who live within Israel, robbing them of the possibility of turning Israel into a state of all its citizens. According to these critics, the Geneva agreement accepts the boundaries of Jerusalem as drawn by the Israeli annexation, legitimizes that annexation, and puts an end to any possibility of returning to the 1967 borders in the city—not to mention sacrificing Palestinian property that remained after 1948 in West Jerusalem.

The Palestinian opposition critique goes further. It notes that the Geneva agreement allows a majority of Israeli settlers to remain where they are, in particular those who live in the neighborhoods that surround Arab Jerusalem. The security arrangements specified in the agreement deal a mortal blow to Palestinian sovereignty and, for all intents and purposes, allow Israel to continue to control the security and economy of a weak Palestinian entity. The document creates disunion at home, weakens international support for the Palestinian cause, and binds the hands of future Palestinian negotiators. In short, the Palestinian critics read the agreement in precisely the opposite way than do its Israeli critics.

The Geneva document is not a complete text. Missing chapters and appendices need to be added. The absence of these appendices led many Palestinians to the conclusion that the Geneva Initiative has secret codicils in which the Palestinian delegation made further concessions.

Neither is it a perfect document. Some of the criticisms leveled against it are valid. For example, there is indeed a danger that the oversight and verification bodies that the agreement establishes will become a sprawling, convoluted, inefficient bureaucracy. When the appendices that will deal with these bodies are prepared, this issue should be addressed. Another valid critique is the decision to leave Alfei Menashe, Ma'aleh Adumim, and Givat Ze'ev as Israeli enclaves within Palestinian territory, with only a narrow corridor linking them to the rest of the country. The question is whether these enclaves will not inevitably be abandoned and deteriorate. The same is true of some problematic twists and turns in the border the Geneva document proposes in Jerusalem—at the compound near the Hyatt hotel on Mt. Scopus, in the Old City, and in Beit Safafa. In these areas it looks as if there will be no choice but to straighten the borders during the official talks.

A shortcoming from the Palestinian point of view is that the document does not include an Israeli apology for the suffering of the Palestinian refugees. Israel needs to acknowledge that it bears part of the responsibility for the suffering that was caused by its expulsion of Palestinians during and after the 1948 and 1967 wars, and by its actions to prevent the refugees from returning to their homes after the wars.

No legal contract can provide for all eventualities, and jurists enjoy searching for holes in texts written by their colleagues. Yet, despite all its deficiencies, the Geneva initiative offers parameters for compromise and maps out the decisions that both sides need to make. Inevitably, people on each side argue that a better agreement could have been achieved. That claim remains unproven, until such time as a better agreement is reached.

One of the critiques of the Geneva agreement leveled by its Israeli opponents is that it does not recognize Israel as a Jewish state. Some even accused the Geneva team of misleading the Israeli public. This issue touches on the state of Israel's fundamental identity.

In fact, the document recognizes the Jewish people's right to a state and, beyond that, it recognizes that the state of Israel is the Jewish people's homeland. Section two, paragraph four of the Hebrew version translates the word homeland as "*bayit le'umi*"—national home, even though there is another Hebrew word, "*moledet*," that is the equivalent of "homeland." This is a far-reaching Palestinian statement, because it recognizes that the state of Israel is not only the state of the Jewish people, but also its homeland. The members of the Jewish nation, who have a right to a state, as the preamble states, are not foreign implants, invaders, or immigrants. The Jewish nation was born here, in the Land of Israel, to which they are returning. In addition, the document recognizes the state of Israel. These three components, taken together, are precisely what the critics seek. The principle was split into three and placed in different locations to make it easier for the Palestinians to market the agreement, but the Palestinians provided the essentials that Israel negotiators wanted. Furthermore, the Palestinians insisted on including a provision specifying that the state's Jewish character does not allow it to infringe on the rights of its ethnic and religious minorities—thereby acknowledging its Jewish character: "this agreement marks the recognition of the right of the Jewish people to statehood and the recognition of the right of the Palestinian people to statehood, without prejudice to the equal rights of the parties' respective citizens." Since Israeli Jewish settlers will not remain in Palestine, this provision is relevant only for Israeli citizens of Palestinian origins. Such a reservation makes sense only if they have recognized the Jewish ethnic-cultural-religious foundation of the state.

It should be noted that the prohibition against discriminating against its Palestinian citizens is hardly an imposition on Israel. It is mandated—even if it has not always been observed—by Israel's Declaration of Independence and basic laws. The explicit requirement that Israel grant equal rights to its Palestinian citizens helps the Palestinians sell the agreement, but the wording is entirely consistent with the Israeli side's own principles and its conception of what constitutes a democratic Jewish state.

There were no Palestinian citizens of Israel on the Israeli negotiating team for the Geneva initiative. Including such a representative would have made it more difficult to market the agreement to the Israeli public. There can be no denying that public relations considerations played a role in choosing the team's members. It should be noted that one of the common questions voiced by the Israeli public has been why the territories to be ceded to the Palestinian state do not include Palestinian-Israeli villages, for example in the Little Triangle region in the center of the country, in exchange for which Israel could retain parts of the West Bank densely populated by settlers. The question itself points to the weakness of Palestinian-Israeli civil status in Israeli consciousness, even among left-wing voters. Indeed, Israeli Palestinians enjoy full legal, individual, and religious rights, but not full equality. Neither do they possess the collective rights of a cultural-ethnic minority. Since 1949, the state has confiscated much of their land, and has restricted their housing construction, planning, and zoning. All Israeli governments have implemented development programs for Jewish settlements, while discriminating against Palestinian citizens in allocating budgets, funds, and services. The resulting frustration felt by Israeli Palestinians pushed many among them to riot in October 2000, in response to the outbreak of the second Palestinian Intifada. Most Israelis would never dream of ceding a Jewish-Israeli settlement within the 1948 borders, with its inhabitants, to Palestine, but many support doing precisely this with Israeli Palestinian settlements. The party that put this program at the top of its platform—Yisrael Beiteinu—won eleven seats in the 2006 elections. The Palestinian-Israelis in the Little Triangle are citizens who live within boundaries of the sovereign state of Israel, and they cannot be ceded any more than Israel's Jewish citizens can. Morally and legally, however, this same principle does not apply to Israel's settlers in the occupied territories. The settlers did not enter the territories after new borders were established, but rather in order to create facts in the field that would change the map. International law defines the transfer of the population of an occupying power into occupied land, and changing the occupied territory's ethnic makeup, as war crimes. The repatriation of the settlers into Israel is not a deportation. Some settlements already contain a third generation born and raised there, but if there is no agreement allowing them to stay where they are, they can be evacuated, despite the human and political difficulty involved.

Israeli critics also charged that the arrangements specified in the Geneva accords would be detrimental to Israeli security and would not allow Israel to defend itself against terror. They noted that, despite Palestinian acts of terror during the Oslo period, and in particular after the outbreak of the second Intifada, the agreement does not explicitly require the Palestinians to fight terror and disarm militias that engage in it.

The drafters of the Geneva document assumed that there would be acts of terror on both sides. This assumption is reasonable given the fierce antagonism with which such an agreement will certainly be received by extremists on both sides—as recent experience proves. While such extreme reactions on the Jewish side would be very small compared to Palestinian terror, neither is it possible to ignore the fact that Israelis have committed terror for the purposes of vengeance or to try to halt the Oslo process.

Indeed, the wording of the Geneva agreement is sweeping and general, in an attempt to cover all eventualities. It seeks to build on the lessons learned from the Oslo agreements, whose implementation was flawed. Article 5 of the Geneva document states that the parties will:

[R]efrain from organizing, encouraging, or allowing the formation of irregular forces or armed bands, including mercenaries and militias within their respective territory and prevent their establishment. In this respect, any existing irregular forces or armed bands shall be disbanded and prevented from reforming at any future date.

[R]efrain from organizing, assisting, allowing, or participating in acts of violence in or against the other or acquiescing in activities directed toward the commission of such acts... .

The Parties reject and condemn terrorism and violence in all its forms and shall pursue public policies accordingly. In addition, the parties shall refrain from actions and policies that are liable to nurture extremism and create conditions conducive to terrorism on either side.

The Parties shall take joint and, in their respective territories, unilateral comprehensive and continuous efforts against all aspects of violence and terrorism. These efforts shall include the prevention and preemption of such acts, and the prosecution of their perpetrators.

To that end, the Parties shall maintain ongoing consultation, cooperation, and exchange of information between their respective security forces.

The fight against terror (including terror against property, land, and institutions!) will be an ongoing battle. It may not be neglected because of disputes with the other side. Furthermore, the text explicitly requires that militias be disarmed, even if they do not act against Israel. The very existence of illegal armed organizations constitutes a breach of the agreement.

Another critique was that the Geneva document does not impose sanctions on the Palestinians if they violate its provisions. This is an odd claim—a peace agreement can hardly be based on attributing bad faith to the other side. If one side believes that the other side is malicious, it would be better off fighting than signing an agreement. Do these critics mean that Israel should impose on the Palestinians a catalog of retaliations, where for example each Qassam rocket will permit Israel to conduct two helicopter attacks on Gaza?

Neither should critics fall into the trap of self-righteousness—the assumption that Israel has only good intentions and Palestinians only bad ones. During the Oslo period, it was not only the Palestinian leadership that obstructed the implementation of that agreement's provisions. To argue that security agreements should be based on an assumption of Palestinian bad faith is to assume that Palestinian leaders will be prepared to sign a document in which they incriminate themselves and declare Israel to be pure.

The curse of the occupation has eaten away at some Israelis so much that some on the right end of the political spectrum have taken the Geneva negotiators to task for not imposing a specific regime structure and governmental operating methods on Palestine, and for not imposing oversight on the ideological parameters of Palestinian public discourse. They also demand sole Israeli security authority over the Palestinian state. The critics who make such demands clearly have learned nothing from the failure of the occupation, and have forgotten whatever they may have once known about the Jewish people's history under foreign rule. The Geneva negotiators do not believe that Israeli military power is omnipotent and do not accept the premise that Israel can achieve security only by force of arms. Neither do they believe that Europe and the United Nations are fundamentally anti-Semitic and anti-Israeli. In Western Europe and the UN there is widespread opposition to Israel's occupation of the West Bank and Gaza Strip and to its repression of the Palestinian people, but not, except on the extreme fringe, to the existence of Israel. Anyone concerned about international legitimacy for Israel's existence should not pour gasoline on the bonfire of the occupation. Western Europe and the UN, after all, played a critical role in the creation of Israel.

The criticism of the Geneva document most frequently leveled by its critics related to the Palestinian refugees of 1948. There were two specific charges: first, that the Palestinians had not abjured their claim that these refuges had a right to return to their former homes within Israel; and, second, that the text specifically cites UN General Assembly Resolution 194—on which the Palestinians base their right of return—as one of the foundations of the solution to the refugee problem.

The proposals for the resolution of the 1948 refugee problem drafted from the end of 2000 onward propose three criteria for differentiating between "permitted" or "preferred" return of refugees and that which is "forbidden" or "tolerable"(Klein 2006b). The first was proposed by President Clinton in December 2000. Using extremely cautious language, Clinton suggested that the Palestinian state would be the focus for Palestinians seeking to return to the area; he thus did not rule out the possibility that Israel would agree to absorb some of them. In other words, Clinton distinguished between preferred return to a focal point, Palestine, and tolerable and peripheral return to Israel.

The second was proposed by Sari Nusseibeh and Ami Ayalon. They distinguished between the return of Palestinians to Palestine and the return of Jews to Israel. They did not categorically reject the right of Palestinian refugees to return, but channeled its implementation into the Palestinian state, in parallel with the Jewish right of return to Israel. Both the Clinton and the Nusseibeh-Ayalon proposals legitimized certain types of return and a right of Palestinian return that are different from the PLO's traditional position.

The Geneva document proposes a third view. It distinguishes between a person's consciousness of his right to return and immigration procedures in Israel for those who choose Israel as a permanent place of residence. The Geneva agreement is constructed as a treaty between countries. State apparatuses make decisions regarding concrete steps and do not address the thoughts of any given individual. They must prevent evildoers from acting on their thoughts. This is precisely what the Geneva initiative does. Article 7, which addresses the refugee issue, states in section 7:

> This agreement provides for the permanent and complete resolution of the Palestinian refugee problem. No claims may be raised except for those related to the implementation of this agreement.

This comes in addition to the general statement in article 1 that the agreement ends all claims by each side against the other:

> The implementation of this Agreement will settle all the claims of the Parties arising from events occurring prior to its signature. No further claims related to events prior to this Agreement may be raised by either Party.

Article 7 also states (section 13) that all bodies established since 1948 to deal with the refugee problem will cease to exist, and that the legal status of "Palestinian refugee" will disappear. An individual refugee who rejects the agreement and continues to maintain his classic right of return will find that no institution recognizes his legal status as a refugee.

To appreciate the change that the Geneva initiative proposes, it is necessary to understand the classic sense of the Palestinian right of return. According to the PLO's longstanding position, the right of return meant that the Palestinian collective as a nation had the right to return to its homeland—and that each Palestinian individual had the right to return to his former home. This right was "sacred" and inalienable, and the PLO demanded that Israel accept and comply with it (Klein 1998). The Geneva document discards this. Even a cursory examination of the Geneva agreement reveals that the way in which a Palestinian refugee would be able to establish Israel as his permanent place of residence is entirely different from the way he would settle in Palestine. Each Palestinian refugee has a vested right to make the Palestinian state his home, while the right to live in the state of Israel can be granted only by Israel itself. A refugee who settles in Israel, under the terms of Israel's immigration laws and procedures, is free to believe that he is returning to his homeland, but the Geneva document provides no legal or institutional expression or backing for that belief. Under the agreement, Israel is a country to which the Palestinian refugee immigrates, just as he might to any other country.

How many such returnees-immigrants will Israel have to admit? According to the text of the agreement (Article 7, section 4),

> Option iv [the option of choosing Israel as the permanent place of residence—MK] shall be at the sovereign discretion of Israel and will be in accordance with a number that Israel will submit to the International Commission. This number shall represent the total number of Palestinian refugees that Israel shall accept. As a basis, Israel will consider the average of the total numbers submitted by the different third countries to the International Commission.

The last sentence refers to International Commission that is to be set up to supervise the solution to the refugee problem. Other countries may suggest to the International Commission the number of refugees they believe Israel should accept. Israel is to consider the average of these numbers in determining the number of refugees it decides to accept, but the final decision will be Israel's alone.

Furthermore, the determination of a refugee's permanent place of residence will not be his decision alone; a technical committee of the international commission will be involved. This commission will include an Israeli representative. The technical committee will be bound by the agreement and the quota of those that Israel will allow to enter. The committee will have no authority to exceed it. The claim, made by

some critics of the Geneva document, that these committees will process refugee cases in ways fundamentally different from the provisions
of the agreement, has no textual basis. It should be kept in mind that
international involvement in the refugee issue is necessary because the
problem cannot be resolved without massive international assistance.
What will be the role of international organizations and the countries
involved? Can they be expected to contribute the large sums of money
necessary for resettlement and to absorb refugees without having some
sort of operative authority? The Geneva agreement offers the countries
prepared to assist Israel and the Palestinians a defined operative role.
The committee will have the authority to decide who among those
wishing to enter Israel will receive the appropriate permission, but it
may not exceed the quota set by Israel.

In the framework of its contribution to solving the refugee problem,
an Israeli government that seeks to act in contradiction of the spirit of
the agreement and to stand on technicalities can base its formal claim
on this provision. But the agreement was not worded in this way to
mislead the Palestinians, but rather to demonstrate that, in contrast
with the classic right of return, Israel here makes a voluntary decision. The hope is that the government of Israel will want to promote
compromise and the resolution of the refugee problem. After all, the
Israeli–Palestinian conflict did not begin in 1967. In 1948, about half
of the Palestinian population became refugees. Israel's interest, in the
opinion of the drafters of the agreement, is not to allow Palestinian
refugees to return to Israel on the basis of the classic right of return.
If the price of a permanent status agreement is finding an apparatus
under which Israel allows some Palestinian refugees to immigrate under parameters it determines or agrees to, the price is worth paying.
This is a compromise between the Palestinian delegation's demand to
impose upon Israel the return of a specific, limited number of refugees,
and the Israel delegation's insistence on Israel's sovereign decision to
permit who will enter, and its refusal to let any of them to enter under
the rubric of "refugee return."

UN General Assembly resolution 194 is cited in the Geneva text as
one of the bases for the resolution of the problem, alongside Security
Council resolution 242 and section two of the Arab peace initiative of
2002. Contrary to popular belief, the text of resolution 194 does not
herald the destruction of Israel, especially when it is placed alongside

resolution 242. Resolution 194 does not specify a right of return, but rather calls on Israel to allow, at the earliest possible time, the return of those refugees who wish to live in Israel in peace. The PLO originally disregarded this decision precisely because it provides for no collective right of return. Similarly, the PLO originally refused to endorse resolution 242, on the grounds that it addresses the Palestinian issue as a refugee problem rather than in terms of a collective's right to self-determination. Once the Palestinian people's right to self-determination was accepted internationally, the PLO accepted both resolution 242 and resolution 194. It argued then that resolution 194 grants each individual refugee an inalienable right of return that Israel must accept (Klein 1998). The PLO's interpretation was overly expansive, since resolution 194 can be read as a request that Israel allow refugees to return, rather than as codification of a right that Israel must accept. Which of these interpretations is valid in terms of the Geneva agreement? It is in this context that the Geneva document cites section 2b of the Arab peace plan of April 2002, which speaks of "a just solution to the Palestinian refugee problem to be agreed upon in accordance with U.N. General Assembly Resolution 194." In other words, the Arab countries also accept the principle that a solution requires Israeli consent—in contradiction of the classic PLO position. In other words, the classic understanding of the right of return is not accepted by the Arab countries. It should be noted that the change in the Arab world preceded the Geneva initiative and made it easier for the Palestinian side to sign it. Arafat gave his prior consent to the wording of the Arab peace plan, before it was officially accepted.

Finally, in the Geneva initiative, the section discussing the end of claims comes together with a permanent and full resolution of the refugee problem. This rules out the possibility that resolution 194 can in the future be used as a basis for claiming a right of return. It is important to note that Palestinian opponents of the agreement decried the provisions on the 1948 refugees and attacked the Palestinian team for signing them.

Legal and diplomatic experts have argued that the Geneva initiative does not end all Palestinian claims against Israel, because it provides for a mechanism for addressing claims that will arise from the agreement. This, they say, provides the Palestinians with a way of reopening subjects that the agreement has already resolved.

The question is, however, to whom the claims on violations will be submitted. Is there any agreement that does not provide for adjudication of disputes regarding the agreement itself? This is not the same as reopening issues that have been agreed upon. Furthermore, even if we accept the charge that subjects could be reopened, then that opportunity would be available to both sides. It is hardly a case, as the criticism suggests, that this provision leaves Israel without recourse.

Another charge has been that the Geneva document is not based on a systemic religious, economic, or ethnic approach, but is merely a political compromise. The opposite is true. The systemic view of the Geneva initiative is expressed, first, in the initiative's structure. The official permanent status talks, in which Israel was the leading and decisive party, were conducted as a zero-sum game. The Intifada created a stalemate, a lose-lose situation. The Geneva initiative proposes, in contrast, a win-win situation, incentives for each side, and a package deal. Second, the Geneva initiative demonstrates that it is not necessary for Israel to continue to occupy the West Bank and Gaza Strip in order to guarantee its security. The more sovereignty the Palestinians received in the West Bank and Gaza Strip, the greater was their willingness to respond to Israel's security needs. Third, the assumption behind the Geneva initiative is that occupation and rule over another nation is not just a democratic problem, but also a Jewish problem. The continuation of the occupation is itself detrimental to the state's Jewish character no less so than is the demographic problem it creates. The challenge that the establishment of the state of Israel presented was whether power and the Jewish religion in its classic form could exist together. Would power not corrupt Judaism? The question mark has loomed larger as the years since 1967 have gone by. The end of the occupation will strengthen the country's Jewish and moral identity no less than will sovereignty over the Western Wall.

Fourth, some of the most important sections of the Geneva document are based on a concept that places the political understanding within a system of civilian action. The refugee provisions call on both civil societies to open themselves to the other's national narrative, beyond the arrangements governments will make for immigration, compensation, resettlement, and rehabilitation. In the religious sphere, the document proposes to establish an interfaith council that will advise both governments and promote dialogue between religions. In my view, the Geneva agreement has considerably more systemic features than do Israel's treaties with Egypt and Jordan.

Finally, the Geneva initiative is founded on the concept that the political agreement is not the end of the process of conciliation and acceptance between the two nations, but rather its beginning. The Geneva initiative does not offer a new Middle East. Instead, it is a first step in a long journey that will change the relations of two nations that have inflicted pain on each other for more than a century. The end of the conflict on the legal and political level does not mean the end of personal antagonism. It does not mean that there will be no feelings of inequity or injustice, or that painful memories will disappear. A diplomatic agreement ensures, however, that these feelings will not lead to action and that they can be dealt with, over the course of years, on the social and personal levels. To make a diplomatic agreement conditional on prior conciliation between the nations is to say that there will be no agreement at all. Hawks who argue that the relations between the nations must be the first thing to change ought to admit that Israel, too, must undergo a mental metamorphosis. Surprisingly, they generally ignore this and clothe themselves in self-righteousness. They do not explain how Israeli society will change its attitudes to the Palestinian nation while the occupation and Jewish settlement activity continue. The end of the occupation is a precondition for any change, and not the result of such change. And the occupation can end, the Geneva agreement says, only by agreement, not as a unilateral move. Zionism's great achievements have come at a horrible price. If we can realize Zionism's objectives while receiving full recognition from the enemy at whose expense those objectives have been achieved, we cannot allow ourselves to miss the opportunity.

GENEVA AVERTS THE BINATIONAL STATE

During the period between the escalation of the Second Intifada and the signing of the Geneva initiative, the idea of a binational Jewish-Arab state came back into fashion among those who had despaired of Israel ever exiting the territories, whether through a diplomatic agreement or through force of arms. Meron Benvenisti, an Israeli who has written extensively about the Palestinian territories, has long argued that the occupation is irreversible and constitutes de facto annexation. But most Israelis and Palestinans have never accepted that view. The resurgence of the concept of the binational state was an expression of distress and despair after Israel reoccupied the territories in the Protective Wall operation of 2002, an occupation that has been far worse for both Palestinian and Israeli society than its predecessor ever was. According to the Israeli human rights organization B'Tselem, from the outbreak of the Intifada in late September 2000, through mid-September 2006, Israel had killed 3,764 Palestinians, and Palestinians had killed 1,011 Israelis. The dead include 764 Palestinian and 129 Israeli minors. After almost six years of fighting, 8,074 Palestinians, including minors, were incarcerated in Israeli detention facilities after being charged with or convicted of violations. Another 708 were under administrative detention, without having been charged or brought to trial. During this period, Israel destroyed 3,884 Palestinian homes and erected hundreds of physical barriers on roads. In the West Bank there are 53 permanent manned roadblocks, plus 16 temporary ones. Of these, 27 lie deep within the territory, 12 are in Hebron and 26 are entry points into Israel. Some 700 kilometers (435 miles) of roads in the West Bank can be freely used by Israelis, but Palestinian use is extremely limited (B'Tselem 2004). According to the Palestinian Red Crescent, between the beginning of the Intifada in September 2000 through August 18, 2006, a total of 30,714 Palestinians had been injured (Palestine Red Crescent undated). The number of Israeli injured from September 29, 2000, through September 18, 2006, is 8,000 (IDF 2006). Palestinian sympathy for the idea of a binational state also grew when Israel smashed the Palestinian Authority and created a governing vacuum there. There was great disappointment with the way the Palestinian Authority functioned during the Oslo period, and impatience with the Palestinian leadership's corruption and failure to build proper governing institutions and agencies. Furthermore, there was disillusionment because of the Palestinian Authority's failure to effect an Israeli withdrawal. In fact, settlements grew; their number doubled after the first Oslo agreement of 1993. According to many Palestinians, their political leadership was disconnected from the people and was fighting among itself for jobs and titles, and for the perquisites of government and of class.

This disenchantment reached a head at two discussions held during November 2002, one in East Jerusalem and the second in Mainz, Germany—the First World Congress for Middle East Studies. On these occasions, Dr. Nazmi Jubeh and Professor Manuel Hassassian, vice-president of Bethlehem University, advocated a binational state as an alternative to the Israeli occupation. Jubeh and Hassassian had long histories of contacts with Israelis, and for years they had worked for a two-state solution—but despair had pushed them toward binationalism. They were not alone. During this difficult period, many Palestinian intellectuals looked to a South African, one-man, one vote, equal civil rights model. They thought that such a solution would have a better chance of success in the international arena than would the partition of Mandatory Palestine. They argued that Israel, supported by the U.S. refusal to intervene had managed to stymie any possibility of partition based on a Palestinian state in the West Bank and Gaza Strip. For these intellectuals, a binational state was the default option. They joined those who from the start had opposed the establishment of a Palestinian ethnic-national state and sought instead full civil equality.

But from the moment the Geneva talks began making progress, Jubeh and Hassassian reverted to their previous support for two states. Jubeh, born in Jerusalem and an archaeologist by profession, was a member of the Palestinian delegation to the Geneva talks; he worked, together with me, primarily on the Jerusalem issue. Hassassian, a political scientist, was brought in to the Palestinian delegation for the Geneva agreement's launching ceremony, and read a letter from Arafat on that occasion.

It is interesting to note that, at the end of March 2004, even Noam Chomsky, the American professor of linguistics who has long been the most prominent intellectual advocate of the binational model, and his personal friend Edward Said, came out in support of the two-state model that the Geneva initiative proposes (Shalom and Podur 2004). Chomsky said he had changed his position because a single-state solution was no longer realistic. Chomsky's support for the Geneva model may grate on many members of Israel's center-left, but its importance should not be discounted. Chomsky is extremely influential among Western elites (in November 2005, a poll by Britain's *Prospect* magazine named him the world's top public intellectual). His support can help unite the left around a plan that has a realistic chance of being accepted in the future by a majority in Israel and in the Palestinian territories.

This plan, which seeks not to dismantle the Jewish national state but rather to strengthen it, also enjoys international support.

There was no reason to despair, because the limit of Israeli power was already apparent on the horizon. The occupation had been defeated because the Palestinians constituted a critical mass of some 4 million people whom the Israelis could not digest or contain in the long run. Any Israeli success in countering the Intifada with military power is momentary, and has a boomerang effect. Furthermore, Israel's increasing need to use military force is evidence of Palestinian society's refusal to reconcile itself to Israeli rule. The days of an inexpensive, "enlightened" occupation are over. Two new generations have arisen: the generation of the 1987 Intifada, and the generation of the al-Aqsa Intifada of 2000. The efforts by the settlers and their collaborators in the government and establishment to preserve and expand their settlements cannot succeed. The appetite for settlement has grown since the Oslo agreement of 1993, but at the same time the ability to incorporate the Palestinians residing on the occupied territories into the Israeli state and society has collapsed. In addition, the majority of Israelis have separated themselves mentally from the Palestinian territories. In responding to the new Intifada, Israel did not go back to the model of occupation it created between 1967 and 1994. It did not reassert control over the Palestinian population's day-to-day affairs. In reoccupying the territories, the Israeli army remained outside Palestinian cities, towns, and villages. It surrounded them and cut them off, not seeing directly the grave consequences this had. According to a World Bank report of April-June 2003, the percentage of Palestinians in the West Bank and Gaza Strip living under the $2-a-day income line grew from 21 percent just before the Intifada to 60 percent (some 2 million people) at the end of 2002. In the Gaza Strip, this figure is even higher—75 percent (World Bank 2003). By any measure, the consequences of the Intifada for the Palestinian population are much harsher than was the direct occupation of 1967.

Israeli society and its leadership have adjusted to this reality. In contrast with the direct and complete occupation of 1967, they do not now see the Palestinians as human beings—they lack close contact with the Palestinians or administrative concern for their everyday needs. In the past, these factors served as agents for humanizing the Palestinian other. If we add to this the low number of Palestinians who now work in the Israeli economy—because of the sieges, curfews, roadblocks, security fences, and refusal to grant permits for entry into Israel—the picture becomes clear. Israel does not intend to create intimate contact with the Palestinians. Instead, it seeks physical and mental separation. The Palestinians are perceived by most Israelis as alien and threatening, people to be kept at a distance, if not imprisoned inside fences. Israeli support for the fence and separation from the Palestinians is not based on concern for morality and civil liberties, but rather on the huge cost of the conflict. This is the opposite of creating a binational state.

Furthermore, a huge majority of Israel's Jews are not prepared to give up their right to a Jewish national state, just as the Palestinian people are not willing to give up their aspiration for their own nation-state. A binational state, in contrast, is one whose institutions are equally divided between two ethnic-national groups. Neither of these options has the support of Israelis, who want a state with a dominant Jewish majority. Jewish dominance will not disappear in a joint Israel-Palestinian state—instead, it will be asserted all the more forcefully. The Israeli Jewish community would dominate such an ostensibly binational or non-national state, thanks to their military, economic, and technological dominance.

The Jewish population would inevitably force the Palestinians into disconnected cantons, on the grounds that this was essential for security. While the justification offered would be different, the practical result would be something similar to South Africa under white rule. The inexorable consequence would be another Palestinian uprising for national liberation. There is no way to predict when this would happen, but experience indicates that each decade a new Palestinian generation matures and seeks a constitutive experience. Because 50 percent of Palestinians in the territories are age fourteen or younger, the potential force of each generation becomes all the more powerful (CIA 2002; Palestinian Central Bureau of Statistics undated). The generation that bore the flag of the Intifada in 1987 is the generation that was born into the occupation of 1987. It never experienced Jordanian rule. Its political consciousness was formed after the Israeli electoral revolution of 1977, when Menachem Begin kept his election promise to create new Israeli settlements in the territories.

Begin also signed a peace treaty with Egypt, in which he recognized the right of the Palestinians in the territories to national self-determination. During Begin's tenure, settlement activity spread from the Jordan valley and the southern West Bank into the northern West Bank and Gaza Strip. The number of settlers grew from about 1,500 in 1972 to 5,023 in 1977, then to 57,840 in 1986 and about a quarter of a million in 2004 (Eldar and Zertal 2005; Foundation for Middle East Peace undated). For the generation that led the al-Aqsa Intifada in 2000, then in their early twenties, the Oslo years were a disappointing, constitutive experience. These young people were in their early teens when the first Oslo agreement was signed, and accompanied their fathers and brothers when they went out into the streets bearing olive branches. Their dashed expectations and the intensification of the occupation led them into an armed, bloody uprising (Klein 2006). Suicide bombers took the place of the stone-throwers of the first Intifada.

If Israel takes advantage of its current strength, and the Palestinian institutional and leadership vacuum, to impose its policies, within a decade it is likely to find itself facing even more severe violence, not to mention the moral price it will pay. The first inklings of this can be seen the Shikaki and Shamir polls of December 2005. While Israeli support for the Clinton parameters remained at the same level as the previous year, 64 percent, Palestinian support declined from 54 to 46 percent. When the pollsters presented the parameters of the Geneva agreement without mentioning it by name, there was a significant decline in Palestinian support and increase in opposition on each item, compared with 2004 (PCPSR 2005). A second expression of this was the massive support for Hamas in the Palestinian Authority's parliamentary elections of 2006. Hamas won 74 of the legislature's 133 seats, as opposed to 55 for Fatah.

Currently, it is possible that an extreme nationalist Israeli party could win significant representation in the Knesset and form the government. This would be especially likely given the failure of the unilateral disengagement from the Gaza Strip and of the second Lebanon war. If there is no breakthrough toward an Israeli–Palestinian permanent agreement, and a new and brutal wave of Palestinian terror breaks out, including rocket attacks on Israel's major urban centers, a great number of Israelis may throw their support to a party of the extreme right. Such a realignment would also be facilitated by the structural weaknesses of Israeli democracy. Israel is a country of immigrants, most of whom come from non-democratic states, where the army carries much weight in the leadership and society. Power plays a large role in popular culture, and political stability is lacking. Hardly any Knesset since the 1980s has completed a full four-year term. Governments have fallen, early elections have been called, and a prime minister has been killed for political-religious reasons. The Intifada brought on an economic crisis, pushed up unemployment, and increased the income gap. The emergence of an extreme right-wing nationalist-religious coalition, one that will declare emergency measures and take harsh, anti-democratic actions, is possible. But a policy of force will not solve any problems, and will only increase the cost of separating into two states.

THE UNILATERAL OPTION:
SEEKING TO EXORCISE THE GENEVA INITIATIVE

Unilateral withdrawal from the Gaza Strip and part of the West Bank, and the construction of a separation fence between Israel and part of the Palestinian territories, was proposed by Israel's center-right and center-left in the wake of the failure of the permanent status talks and the escalation of the Intifada. Prime Minister Ariel Sharon's disengagement program received broad support from Israelis who were not prepared to pay the price of an Israeli–Palestinian agreement based on a two-state solution, those who believed the Palestinian leadership to be unreliable, and those who also sought to ease the burden of the occupation and/or military confrontation with the Palestinians. Unilateralism's advocates seek to use it to exorcise the Geneva initiative and remove it from the public agenda. The Sharon government's original plan was a 786 km (488 miles) long border, in addition to another border of 143 km (89 miles) along the Jordan River, for a total of 929 km (577 miles)—three times the length of the Green Line. With this border, Israel would annex, de facto, 43 percent of the West Bank's territory and 346,650 of its inhabitants, as well as 86 Israeli settlements with 367,427 (including East Jerusalem) inhabitants. In the summer of 2003, the cabinet approved a border that would annex to Israel about 20 percent of the West Bank, on which 270,000 Palestinians live, not including the 200,000 who live in East Jerusalem. At the same time, the plan left 58 Israeli settlements, with a population of 70,000, outside the fence, as well as some 700 km (435 miles) of roads used exclusively by the settlers. This number does not include some 80 unlicensed outposts that were never dismantled by the government, apparently not by coincidence. If these outposts are brought inside the fence, the annexed area will revert to that of the original plan, 43 percent of the West Bank under exclusive Israeli control. This is virtually identical to Sharon's map for a permanent settlement in the 1980s, and in 2000 it was Israel's opening position in the permanent status talks (Klein 2003b:68). In contrast, the border proposed by the Geneva agreement between Israel and the West Bank is 445 km (277 miles) long, and does not annex a single Palestinian individual or residence. The Geneva plan annexes 110,000 Israeli settlers and 21 settlements, on only two percent of the West Bank's land, not including East Jerusalem.

The Israeli Supreme Court, the International Court of Justice in the Hague, and moderate international pressure forced Israel to make changes in the fence's route. The length of the fence line approved by the cabinet in February 2005 was 644 km (400 miles). It leaves about eight percent of the West Bank on the Israeli side of the fence, with a Palestinian population of 206,000 (again, this does not include East Jerusalem). About 341,000 Israeli settlers will be on the Israeli side of the fence, including the inhabitants of Ma'aleh Adumim and Ariel. The line is similar to the one that appeared on the map that Israel presented in the permanent status talks at Taba, in January 2001. At Taba, however, there were negotiations, whereas the line of the fence is a unilateral act intended to impose on the Palestinians a border drawn according to Israeli interests. In its affidavit to the Supreme Court, the state admitted that the fence line was intended to expand the areas of the settlements (Ha'aretz, July 4, 2005). The same document declared that the fence was not temporary, in contradiction of previous claims (Ha'aretz, July 4, 2005). The cost of construction—approximately $1 million per kilometer—proves this. Finally, in its proposal for the Taba talks, Israel did not leave settlers or military forces beyond the border it proposed, while Sharon's plan leaves the Israeli army and many settlers on the far side of the fence, as means of pressure on and control of the Palestinians. In other words, so long as there is not a complete evacuation of Israeli forces and citizens from the area to the east of the fence, it is impossible to see it as a border. Instead, it is an aggressive means of control meant to force the Palestinians to agree to it as a border at some point in the future.

Rulings by Israeli and international courts have required Israel to find solutions for humanitarian problems, transport difficulties, and access for 200,000 Palestinians who today live imprisoned in fenced-off enclaves—in addition to the problems in East Jerusalem discussed above. Israel has found it difficult, and will continue to find it difficult, to find solutions that resolve these problems adequately, and to enlist the personnel and budgetary resources to maintain such a problematic border. Furthermore, such a policy is unlikely to be practicable. Increasing pressure on the Palestinian population can temporarily repress Palestinian violence, but in the long run it is an incentive to terror. It simply reinforces the Palestinians' conviction that they cannot live with Israeli settlements or accept the de facto annexation of some eight percent of the West Bank and Israeli control of the rest of the West Bank. When Israel proposed to withdraw unilaterally from the Gaza Strip, Hamas gained strength and defeated Fatah in the Palestinian elections. The Palestinian public has come to see the Hamas strategy of expelling Israel from Palestinian lands by force as more effective than the strategy promoted by Fatah's central stream, ending the occupation through diplomacy. At the same time, Fatah's radical wing is preparing to cooperate with Hamas against Israel, when Palestinian hopes for a negotiated agreement vanish entirely. But a pragmatic trend in Hamas could grow stronger and grant legitimacy to a permanent agreement based on a Palestinian national and pan-Arab consensus. Abbas has tried to push in this direction by proposing a joint political platform with Hamas. He proposes the formation of a national unity government that accepts the Arab League peace plan of 2002 and the agreements the PLO has signed with Israel. To reinforce this latter possibility, Israel must cooperate and display its willingness to carry out a larger withdrawal than the government has so far approved. But the fact is that Israel's recent governments see as an enemy any central Palestinian leadership that demands full independence on all the 1967 territories.

THE GENEVA AGREEMENT—PRELUDE TO A NEW ZIONISM

A permanent status agreement like the Geneva agreement will not be easy. In fact, it will be painful and traumatic. It will come almost as a necessity, when all other alternatives, including unilateral withdrawal, have failed. Israel's painful divorce from the West Bank and Gaza Strip will probably bring on a national crisis and an identity crisis. It will create a charged atmosphere of negative emotions toward the other side and toward the agents of the change (people of the left, the government that negotiates and carries out the agreement, and the international actors that mediate it). These crises are likely because the state's national project of the last forty years, that of using settlements to demarcate its eastern border, will come to an end. Israel may have to deal with internal violence perpetrated by extremist forces that refuse to accept the democratic decision to reach accommodation with the Palestinians.

The Palestinians will undergo a similar crisis. They will have to face down their extremists who refuse to accept the necessary concessions. Beyond that, however, Palestine will have to build itself while coping with the internal problems of a young, densely populated, poor, and small country. Palestinian society will have to emerge from its passivity and stop blaming Israel for all its own flaws. The activism of the Palestinian armed struggle and diplomatic effort will have to be turned toward building a country and its institutions. The end of the occupation is a precondition for these processes, not a result of them.

The implementation of the Geneva agreement, or any other permanent agreement between Israel and the Palestinians, will require a redefinition of Zionism's goals. Classical Zionism was based on three foundations: immigration to the historic Jewish homeland, acquisition of land, and establishment of a democratic Jewish national home. Immigration was aimed at creating a critical demographic mass of Jews in the historic land of Israel; land acquisition was meant to create a continuous territorial entity where the Jewish state would be sovereign; the establishment of a democratic and Jewish state was meant to create a well-governed society in which Jews from the Diaspora would want to live. The Zionist movement acquired land by purchase, settlement, military conquest, and administrative fiat—the nationalization of land. In 1948, at the end of the war that established Israel's recognized de facto borders, it looked as if purchase and military conquest would become things of the past. Thereafter, Israel used settlement and administrative means to achieve its classic Zionist goals. But the 1967 war opened up new territories for the pursuit of classic Zionism. The settlement of the occupied territories became Israel's national project. The state encouraged Jews to move to the new territories, with the purpose of gaining control of the land there and redefining the state's borders. Since most of the territories occupied in 1967 (the exception being East Jerusalem) were not formally annexed to Israel, the military administered them and became the dominant factor in day-to-day life of the Palestinian inhabitants. As Israel became more ensconced in the territories and broadened the settlement project, the links between the settlements, the army, and the state bureaucracy grew tighter, to the point that it is difficult to make out where one ends and the other begins. A military-settlement-bureaucracy complex arose that suffocates not only the Palestinian inhabitants of the territories, but also the future of the state of Israel (Gorenberg 2006).

It is a mistake to see the settlement movement as the process of repeated waves of young enthusiasts, or as a marginal group of religious eccentrics dragging the country along behind it. Even though the inner kernel of the settlement movement is motivated by a messianic Jewish ideology, settler leaders are correct when they say that they acted in the name and with the help of the Israeli government. In their view, they are the manifestation of classic Zionism. It is interesting that, in the era in which classic Zionism has reached the limit of its abilities, religious fundamentalism has grown among extremist settlers, their reservations about the state are increasing, and the first signs of a messianic post-Zionism are appearing.

When a permanent agreement is reached, there will be no time to recover from the amputation and to go through physical therapy and rehabilitation. Israeli society will have to redefine its identity. Its withdrawal from parts of its historical homeland, and the end of the national project it spent four decades pursuing, will produce a crisis of identity. A significant part of the society will undergo a severe ideological crisis brought on by the failure of its messianic vision of a Greater Israel. To some extent, the Palestinian uprising mitigates this crisis, because it demonstrates the need to compromise with the Palestinians so that the cycle of violence will come to an end. On the other hand, the bloody conflict, terror, and the emotions that come in their wake make it more difficult for these Israelis to accept the need to compromise. The withdrawal will be especially difficult for groups on the religious right that have a high commitment to ideology, social cohesiveness, and an authoritative or charismatic leadership in the form of extremist rabbis who head yeshivot (religious seminaries). These same groups possess a culture of personal sacrifice and a scale of values in which the imaginary national collective is supreme. Settlement Zionism will have to concede its place to neo-Zionism. Even though the settlement project has scored some successes, it cannot avoid the crisis that withdrawal will cause. The eschatological expectations of messianic ideological movements on the right have gone sky-high, so they will have that much farther to fall—and their opposition to the withdrawal will be proportionately strong. Commitment to democratic and liberal values is weak on the religious right. Opinion polls, studies, and voting patterns show that the most important factor in determining right-wing, nationalist sentiments is the level of religious observance. It is sad to see how Judaism, with its rich tradition of universal values, has in Israel become simplistic, one-dimensional, territorial, and xenophobic. After 1967, religious Judaism became identified with the land of Israel, and the land of Israel became identified with only that 22 percent of it that made up the territories conquered in 1967. Evacuation of a large proportion of the settlements is liable to push the extremists to armed resistance. It is difficult to estimate how many of the 200,000 settlers would take part—it could be 2,000, or just 200. Past experience of confrontations between the Israeli army and settlers indicates that the settlers will be aided by an ideological and organizational rear constituting a pool of supporters within Israel. No one should take lightly the settlers' ideological commitment, their economic and emotional resources, and the price in blood they paid during the Intifada, nor the fact that they are networked closely into the Israeli public and leadership, including the military. Similar situations have led in other countries to civil wars or armed uprisings.

The crisis will not be restricted to religious Zionism. The entire nation will face it. Classic Zionism, more than a century old, has reached the point where its territorial success endangers the state. It is a difficult fact to face, but it must be faced. Zionism and the state of Israel, which elicited the world's wonder and admiration in 1948 and 1967, have lost both as it invested itself in the settlement enterprise and the occupation. What has Israel given to human culture since 1967?

The society of colonizers intends to be a managing society and works hard to give that appearance.... On examining the situation more closely, one generally finds only men of small stature beyond the pomp of simple pride of the petty colonizer. With practically no knowledge of history, politicians given the task of shaping history, are always taken by surprise or incapable of forecasting events. Specialists responsible for the technical future of a country turn out to be technicians who are behind the time because they are spared from all competition. As far as administrators are concerned, the negligence and indigence of colonial management are well known. It must truthfully be said that better management of a colony hardly forms part of the purpose of colonization... .

Even if every colonialist is not mediocre, every colonizer must, in a certain measure, accept the mediocrity of colonial life and the men who thrive on it.

(Memmi 1991:49, 51).

The state of Israel faces more than the physical removal of the settlers from their homes. The much greater challenge is to create the Zionism of the day after. It is not sufficient to legislate compensation packages for the settlers, nor is the legitimacy granted the withdrawal by a decision of the Knesset or elections sufficient. Israel must create a new Zionist identity and redefine Zionism's goals for the twenty-first century. A new complex of ideals, Israeli, civilian, and Jewish, will be at its center. Zionism will no longer be a matter of gaining one acre after another, no longer a matter of settlers and uniforms. It will be a Zionism that places the human being at the center, and that gives priority to education, health, public welfare, culture, physical infrastructure, and environmental quality. The Oslo agreements were meant to set this process of change going, but the settler-military complex blocked it. A permanent agreement with the Palestinians will have to overcome this obstacle and bring about a change in national identity.

Israel's withdrawal from the 1967 territories will be accompanied by a need to preserve Israel's character as a Jewish country and to concentrate the Jewish population in a territory in which it has a solid majority. Historical territories will be given up for a Jewish need. But, as soon as Israel returns to its 1949 borders, it will have to face the challenge of the Palestinian Israelis, who today already find it difficult to accept the inequity they have experienced for so long. When there is a permanent agreement with the Palestinians, Israel will no longer be able to view its Palestinian citizens as permanently suspect, unofficial enemy agents.

They, in turn, will amplify their demands for civil equality, recognition of Palestinian Israelis as a unique group not only religiously, but also as a cultural minority with its own ethnic origins. Some may call more forcefully for a redefinition of Israel as a state of all its citizens rather than a Jewish state. If the ground is not prepared, it will be difficult for the Jewish majority to address this challenge. Israel's Jews will have withdrawn from parts of their historical homeland, but will still face a demographic threat from the high rate of natural increase among its own Palestinian citizens. It may also face the national trauma of an armed uprising by the settlers and extreme right, and perhaps also a civil war. The danger is that Israel will turn from repression of the Palestinians in the territories it acquired in 1967 to a narrow ethnic nationalism that will lead it to repress its own Arab citizens. This would be detrimental both to the country's democratic and to its Jewish character. We should take note of the South African experience and begin a process of changing our national identity now, in parallel to paving the way for a permanent status agreement with the Palestinians of the West Bank and Gaza Strip.

Epilogue

In the years that have passed since the Geneva initiative was signed, its most notable achievement is to have become the reference framework for any discussion about the shape of an Israeli–Palestinian agreement. The Geneva initiative stands out in such discussions alongside President Clinton's parameters, United Nations Security Council resolutions 242 and 338, and the Arab League's peace initiative. The political and public standing that the Geneva initiative achieved within a few months of being signed led Prime Minister Ariel Sharon to announce his unilateral disengagement plan from the Gaza Strip and northern West Bank in mid-2004, and to begin the construction of a separation wall and security fence within the West Bank.

In contrast with the Geneva initiative, which is based on direct talks between the two sides, Sharon maintained that Israel had to take unilateral steps and impose, with the help of the Bush administration, Israel's approach on the Palestinians. Sharon and his government knew that there was no Palestinian partner for the map they had to offer, so their approach was one-sided. In the summer of 2005, Israel evacuated its settlements and bases in the Gaza Strip and northern West Bank. Sharon won broad international praise for this move. But within a year the policy proved its bankruptcy. Withdrawal from these territories in the absence of negotiations with the Palestinians, and sometimes while displaying public disdain for them, brought home to the Palestinians that they could expect nothing from talks, nor could they expect any support from the West. The result was the decline of Fatah—which had since the 1980s advocated a negotiated solution—and the ascent of Hamas—which promised clean government, in contrast to the corruption of the PLO and Palestinian Authority establishment. It also promised to end the occupation by force of arms. With a great deal of justification, Hamas attributed the Israeli withdrawal to the terror and guerrilla operations it had conducted against Israeli solders and civilians, and to the heavy cost that Israeli incurred in occupying the Gaza Strip.

Lacking an Israeli partner, Fatah, led by President Mahmoud Abbas, sought talks with Hamas. Fatah's and Hamas's positions began to grow closer during Abbas's campaign for the presidency in January 2005. The process continued with the Cairo understandings and the cease-fire agreement he reached with Hamas in January 2005. At this writing, the two Palestinian factions have reached tentative agreement on a national unity government. In parallel, Fatah's activist wing (Tanzim and the al-Aqsa Martyrs' Brigades, the movement's military arm) has grown closer to Hamas. While the Geneva initiative offers a model for negotiation and agreement between the peace camps on both sides, the larger public and principal political organizations on each side have distanced themselves from each other and turned inward. Hamas's victory in the Palestinian parliamentary elections of 2006, the continuation of Palestinian Qassam rocket attacks from the Gaza Strip on Israeli villages and towns, ongoing Palestinian governmental chaos, and the economic strangulation of the Gaza Strip have proved that the unilateral disengagement program was a mistake. Palestinians have been further frustrated by more Israeli unilateral actions in the West Bank—the expansion of the settlements, roadblocks, the cordoning off of Palestinian cities, the imprisonment of thousands of Palestinians, and the difficulties that the separation wall and fence have created for the daily lives of hundreds of thousands of Palestinians. The hollowness of unilateralism is also evident in the failure of Israel's earlier unilateral withdrawal from Lebanon, demonstrated by Israel's second war there in the summer of 2006.

As this book goes to press, the two sides are again at a crossroads. President Bush's road map has not succeeded in gaining momentum because it does not lead in any clear direction. It was primarily a guide for interim arrangements, and for containment of the Israeli–Palestinian conflict in a framework that was extremely foggy with regard to a final agreement and the end of the conflict. In this situation, the Geneva initiative stands out as an alternative to the poverty of current policy. The question is whether the Israeli and American governments will have sufficient energy and political courage to change direction. Another open question is whether the two sides can renew negotiations given their current lack of faith in each other. Attempts to achieve a partial final status agreement, in keeping with the Road Map, have failed. Once again, the Geneva initiative is relevant as a model for a final Israeli–Palestinian agreement, and as a possible basis for renewal of negotiations.

BIBLIOGRAPHY

Ackleson, Jason M. 2000. "Discourse of Identity and Territoriality on the US-Mexico Border." In Nurith Kliot and David Newman, eds., *Geopolitics at the End of the Twentieth Century: The Political Map of Changing World*, pp. 155–79. London: Frank Cass.

Adam, Heribert, Kanya Adam, and Kogila Moodley. 2004. "Conditions for Peacemaking: Negotiating the Non-negotiable in South Africa and in the Middle East." In Ulrich Schneckener and Stefan Wolf, eds., *Managing and Settling Ethnic Conflicts: Perspectives on Success and Failures in Europe, Africa and Asia*, pp. 220–47. London: C. Hurst.

Adwan, Sami and Dan Bar On, eds. 2004. *Peace Building Under Fire: Palestinian/Israeli Wye River Projects.* Tel Aviv and Jerusalem: Peace Research Institute in the Middle East, The American Embassy and The Consulate General of the United States.

Agha, Hussein and Robert Malley. 2001. "Camp David: The Tragedy of Errors." *New York Review of Books.* August 9.

Agha, Hussein and Robert Malley. 2002a. "Camp David and After: An Exchange 2, A Reply to Ehud Barak." *New York Review of Books.* June 13.

Agha, Hussein and Robert Malley. 2002b. "Camp David and After Continued: Reply by Hussein Agha, Robert Malley." *New York Review of Books.* June 27.

Agha, Hussein, Shai Feldman, Ahmad Khalidi, and Zeev Schiff. 2003. *Track 2 Diplomacy Lessons from the Middle East.* Cambridge, Mass.: MIT.

Al-Awda. 2003. "Regarding Geneva." At http: //leb.net/~al-awda/regardinggeneva.

Almagor, Dan. 2005. "Yerushalayim Shel Az." ("Jerusalem of Then"). *Kol Ha-Ir.* Oct. 7.

Al-Quds. 2002. "Urgent Appeal to Stop Suicide Bombings" (Arabic). June 19.

Arieli, Shaul, and Ron Pundak. 2004. *Ha-Hebet Ha-Teritoriali Be-Masa U-Matan Ha-Yisraeli-Falastini Al Hesder Qeva (The Territorial Aspect of the Israeli–Palestinian Negotiations on a Permanent Agreement).* Tel Aviv: Peres Center for Peace.

Avineri, Shlomo. 2004. "Fatal Flawed Peace Proposal: The Geneva Proposal Fails to Commit Palestinians to Accepting Israel as a State or to Giving Up Their Right of Return." *Los Angeles Times*. Jan. 4.

Ayalon, Ami and Sari Nusseibeh. 2002. Statement of Principles. http: //www. mifkad.org.il/en/principles.asp.

B'Tselem. 2004. "Forbidden Roads: The Discriminatory West Bank Road Regime." At www.btselem.org.

Bar Siman Tov, Ya'akov, Efraim Lavie, Kobi Michael, and Daniel Bar-Tal. 2005. *Ha-'Imut Ha-Alim Ha-Yisra'eli-Falastini 2000–2004, Ha-Ma'avar Mi-Yishuv Sichsuch La-Nihul Sichsuch (The Violent Israeli–Palestinian Confrontation 2000–2004, The Transition from Conflict Resolution to Conflict Management)*. Jerusalem: Jerusalem Institute for Israel Studies.

Bayat, Asef. 2000. "From Dangerous Classes to Quiet Rebels: Politics of the Urban Subaltern in the Global South." *International Sociology* 15 (3): 533–57.

Beilin, Yossi. 2001. *Madrich LeYona Petzu'ah (Guide for a Wounded Dove)*. Tel Aviv: Yediot Aharonot.

Beilin, Yossi. 2004. *The Path to Geneva: The Quest for a Permanent Agreement, 1996–2004*. New York: RDV books.

Ben-Ami, Shlomo. 1998. *Maqom Le-Kulam (A Place for Everyone)*. Tel Aviv: Ha-Kibbutz Ha-Me'uchad.

Ben-Ami, Shlomo. 2004. *Hazit Le-Lo 'Oref: Masa' El Gevulot Tahalich Ha-Shalom (A Front with No Rear: A Journey to the Boundaries of the Peace Process)*. Tel Aviv: Yediot Aharonot.

Benn, Aluf. 2003. "AMA"N Ke-To'alman Shel Ha-Memshala" ("Army Intelligence as Propagandist for the Government"). *Ha'aretz*. Feb. 6.

Bollens, Scott. 1998. "Urban Planning Amidst Ethnic Conflict: Jerusalem and Johannesburg." *Urban Studies* 35(4): 729–50.

Bollens, Scott. 1999. *Urban Peace Building in Divided Societies: Belfast and Johannesburg*. Boulder, CO and Oxford: Westview.

Brainstorming Team on the Jerusalem Issue. 2000. *Hesderei Shalom Be-Yerushalayim (Peace Arrangements in Jerusalem)*. Jerusalem: Jerusalem Institute for Israel Studies.

Centro Italiano per la Pace in Medio Oriente. 2001. *Israelis Palestinians Coexisting in Jerusalem*. Milan.

Chigas, Diana V. 1997. "Unofficial Intervention with Official Actors: Parallel Negotiation Training in Violent Intrastate Conflicts." *International Negotiation* 2 (3).

Chufrin, Gennady I. and Harold H.Saunders. 1993. "A Public Peace Process." *Negotiation Journal* 9 (2): 155–78.

CIA. (Central Intelligence Agency). 2002. *The World Factbook*. https: //www. cia.gov/cia/publications/factbook/index.html.

Connelly, Matthew. 2002. *A Diplomatic Revolution: Algeria's Fight for Independence and the Origins of the Post-Cold War Era.* Oxford: Oxford University Press.

Council for Peace and Security. 2005. Hoda'a VeTeguva LeBaga'tz—Atirat a-Ram (Statement and Response to Supreme Court—a-Ram Petition), Section 11. http: //www.peace-security.org.il/NewsInner.asp?Acat = 1&ArticleID = 310, accessed Oct. 10, 2006.

Cristal, Motti. 2004. "The Geneva Accords: A Step Forward in the Wrong Direction?" *Strategic Assessment* 6 (4) (February).

Dajani, Omar M. 2005. "Surviving Opportunities: Palestinian Negotiating Patterns in Peace Talks with Israel." In Tamara Cofman Wittes, ed., *How Israelis and Palestinian Negotiate: A Cross-Cultural Analysis of the Oslo Peace Process,* pp. 39–80. Washington D.C.: United States Institute of Peace Press.

Davis, John and Edy Kaufman. 2002. "Second Track/Citizens' Diplomacy: An Overview." In John Davis and Edy Kaufman, eds., *Second Track/Citizens' Diplomacy: Concepts and Techniques for Conflict Transformation,* pp. 1–14. Lanham, MD: Rowan and Littlefield.

Drucker, Raviv and Ofer Shelah. 2005. *Bumerang: Kishalon Ha-Manhigut Ba-Intifada Ha-Sheniya (Boomerang: The Failure of Leadership in the Second Intifada).* Jerusalem: Keter.

Eldar, Akiva and Idith Zertal. 2005. *Adonei Ha-Aretz: Ha-Mitnachalim U-Medinat Yisra'el, 1967–2004 (Lords of the Earth: The Settlers and the State of Israel, 1967–2004).* Tel Aviv: Dvir.

Eldar, Akiva. 2004. "Partzufo Ha-Amiti: Re'eyon 'Im Amos Malka" ("His Real Face: An Interview with Amos Malka"). *Ha'aretz.* June 11.

Eliade, Mircea. 1959. *The Sacred and the Profane,* New York: Harcourt Brace.

Enderlin, Charles. 2003. *Shattered Dreams: The Failure of the Peace Process in the Middle East, 1995–2002.* New York: Other Press.

Eran, Gideon and Zali Gurevitch. 1991. "'Al Ha-Maqom" ("On the Place"). *Al-payim* 4: 9–44.

Falah, Ghazi and David Newman. 1995. "The Spatial Manifestation of Threat: Israelis and Palestinians Seek a 'Good' Border." *Political Geography* 14: 689–706.

Fisher, Ronald J. 1997a. *Interactive Conflict Resolution.* Syracuse: Syracuse University Press.

Fisher, Ronald J. 1997b. "The Potential Contribution of Training to Resolving International Conflict." *International Negotiation* 2 (3).

Fisher Ronald J. 2002. "Historical Mapping of the Field of Interactive Conflict Resolution." In John Davis and Edy Kaufman, eds., *Second Track/Citizens' Diplomacy: Concepts and Techniques for Conflict Transformation,* pp. 61–80. Lanham, MD: Rowan and Littlefield.

Foundation for Middle East Peace. Undated. "Settlement Database and Suitability Assessment." At http: //www.fmep.org/settlement_info/settlement_database.html.

Gidron, Benjamin, Stanley N. Katz, and Yeheskel Hasenfeld. 1994. *Mobilizing for Peace: Conflict Resolution in Northern Ireland, Israel/Palestine, and South Africa.* New York: Oxford University Press.

Golani, Motti. 1998. "Kissufim LaChud Ma'asim LaChud: Mediniyut Yisra'el Be-She'elat Yerushalayim 1948–1967" ("Longings Separately and Actions Separately: Israeli Policy on the Jerusalem Question, 1948–1967"). In Anita Shapria, ed., '*Atzma'ut: 50 Ha-Shanim Ha-Rishonot,* pp. 267–96. Jerusalem: Zalman Shazar Center.

Gorenberg, Gershom. 2006. *The Accidental Empire: Israel and the Birth of the Settlements, 1967–1977.* New York: Times Books.

Gurr, Ted R. and John Davis. 2002. "Dynamics and Management of Ethnopolitical Conflicts." In John Davis and Edy Kaufman, eds., *Second Track/Citizens' Diplomacy: Concepts and Techniques for Conflict Transformation,* pp. 31–48. Lanham, MD: Rowan and Littlefield.

Ha'aretz. Undated. "Mechir Ha-Hitnachluyot" ("The Price of the Settlements"). At http://www.haaretz.co.il/hasite/pages/LiArtSR.jhtml?objNo = 53757.

Hanieh, Akram. 2001. "The Camp David Papers." *Journal of Palestine Studies* Vol. 30: 75–97.

Hanssen–Bauer, Jon. 2005/6. "Bustling Backwards: Lessons from the Norwegian Sponsored Israeli–Palestinian People-to-People Program." *Palestine–Israel Journal* 12 (4): 39–52.

Hassner, Ron. 2003. "To Halve and Hold." *Security Studies* 12 (Summer): 1–33.

Henriksen-Waage, Hilde. 2004. *Peacemaking Is a Risky Business: Norway's Role in the Peace Process in the Middle East, 1993–96.*Oslo: PRIO—International Peace Research Institute.

Hepburn, Stanley A.C.H. 1994. "Long Division and Ethnic Conflict: The Experience of Belfast." In Seamus Dunn, ed., *Managing Divided Cities,* pp. 88–104. Kiel: Kiel UP.

Hirshfeld, Yair. 2000. *Oslo: Nusha Le-Shalom (Oslo: A Formula for Peace).* Tel Aviv: Yitzhak Rabin Center for Israel Studies and Am Oved.

IDF (Israel Defense Forces). 2006. "General Info [sic] and Statistics: Ebb and Flow: Summary of Terror Attacks in the Last Five Years." http://www1.idf.il/dover/site/mainpage.asp?sl = EN&id = 22&docid = 52616, accessed Oct. 3, 2006.

IPCRI (Israel Palestine Center for Research and Information). 2002. *Yes PM: Years of Experience in Strategies for Peace Making, Looking at Israeli–Palestinian People to People Activities, 1993–2002.*

Kaspit, Ben. 2000. "Shenatayyim Le-Intifada" ("Two Years of the Intifada"). *Ma'ariv.* Part I September 6, Part II September 13.

Kassisiyyeh Issa. 2002. "Second Track Negotiations: The Jerusalem File." *Jerusalem Quarterly* (15).

Kaufman, Edy and Walid Salem, eds. 2006. *Bridging the Divide: Peace-Building in the Israeli–Palestinian Conflict.* Boulder, CO: Lynne Reinner and The European Centre for Conflict Prevention in Utrecht.

Kaufman, Edy. 2002. "Sharing the Experience of Citizens' Diplomacy with Partners in Conflict" and "Towards Innovative Solutions." In John Davis and Edy Kaufman, eds., *Second Track/Citizens' Diplomacy: Concepts and Techniques for Conflict Transformation,* pp. 183–264. Lanham, MD: Rowan and Littlefield.

Kelman, Herbert C. 1992. "Informal Mediation by the Scholar/Practitioner." In Jacob Bercovitch and Jeffrey Z. Rubin, eds., *Mediation in International Relations: Multiple Approaches to Conflict Management,* pp. 64–69. New York: St. Martin's Press.

Kelman, Herbert C. 1994. "Promoting Joint Thinking in International Conflicts: An Israeli–Palestinian Continuing Workshop." *Journal of Social Issues* 50 (1): 157–78.

Kelman, Herbert C. 1996. "Negotiation as Interactive Problem Solving." *International Negotiation* 1: 99–123.

Kelman, Herbert C. 1998. "Interactive Problem Solving: An Approach to Conflict Resolution and its Application in the Middle East." *PS: Political Science and Politics* 31: 190–98.

Kelman, Herbert C. 2002. "Interactive Problem Solving as a Tool for Second Track Diplomacy." In John Davis and Edy Kaufman, eds., *Second Track/ Citizens' Diplomacy: Concepts and Techniques for Conflict Transformation,* pp. 81–106. Lanham, MD: Rowan and Littlefield.

Kleiman, Aharon. 2005. "Israeli Negotiating Culture." In Tamara Cofman Wittes, ed., *How Israelis and Palestinian Negotiate: A Cross-Cultural Analysis of the Oslo Peace Process,* pp. 81–132. Washington, D.C.: United States Institute of Peace Press.

Klein, Menachem. 1998. "Between Right and Realization: The PLO Dialectics of 'The Right of Return.'" *Journal of Refugee Studies* 11 (1): 1–19.

Klein, Menachem. 2001. *Jerusalem: The Contested City.* New York: New York University Press; London: C. Hurst.

Klein, Menachem. 2003a. "Mezima? Tzeiruf Miqrim!" ("Plot? Coincidence!"). In Avraham (Rami) Friedman and Shlomo Hasson, eds., *Keitzad Mashpi'im: Choqrim Ve-Qov'ei Mediniyut,* pp. 165–88. Jerusalem: Jerusalem Institute for Israel Studies.

Klein, Menachem. 2003b. *The Jerusalem Problem: The Struggle for Permanent Status.* Gainesville: University Press of Florida.

Klein, Menachem. 2004a. "Jerusalem Without East-Jerusalemites? The Palestinians as the 'Other' in Jerusalem." *Journal of Israeli History* 23 (2): 174–99.

Klein, Menachem. 2004b. "Jerusalem: Constructive Division or Apartheid?" In Dan Leon, ed., *Who's Left in Israel: Radical Political Alternatives for the Future of Israel*. Brighton: Sussex Academic Press.

Klein, Menachem. 2004c. "Answers to Geneva Agreement Critiques." *Strategic Assessment* 7 (2) (July): 38–43.

Klein, Menachem. 2004d. "The Logic of Geneva Agreement." *Logos: A Journal of Modern Society and Culture* 3 (1) (Winter), at http: //www.logosjournal. com/klein.htm. Also in Stephen Eric Bronner and Michael J. Thompson, eds., *The Logos Reader: Rational Radicalism and the Future of Politics*. Lexington: University Press of Kentucky (2006).

Klein, Menachem. 2004e. "A Path to Peace: Sharon's Disengagement Plan or the Geneva Accord?" *Logos: A Journal of Modern Society and Culture* 3 (3) (Summer), at http: //www.logosjournal.com/klein_sharon.htm.

Klein, Menachem. 2005. "Old and New Walls in Jerusalem." *Political Geography* 24 (1): 53–76.

Klein, Menachem. 2006a. "The Intifada: The Young Generation in the Front." In Charles W. Greenbaum, Philip Veerman and Naomi Bacon-Shnoor, eds., *Protection of Children During Armed Political Conflict: A Multidisciplinary Perspective*, pp. 45–56. Antwerp and Oxford: Intersentia.

Klein, Menachem. 2006b. "The Palestinian 1948 Refugees: Models of Allowed and Refused Return." In Michael Dumper, ed., *Palestinian Refugee Repatriation in Global Perspective*. London: Routledge.

Klein, Menachem. 2007. "The Negotiations for the Settlement of the 1948 Refugee Problem." In Eyal Benvenisti, Chaim Gans and Sarri Hanafi, eds., *Israel and the Palestinian Refugees*. Heidelberg: Max Planck Institute for Comparative Public Law and International Law.

Konrad Adenauer Foundation, The Harry S. Truman Research Institute at the Hebrew University and the Palestine Consultancy Group, East Jerusalem. 1998. *Is Oslo Alive?* Panel Held at the Notre Dame Center, Jerusalem, November 24, 1997.

Lein, Yehezkel and Alon Cohen-Lifshitz. 2005. *Under the Guise of Security: Routing the Separation Barrier to Enable the Expansion of Israeli Settlements in the West Bank*. Jerusalem: B'Tselem, Bimkom. http://www.btselem.org/ Download/200512_Under_ the_Guise_of_Security_Eng.doc. Accessed Oct. 10, 2006.

Machsomwatch. 2004. "A Counter View: Checkpoints 2004." www.machsom-watch.org/docs/counterview.pdf.

Malka, Amos. 2004. "Shichtuv Be-De'avad" ("Ex Post Facto Rewriting"). *Yediot Aharonot*. June 30.

Matz, David. 2003. "Why Did Taba End?" *Palestine-Israel Journal* 10 (3): 96–105, and (4): 92–104.

McDonald, John W. 1991. "Further Exploration of Track Two Diplomacy." In Louis Kriesberg and Stuart J. Thorson, eds., *Timing the De-escalation of International Conflicts*, pp. 201–20. Syracuse: Syracuse University Press.

McDonald, John W. 2002. "The Need for Multi-Track Diplomacy." In John Davis and Edy Kaufman, eds., *Second Track/Citizens' Diplomacy: Concepts and Techniques for Conflict Transformation*, pp. 49–60. Lanham, MD: Rowan and Littlefield.

Meital, Yoram. 2004. *Shalom Shavur: Yisra'el, Ha-Falastinim, Ve-Ha-Mizrach Ha-Tichon (Broken Peace: Israel, the Palestinians, and the Middle East)*. Jerusalem: Carmel.

Memmi, Albert. 1991. *The Colonizer and the Colonized*. Boston: Beacon Press.

MEMRI. 2003. "Palestinian Reactions to the Geneva Understandings." November 11. At http://www.memri.org.il/memri/loadallarticlespage.asp?language = hebrew&iPage = 14.

Montville, Joseph. 1987. "The Arrow and the Olive Branch: A Case for Track Two Diplomacy." John McDonald and Diane Bendahmane, eds., *Conflict Resolution: Track Two Diplomacy*, pp. 5–20. Washington D.C.: Foreign Service Institute, Department of State.

Morris, Benny. 2002. "Camp David and After: An Exchange 1, An Interview with Ehud Barak" and "Camp David and After Continued." *New York Review of Books*. June 13, June 27.

Nassar–Najjab, Nadia. 2005/6. "Post Oslo Dialogue: An Evaluation." *Palestine–Israel Journal* 12 (4): 22–33.

Newman, David and Anssi Passi. 1988. "Fences and Neighbours in the Post-Modern World: Boundary Narrative in Political Geography." *Progress in Human Geography* 22: 186–207.

Oz, Amos. 1983. *Po VeSham Be-Eretz Yisrael Be-Stav 1982 (Here and There in the Land of Israel, Fall 1982)*. Tel Aviv: Am Oved.

Palestine Red Crescent. Undated. "Tables of Deaths and Injuries." At http://www.palestinercs.org/crisistables/table_of_figures.htm.

Palestinian Center for Policy and Survey Research. 2003. "While a Majority Opposes the Geneva Document, Palestinian Attitudes Vary Regarding Its Core Components." December 16. At http://www.pcpsr.org/survey/polls/2003/p1oejoint.html.

Palestinian Center for Policy and Survey Research. 2005. "In the Post Arafat Era, Palestinians and Israelis Are More Willing to Compromise." Jan. 18. At http://www.pcpsr.org/survey/polls/2005/jointpreelections05.html.

Palestinian Central Bureau of Statistics. Undated. "Population by Age Groups in Years, Region and Sex." http://www.pcbs.gov.ps/Portals/_pcbs/phc_97/phc_t2.aspx. Accessed Oct. 3, 2006.

Passi, Anssi. 1999. "Boundaries as Social Process: Territoriality in the World of Flows." In David Newman, ed., *Boundaries, Territoriality and Post-Modernity*, pp. 69–88. London: Frank Cass.

PCPSR (Palestinian Center for Policy and Survey Research). 2005. "Press Release: Joint Palestinian-Israeli Public Opinion Poll. Dec. 21. http: //www. pcpsr.org/survey/polls/2005/p18ejoint.html.

Peace Now. Undated. "Settlements in Focus." At http: //www.peacenow.org. il/site/en/peace.asp?pi = 51.

Pedatzur, Reuven. 2004. "Terumato Shel TzaHa"L La-Haslama" ("The IDF's Contribution to the Escalation"). *Ha'aretz*. June 30.

Peters, F. E. 1986. *Jerusalem and Mecca: The Typology of the Holy City in the Near East*. New York: New York University Press.

Porath, Yehoshua. 1995. *The Emergence of the Palestinian Arab National Movement, 1918–1929*. London: Frank Cass.

Pratt, Martin and Janet Alison Brown, eds. 2000. *Border Lands Under Stress*. London: Kluwer.

Pressman, Jeremy. 2003. "Visions in Collision: What Happened in Camp David and Taba?" *International Security* 28: 5–43.

Pundak, Ron. 2001. "From Oslo to Taba: What Went Wrong?" *Survival* 43: 31–45.

Rabinowitz, Itamar. 2004. *Chevelei Shalom: Mishalat Lev O Medina'ut? (Peace Agonies: Wish or Statesmanship?)*. Tel Aviv: Kinneret, Zemora Bitan Dvir.

Rapoport, Meron. 2005. "This Land Is Your Land, This Land Is My Land." *Ha'aretz* Friday Magazine. March 4.

Ross, Dennis. 2004. *The Missing Peace: The Inside Story of the Fight for Middle East Peace*. New York: Farrar Straus and Giroux.

Rouhana, Nadim. 1995. "Unofficial Third Party Intervention in International Conflict: Between Legitimacy and Disarray." *Negotiation Journal* 11 (3): 255–71.

Rouhana, Nadim. 2000. "Interactive Conflict Resolution: Theoretical and Methodological Issues in Conducting Research and Evaluation." In Paul Stern, Alexander George, and Daniel Druckman, eds., *International Conflict Resolution: Techniques and Evaluation*, pp. 294–337. Washington, D.C.: National Academy Press.

Rubinstein, Dani, Robert Malley, Hussein Agha, Ehud Barak, and Benny Morris. 2003. *Kamp David 2000: Ma Be-Emet Qara Sham? (Camp David 2000: What Really Happened There?)*. Tel Aviv: Yediot Aharonot and Sifrei Aliyat Ha-Gag.

Rubinstein, Dani. 2004. "Ha-Ha'Aracha Ha-Mut'et Higshima Et 'Atzma: Ra'ayon 'Im Matti Steinberg" ("The Mistaken Evaluation Fulfilled Itself: An Interview with Matti Steinberg"). *Ha'aretz*. June 16.

Saunders, Harold H. 1985. "We Need a Later Theory of Negotiation: The Impact of Pre-Negotiation Phases." *Negotiation Journal* 1 (3): 249–62.

Saunders, Harold. H. 1995. "Possibilities and Change: Another Way to Consider Unofficial Third Party Intervention." *Negotiation Journal* 11 (3): 271–76.

Sayigh, Yezid. 1997. *Armed Struggle and the Search for State: The Palestinian National Movement, 1964–1993*. Oxford: Clarendon.

Segev, Tom. 2005. *1967: Ve-Ha-Aretz Shinta Et Paneha (1967: And the Face of the Land Changed)*. Jerusalem: Keter.

Shalom, Stephen R. and Justin Podur. 2004. "Justice for Palestine?" *Znet*, March 30. At http://www.chomsky.info/interviews/20040330.htm.

Shamir, Shimon and Bruce Maddy-Weitzman, eds. 2005. *The Camp David Summit: What Went Wrong? Americans, Israelis and Palestinians Analyze the Failure of the Boldest Attempt Ever to Resolve the Palestinian-Israeli Conflict*. Brighton and Portland: Sussex Academic Press.

Shamir, Shimon, ed. 2005. *Diplomatia Ezrachit Be-Maslul Shtayyim: Ha-Im Yesh Le-Ezrachim Cheleq Be-Tahlichei Yishuv Sichsuchim (Citizens' Diplomacy in Track Two: Is There a Role for Citizens in Conflict Resolution?)*. Tel Aviv: Ramot.

Shavit, Ari. 2004. "Be-Shem Marsho" ("In the Name of His Client"). *Ha'aretz* Friday Magazine. Oct. 8.

Shenhav, Yehuda, ed. 2004. *Qolonialiyut Ve-Ha-Matzav Ha-Postqoloniali (Colonialism and the Post-Colonial Situation)*. Jerusalem: Van Leer Institute and Ha-Kibbutz Ha-Me'uchad.

Sher, Gilad. 2001. *Ba-Merchaq Negi'a: Ha-Masa U-Matan Le-Shalom 1999–2001, 'Edut (At Touching Distance: The Peace Process 1999–2001, Testimony)*. Tel Aviv: Yediot Aharonot.

Shlaim, Avi. 2000. *The Iron Wall: Israel and the Arab World*. London: Penguin.

Stern, Yoav. 2004. "Re'eyon 'Im Efrayim Lavie" ("Interview with Efrayaim Lavie"). *Ha'aretz*. June 13.

Susser, Asher. 2003. "A Shaky Foundation." *Ha'aretz*, Dec.15.

Susskind, Lawrence E., Abram Chayes Abram, and Janet Martinez. 1996. "Parallel Informal Negotiation: A New Kind of International Dialogue." *Negotiation Journal* 12 (1).

Swirsky, Shlomo. 2005. *Machir Ha-Yohara: Ha-Kibush, Ha-Machir She-Yisra'el Meshalemet (The Price of Arrogance: The Occupation, The Price Israel Pays)*. Tel Aviv: Adva Center and Mapa.

Swisher, Clayton. 2004. *The Truth About Camp David: The Untold Story About the Collapse of the Middle East Peace Process*. New York: Nation Books.

Truman Institute. 2005. "Joint Palestinian-Israeli Public Opinion Poll: Stable Majority Support for Clinton's Final Status Package Among Israelis But Decline in Support Among Palestinians." At http://truman.huji.ac.il/polls.asp.

Turner, Victor. 1971. "The Centre Out There: Pilgrim's Goal." *History of Religion* 12 (3): 191–230.

Wanis-St. John, Anthony. 2001. "Back Channel Diplomacy: The Strategic Use of Multiple Channels of Negotiation in Middle East Peacemaking." Ph.D. diss., Fletcher School of Law and Diplomacy, Tufts University.

World Bank. 2003. "West Bank and Gaza Update: World Bank Report on Impact of Intifada. April-June." http://lnweb18.worldbank.org/mna/mena.nsf/Attachments/Update+May+2003+English/$File/may+lay-en-Blue03.pdf

INDEX

Abbas, Mahmoud (Abu-Mazen), 4,
    16, 22, 32, 47, 48, 55, 60, 65, 178,
    179, 202, 210
'Abd al-Razeq, Hisham, 17, 26, 41, 45,
    54, 55, 61
al-'Abd, Samih, 17, 32, 50, 52, 53, 68,
    69–72, 78, 120, 132, 163
'Abd-Rabbu, Yassir, 3, 6–7, 8, 9, 11, 12,
    18, 22, 32, 33–34, 44, 47–48, 55, 77,
    119, 128, 129, 162–63, 166, 175, 176,
    178; at London talks, 17, 50, 61, 69;
    meeting with Israeli team, 26–27
Abu-Mazen. See Abbas, Mahmoud
Abu-Safiyya, Yussuf, 22, 23
Abu-Zayyad, Ziyyaad, 22
Adam, Heribert, 151
Adam, Kanya, 151
Adam Smith Institute, 168
African National Congress, 22–23,
    24–25
Agha, Hussein, 4, 177
Alfei Menashe settlement, 49, 53, 73,
    76, 78, 183
Algeria, 57
Algerian independence movement,
    152–56
al-'Amiry, Su'ad, 26
Apartheid regime, 22, 25
Aqaba summit of June, 2003, 48, 178

al-Aqsa Martyrs' Brigade, 210
al-Aqsa mosque, 106
Arab peace initiative of 2002, 191,
    192, 202, 209
Arafat, Yassir, 4, 6, 16, 21, 36, 41,
    60, 145, 192, 196; declaration,
    state of Palestine, 5; and Geneva
    initiative, 43, 44, 47, 147–48, 158,
    163; Israeli view of, 43; Muqata
    discussion, 47
archeological excavations, 106, 112,
    113, 141
Ariel settlement, 53, 201
Arieli, Shaul, 17, 31–32, 33, 34, 50, 52,
    53, 54, 68, 69, 70, 72, 77, 78, 127
Armenian Patriarchate, 126
Arnon, Arieh, 40
al-Asad, Hafez, 6
Ayalon, Ami, 13, 27, 28, 30, 31, 172,
    173, 188
Ayalon–Nusseibeh document, 18,
    27–31, 172–73
al-Ayam (newspaper), 14

Barak, Ehud, 42, 53, 67, 100, 101,
    119, 151, 161, 173; Taba talks, 1–3;
    Camp David summit, 4–6, 20, 35;
    Jerusalem negotiations, 36, 87,
    103, 114, 115, 116

Barak government, 20, 21, 23, 40, 52, 96, 99, 107

Barakeh, Mohammad, 27

Baram, Uzi, 38

Barghouti, Marwan, 44

Bar Navi, Eli, 51, 101

Barnea, Nachum, 13

Bayat, Asef, 97

al-Baz, Usama, 9

Bedouin of the Negev, 86

Begin, Menachem, 58, 198–99

Begin highway, 121, 130, 139–40

Beilin, Yossi, 1, 2, 3, 4, 6–7, 8, 9, 11, 12, 14, 18, 19, 22, 26, 30, 31, 32, 33, 34, 35, 38, 39, 40, 43, 44, 47, 48, 55, 62, 73, 74, 77, 78, 100, 121, 129, 166, 175, 178

Beilin–Abu-Mazen agreement, 4–5, 6, 8, 16, 18, 71, 104

Beitar Elit, 75, 128

Beit Jala, 93

Beit Jubrin, 72, 135

Belfast, 85

Ben-Ami, Shlomo, 2, 4, 20, 33, 36, 42, 100, 101, 102, 103, 109, 112, 114, 119

Ben-Shachar, Haim, 38

Benvenisti, Meron, 194

Bethlehem, 91, 93, 128–29, 132

Bethlehem–Hebron road, 73

Bethlehem University, 196

Biblical Zoo, 133

borders: Green Line, 53, 63, 64, 73, 200; Israel–West Bank, 143, 201; nature of, 142–43. *See also* Jerusalem, borders and boundaries; security fence and wall

Botha, Pik, 23, 25

British mandate, 41. *See also* Mandatory Palestine

Brom, Shlomo, 31, 32, 52, 72, 78

B'Tselem, 195

Burg, Avraham, 22, 36, 37, 62, 114

Bush, President G. W., 48, 178, 179, 209

Cairo understandings, 210

Calmy-Rey, Micheline, 12

Cambridge University, 32

Camp David summit (2000), 1, 4–6, 35, 41, 56, 149; American compromise, 109, 110; and Barak government, 20, 21; Jerusalem issues, 29, 84, 92, 98, 108–10, 111, 113, 114–15, 117; Palestinian strategy at, 148–49; territorial negotiations, 67–68

Cape Town seminar, 22–25. *See also* South African peace talks

Carter, President, 38–39

cease-fire agreement of 1949, 133

Cemeteries: Christian, 105, 125, 133; Jewish, 81, 132; Muslim, 105

Chomsky, Noam, 196

Church of the Holy Sepulcher, 103, 106

citizens' diplomacy, 158–59, 161–62, 171. *See also* Track-two talks

civil society, 38, 58, 60, 61, 159, 193

Clinton, President, 3, 5–6, 22, 67, 101, 112, 117, 133, 188

Clinton parameters, proposals of December 2000, 3, 6, 27, 67, 209; Jerusalem issue, 34, 111–12, 117, 121; refugee issue, 57, 61, 188; support for, 199

Cohen, Ron, 39

Communist party, 27, 54

Conference center event, 33–34

Dahlan, Mohammad, 55

Dajani, Omar, 145, 146, 148, 156

David, King, 84

Dayan, Ilana, 13
Dayan, Moshe, 82, 151
Dead Sea meetings. *See* Jordan talks
de Gaulle, Charles, 152, 153
Deheishe refugee camp, 73
Democratic Front for the Liberation
  of Palestine, 44, 54
demographic issue, 64, 137, 207; in
  Jerusalem, 79, 83, 87, 89, 96,
  97–98
Dome of the Rock, 106
Duek, Nissim, 7, 10

early-warning stations, 56
Economic Cooperation Foundation
  (ECF), 2, 14, 22, 33, 35, 105–6, 167
economic gap, 137
Efrat, 49, 53, 73, 75
Egypt, 41
Egyptian-Israeli peace agreement, 58,
  65–66, 154, 198
Eldar, Akiva, 3, 20
elections, 153; American 2000, 5;
  Israeli 1977, 198; Israeli 2002,
  1, 39, 48, 179; Israeli 2003, 18;
  Palestinian 2006, 199, 202, 210
Erekat, Saeb, 22, 47, 179
Etzion block, 73
extraterritorial status, 103, 105
Eyal, Nadav, 10

Fares, Kadura, 26, 41, 43, 44, 45, 46,
  54, 75, 77, 127
Fatah, 9, 10, 23, 28, 152, 181, 209;
  central committee, 46; generation
  of, 46; and Geneva initiative, 46,
  47, 77, 163; Hamas agreement,
  65, 210; and Palestinian 2006
  elections, 199, 202; terror
  campaign, 21
Feldman, Shai, 177
FIDA party, 44, 162

First World Congress for Middle East
  Studies, 196
France, 152–56
freedom of worship, 81
Friedlander, Jonathan, 33
"From Oslo to Taba: What Went
  Wrong" (Pundak), 21
fundamentalism, Jewish, 114–15, 204

Galnor, Yitzhak, 19
Galon, Zahava, 39
Gaza Strip, 135, 210; evacuation of
  settlements, 15, 65
General Security Services (Shin Bet),
  20, 63
Geneva initiative: activists, 15, 47;
  American involvement, 146, 148;
  al-Awda petition, 182; Cape Town
  seminar, 22–25; coalitions, 157;
  context of, 177–81; criticisms of,
  164, 181–94; experts, assistance
  of, 134–35, 147, 148, 149, 156, 167–
  68, 170; funding, 12, 17, 18, 19;
  international support, 48, 175–76,
  181; intimacy of negotiations,
  165–66; and Israeli press, 6–7, 10,
  12–13; and Israeli public, 34–35,
  48; leaders of, 168–69, 171, 175,
  176, 178–79; legitimacy of, 171,
  173, 174; maps used, 2, 17, 63, 68,
  69–70, 76, 136; media interest,
  11, 13–14, 174; MEMRI summary
  of, 182; and Meretz party, 40;
  Movenpik Hotel, Jordan, meeting
  at, 77; peace camps, 11, 42–43, 162;
  peace coalition, 11, 15, 22, 25–26;
  politicians involvement, 38–39,
  156, 161–62; private meetings,
  166; public relations, marketing
  campaign, 7–8, 17, 35, 46, 175,
  176–77; public support, 45, 164,
  174–75; security issues, 49, 56–57,

183, 186; and Sharon government, 173; success, reasons for, 156–58; Swiss mediators, 128, 164, 165; territorial negotiations, 31, 53, 62–79; territorial compensation, 45, 62, 66, 67, 71, 109, 134–35; tour of Jerusalem seam, 130, 131, 132, 134; video conference on refugees, 38, 57, 61; World Bank building meetings, 18–19, 26, 45, 48, 52, 77. *See also* Jordan talks; London talks; Taba talks

document, 4, 8, 31, 37, 57, 77, 173–74, 177; appendices, 138, 183; Articles, 186–87, 189–90; claims, end of, 189, 192–93; draft, 10, 39, 169; interfaith council, 193; Israel, recognition of, 184; Jewish right to a state, 27, 43, 184; militias, 186–87; Palestinian right to a state, 184; publication, distribution of, 13–14; release of prisoners, 54–55; right of return, 30, 182, 188–89; side letter to, 180; signers of, 182; signing ceremony, 8, 9

Israeli team, delegation, 31–40, 41, 48–50, 70, 124, 126, 135, 163–64, 179–80; and Israeli national leadership, 160; Meretz delegation, 39–40; military officers, 31–32, 149; public relations staff, 12; working procedures, 108, 148–51

Palestinian team, delegation, 9, 40–48, 78, 115, 121, 124, 128, 129, 134, 145–48, 162–64, 178–80; Arafat's involvement, 43, 44, 47, 147–48, 158, 163; concessions made by, 43, 56–57, 174, 175, 180; experts, assistance of, 134–35, 147, 148, 149, 168; and Fatah, 47, 77, 163; flexibility of, 42, 148; leaders of, 178–79; legitimacy of, 146, 147; and Palestinian national leadership, 160, 162, 175, 182; Tanzim representatives, 43–46, 55, 77, 78; travel permits for, 9, 17, 57, 180; working procedures, 14–15, 41, 145–48

Germany, Jewish attitude toward, 60–61

Gilad, Amos, 9, 20

Ginat, Yossi, 172

Givat Ze'ev, 45, 53, 74–76, 77–78, 94, 102, 128–29, 183; annexation of, 37, 49, 73, 87, 108, 134

Golan, Galia, 26

Golan Heights, Israeli withdrawal from, 6, 66

Goldstein, Baruch, 16

Good Friday Agreement, 33

Greater Israel Movement, 21, 204

Greenfield, Tzvia, 21, 35, 37

Green Line, 53, 63, 64, 73, 200

Grinstein, Gidi, 2

Grossman, David, 21, 35, 60

Guardian, 33

Gush Etzion settlement, 53, 75, 93, 102, 108

Ha'aretz, 3, 13, 16, 20, 21, 33, 64, 115

Habash, Sahar, 46

Hadash faction, 27

HaLevy, Rabbi Yehuda, 88

Halutza sands, 71

Hananiyya, Ghazi, 22

al-Haram al-Sharif, 28–29, 109, 120; al-Aqsa mosque, 106; archeological excavations, 112; Dome of the Rock, 106; Sharon's visit to, 29; sovereignty over, 29, 110, 112; Waqf administration of, 102; Western Wall as part of, 123. *See also* Temple Mount

Har Gilo settlement, 93
Har Shmuel settlement, 75, 76
Harvard University, 31
al-Hasan, Hani, 10, 46
Hassassian, Manuel, 196
Hazan, Naomi, 22
Hebrew University of Jerusalem, 19,
    21, 31, 131
Hebron, 16, 44, 73, 124
Hebron road, 132, 134
Hesder yeshiva, 54
Hirschfeld, Yair, 22, 33, 167
Holocaust, 61
Holy Basin, 105, 111, 113–14;
    sovereignty over, 105–6, 109, 110
Hourani, Mohammad, 26, 41, 43, 44,
    45, 46, 54, 72, 75, 77, 78, 129
al-Husseini, Faisal, 92
Husseini, Kamel, 7

Ibrahim, George, 26
Inbar, Giora, 12, 31, 50, 54
Interim Agreement Administration,
    31
international community, 15
International Court of Justice, 201
international law, 147
International Red Cross, 19
Intifada, first, 46, 63, 84, 99, 197,
    198; generation of, 197, 198
Intifada, second (al-Aqsa), 1, 16, 17,
    29, 35, 63, 64–65, 86, 116, 185;
    consequences of, 89, 90, 118, 195,
    197, 200; generation of, 197, 199
Iran, 23
Iraq, 41, 57; American war in, 177, 178
Islamicists, 21
Israel: army, 46, 64, 65, 197, 201,
    205; citizenship, 92; colonialism,
    21; Declaration of Independence,
    185; defense establishment, 150;
    democracy, weakness of, 199–200;

Egypt, peace negotiations with,
    152; elites, 107; foreign ministry,
    150; founding narrative, 59;
    General Security Services (Shin
    Bet), 20, 63; as homeland of
    Jewish people, 184; international
    legitimacy, 188; as Jewish state, 27,
    184, 203, 207; Knesset, 31, 36, 100,
    149, 199, 200; military subculture,
    150–51; Palestinian nation, recog-
    nition of, 152; political left, 20,
    21, 48, 160, 179; political right, 15,
    23, 107; religious right, 204, 205;
    self-determination, right to, 59;
    Supreme Court, 93, 94, 95, 201;
    war crimes, 59
Israel Defense Forces (IDF), 20, 23,
    68
Israel-Jordan peace treaty, 66, 154
Israel-Palestine Center for Research
    and Information, 140–41
Israeli intelligence, 9, 20
Israelis: conformism of, 51; national
    identity, 52, 81, 82, 137, 204;
    Palestinian-Israelis, 27, 183,
    185–86, 206–7; peace camp, 11, 42;
    sense of security, insecurity, 42,
    56, 137; sense of superiority, 137;
    view of Palestinians, 51, 124, 150,
    197–98

Jebusites, 84
Jerusalem: American compromise,
    109; annexations to, 18, 37, 75, 79,
    81, 93–94, 108, 111, 133, 183;
    archeological excavations, 106, 112,
    113, 141; cemeteries, 81, 105, 125, 132,
    133; Biblical Zoo, 133; City of David,
    105, 112, 125; demographic issue,
    79, 83, 87, 89, 96, 97–98; de-
    territorialization of, 99; freedom
    of worship, 81; government

buildings, 131; Holy Basin, 105–6, 109, 110, 111, 113–14; holy sites, 140; and identity, 85–86; Israeli public debate on, 107; Jerusalem Day, 81, 84; Liberty Bell Park, 89; Monastery of the Cross, 140; Mount of Olives, 81, 105, 112, 125, 132; Mt. Zion, 105, 125, 133, 140; Municipal Route 1, 131, 138, 140; as open city, 104, 122; Palestinians, marginality of, 86; partitioning of, 34, 85, 89, 111, 118, 119–21, 122, 132, 136–37, 140–42; partitioning proposal, three rings, 101–2, 109; permanent status agreement for, 92, 96, 140, 142, 143, 172; police academy building, 129, 131; police headquarters, 131; poor, encroachment of, 97; security fence and wall, 87, 93–96, 141; segregation of, 88–89; sovereignty, Israeli supreme, 103, 104; special regime proposal, 113–14; as symbol, 88, 99–100, 144; Talpiot shopping area, 89; tourism, 89, 120, 127; track-two proposals for, 103–7; umbrella municipality, 102, 103–4, 108, 111, 118, 137; united, 81–82, 87, 102, 107

borders and boundaries, 89–94, 130–36; administrative, 104, 111; annexation line (1967 line), 82, 83, 90–91, 93–94, 108, 138, 183; border regime, 137, 139–40; border strip proposal, 138; crossings and checkpoints, 119, 139–40; demographic, 89–90; fence and wall, 87, 93–96, 141; Geneva agreement map, 136; "hard," 111; international, 90, 104, 119; of Israeli control, 90; "Jerusalem envelope," 73, 96; metropolitan, 91; municipal, 18; physical, 104, 135–37, 138–39, 183; political, 92; politicization of, 98; pre-1967, 103; seam between East-West, 89, 130, 131, 136, 141, 139; "soft," 111, 119, 122; with West Bank, 82, 94

East, 66, 67, 71, 74, 78, 79, 87, 117, 118, 137, 195, 200; Abu-Dis, 132; annexation of, 81–83, 91, 98; Arab neighborhoods, 88, 96, 109, 118; Beit Hanina, 94, 101, 109, 130, 131, 140; Beit Safafa, 78, 133–34, 136, 140, 183; border crossings to West Bank, 94; business center, 132; expansion of, 83, 91, 93; French Hill, 130, 131, 138; Gilo, 133, 134; Givat HaMatos, 133; Har Homa, 87, 93, 111, 133, 134; house demolitions, 83, 141; identity cards, confiscation of, 83, 141; infrastructure, 140; Israeli control over, 87, 90, 96, 107; Israeli institutions, 90; Israeli law in, 82, 87, 107; Jewish neighborhoods, 71, 78, 87, 93, 96, 97, 109, 118, 123–24, 130, 134–35, 138; Jewish population, 79, 108; municipal services, 102, 106, 136; Neve Ya'akov, 93, 94, 102, 130–31, 140; occupation, benefits of, 82; Palestinian institutions, 86, 92; Palestinian leadership, 134; PLO in, 33, 92, 107; Palestinian sovereignty, 87, 92, 108, 122, 124; Palestinians, 82–84, 86, 92, 94–95, 97–98, 141; Palestinians, Israeli discrimination against, 84, 85; Pisgat Ze'ev, 93, 129, 130–31; al-Quds, 29, 74, 101, 102, 111, 118, 119, 121, 122, 127, 135, 142, 144; Ramot Eshkol, 131; Ramot, 75, 78; Ras al-Amud, 132; right of association,

141; roadblocks, 91, 94, 96; security 109, 141, 142; settlers, 89–90, 141; Sharafat, 133, 134; Sho'afat, 101, 109, 130, 131; social security system, 121, 122, 141; surveys of, 95, 121–23; Sha'ar Mizrach, 87; suburbs, 101; territorial powers in, 127–28. *See also* Al-Quds

Old City, 78, 83, 85, 86, 88, 100, 102, 104, 109–12, 114, 136, 183, access to, 126–27; checkpoints, 120–21; Church of the Holy Sepulcher, 103, 106; city wall, 129, 132; division of, 120–21; Dung Gate, 125, 127; Golden Gate, 105; Herod's Gate, 125; international security force, 118, 125, 126, 129–30, 141; Jaffa Gate, 78, 126, 127, 128–30, 132; Jaffa-Zion Gate road, 78, 126, 129, 164; Kishla compound, 130; Lion's Gate, 125, 132; as living museum, 120; Nablus Gate, 125, 132; New Gate, 125; as open city, 118–19, 120, 125; Quarter, Armenian, 105, 109, 112, 118, 126, 136; Quarter, Christian, 105, 109, 112, 118, 126; Quarter, Jewish, 105, 109, 110, 112, 114, 118, 119, 120, 126, 127, 136; Quarter, Muslim, 105, 109, 110, 112, 118, 120, 126, 136; *shuk*, 83, 120, 126, 136; sovereignty, 78, 118; sovereignty over city gates, 125; special regime proposal, 110, 112, 113–14; Tower of David, 126–30; traffic in, 127, 131, 132; Western Wall, 28–30, 81–82, 106, 110, 112, 114, 118, 119, 123, 124; Zion Gate, 78, 125, 126. *See also* al-Haram al-Sharif; Temple Mount

West, Jewish-Israeli, 87, 88–89, 96, 103, 121, 122, 130, 134–35, 137, 183; Arab neighborhoods, former, 117; Israeli investment in, 87; Jewish neighborhoods, 121; Mevasserat Yerushalayyim, 75; Mt. Scopus, 78, 131, 136, 140, 183; sovereignty over, 108, 119

Jerusalem: The Contested City (Klein), 101

"Jerusalem: A Mutual Israeli-Palestinian Embrace," 101–2

Jerusalem–Bethlehem road, 133

Jerusalem Day, 81, 84

Jerusalem Institute for Israel Studies, 32, 95, 101, 167

Jerusalem Mall in Malha, 89, 133, 135

Jerusalem–Ramallah highway, 18

Jerusalem–Tel Aviv road, 37, 72

Jerusalem–Tel Aviv train route, 133

Jewish fundamentalists, 113, 114–15

Jewish religious discourse, 114

Jewish state, 26–27, 184–85; Israel as a, 27, 184, 203, 207; Jewish peoples' right to a state, 27, 43, 59, 184, 198

Jews of Diaspora, 106, 203

Jordan, 41, 66, 68, 81

Jordan talks, 9–13, 124, 127–28, 131, 156, 180; refugee issue, 61–62; Temple Mount issue, 36–37

Jordan Valley, 56, 71

Jubeh, Dr. Nazmi, 26, 34, 50, 54, 120, 196

Judaism, 27, 113, 116, 193, 205

Jum'ah, Bashar, 32

Kadmiel, Doron, 31

Karin A, Israeli interception of, 23

Karni, Boaz, 33

Kaspit, Ben, 13

Katzir, Yehudit, 60

Keller, Alexis, 19, 34, 57, 178

Kfar Etzion, 62

Khalidi, Ahmad, 4, 177

Khoury, Saman, 26
Kibbutzim, 72, 135
Kimmerling, Baruch, 21
Kleiman, Aharon, 149, 151, 156
Knesset, 31, 36, 100, 149, 199, 200;
    elections of 2003, 18; Hadash
    faction, 27
Kollek, Teddy, 81

Labor party, 18, 36, 39, 48, 52, 100–
    101
Labor Zionist movement, 52
Landau, Minister, 173
Lang, Nicholas, 19, 57
Lapid, Minister, 173
Lapidot, Ruth, 31
Latrun, 72, 128
Lautman, Dov, 38
law, international, 186
League of Nations, 20
Lebanon, 66
Lebanon war, second, 199, 210
Leibowitz, Yeshayahu, 37
Levy, Daniel, 2, 22, 26, 32, 33, 34, 44,
    50, 166
Levy, David, 4
Lieberman, Avigdor, 173
Lifta, 134
Likud: government, 17, 31, 107; party,
    9, 15, 16, 31, 48, 58, 62, 73, 179
Little Triangle region, 185–86
Livnat, Limor, 173
Livni, Eti, 35, 38
London channel, 33
London talks, 13, 17, 41, 45, 50, 69–
    70, 178; Jerusalem issues, 125–26,
    130; prisoner release issue, 55, 61;
    public relations campaign, 7–8;
    territorial negotiations, 71–74

Ma'aleh Adumim, 45, 53, 70, 76,
    77, 78, 102, 128–29, 131, 183, 201;

annexation to Jerusalem, 73–74,
    87, 93, 108, 134
Ma'aleh HaHamisha hotel meetings,
    20, 21–22
Ma'ariv, 10, 13, 174
Madrid document, 103
Madrid non-paper, 109
Maimonides, 88
Makhoul, Issam, 27
Malley, Robert, 22, 34
Manasra, Zuhir, 54, 72, 78, 128, 129
Mandatory Palestine, 65, 141, 147, 196.
    See also British mandate
Mars al-Kabir, 153, 155
Matalon, Ronit, 21, 60
Mbeki, President Thabo, 22, 23, 25
Melchior, Rabbi Michael, 114
MEMRI, 182
Merchav, Reuven, 22
Meretz party, 1, 3, 18, 39–40, 101
Meridor, Dan, 2
messianic ideology, theology, 62,
    204, 205
Mevasserat Tzion, 87
Michael, Sami, 60
military subculture, 150–51
militias, 20, 23, 181, 186–87
Mishor Adumim, 70, 74
Mitchell, George, 181
Mitzna, Amram, 9, 32, 39, 52, 72, 77,
    78, 129, 166
Modi'in, 37
Mohammad, Prophet, 29
Monastery of the Cross, 140
Moodley, Kogila, 151
Moratinos, Miguel, 3
Moratinos document, 3
Morocco, 57, 88, 154
Mount of Olives, 81, 105, 112, 125, 132
Mt. Zion, 105, 125, 133, 140
Movenpik Hotel in Jordan, meeting
    at, 77

Mubarak, Hosni, 9
Muqata, discussion at, 47
Musa al-'Alami compound, 133, 134

Nabi Samuel, 75, 76, 140
Nakba of 1948, 72
National Security Council, 22
negotiation practices and tactics:
    "adequate consensus," 25;
    "concessions," 68–69, 70; divide-
    and-rule, 150, 157; informal talks,
    166; Israeli, 149–51; press leaks,
    7; reciprocity, 117; "red lines," 44,
    66, 148, 149, 157, 163; reopening
    issues, 41, 69–70, 129; salami
    method, 69, 77; "walking in the
    woods," 32; zero-sum game, 51,
    66, 143–44, 193
1948 narrative, 58–59, 61
1948 territories, 65
1948 war, 58, 59, 184, 203
1967 territories. See West Bank and
    Gaza Strip
1967 war, 62, 72, 75, 81–82, 85, 184,
    203
Netanyahu, Binyamin, 107
NGOs, 159
Nobel Prize ceremony, 38–39
Nusseibeh, Sari, 13, 27, 28, 31, 43, 172,
    173, 188

Occupation, Israeli, 15, 59, 64, 65, 82,
    188, 193, 194, 195, 197, 198, 199,
    202, 203, 210
Oklahoma channel, 172–73
Olmert, Ehud, 36, 173
al-Omari, Ra'ith, 22, 26, 32, 50, 166
Ophel Road, 132
Orient House, 33, 92, 167
Oron, Haim, 22, 23, 39, 40, 62, 129
Oslo accords, agreements, 1, 17, 31,
    41, 47, 63, 67, 85, 96, 111, 134,

152, 206; implementation of,
    43, 149, 151, 159, 186, 187; and
    Jerusalem borders, 91–92; Likud
    opposition, 17; period, years of,
    46, 74, 86, 146, 148, 155, 159; PLO
    concessions, 149; process, 16, 18,
    20; negotiations, 161, 177;
Oxford University, 32, 33;
Oz, Amos, 13, 21, 35, 124, 133

Palestinian Authority, 6, 11, 24, 32,
    47, 90, 91, 92, 98, 164, 179, 210;
    organizational shortcomings, 20,
    41–42, 145–46, 148; destruction of,
    46, 86, 92, 175, 195; reforms in, 17,
    65; on Temple Mount issue, 116–17
Palestinian Communist Party, 54
Palestinian-Israelis, 27, 183, 185–86,
    206–7
Palestinian Legislative Council, 4,
    22, 44
Palestinian Liberation Organization
    (PLO), 42, 59, 109, 145–46,
    154, 156, 210; African National
    Congress, compared to, 25;
    in East Jerusalem, 92, 107;
    executive committee, 44, 176;
    Israel, agreements with, 202;
    Israel, recognition of, 113, 116,
    149; negotiations department, 33,
    145, 147, 148, 168; organizational
    shortcomings, 41, 145–46;
    Orient House, 33, 92, 167; Oslo
    concessions, 149; on right of
    return, 30, 189
Palestinian national leadership,
    5, 36, 60, 115, 149, 200, 202;
    organizational shortcomings, 41,
    46, 47, 146, 195; and Sharon, 48,
    178, 179
Palestinian Peace Movement, 26
Palestinian Red Crescent, 195

Palestinians: collective institutions, 86, 92; contradictions, 137–38; Israeli discrimination against, 84, 85, 185; national movement, 58, 65; Palestinian-Israelis, 27, 183, 185–86, 206–7; peace activists, 43; peace opponents, 152; right to self-determination, 59, 192, 198; right to a state, 184; rights, 27, 141, 185; security agencies, 141; sovereignty, 56, 65,156, 183; terror used by, 20, 23, 34, 64, 65, 186, 199; view of Israelis, 124; war crimes, 59

Palestinian state, 2, 5, 59, 61, 88, 101, 142, 147, 149, 154, 196; Israeli authority over, 188; settlements as obstacle to creating, 63, 90

Paritzki, Joseph, 173

Pat neighborhood, 133, 138

Peace Administration, 32

peace camps, 11, 42–43, 162

Peace coalition, 11, 15, 22; declarations, 25–26; and elites, 25

Peace Now, 13, 26, 40, 63

people-to-people activities, 159

Peres, Shimon, 1, 2, 16, 19, 36, 100

permanent status agreement, 2, 4, 5, 6, 13, 17, 38, 42, 43, 52, 68, 73, 161, 167, 169, 180, 181, 202; binational model, 27, 194–96, 198; civil rights model, 196; in Jerusalem, 92, 96, 107, 136, 140, 142, 143, 172; negotiations, talks, 3, 53, 67, 74, 98, 107, 146, 151, 152, 163, 193, 200, 201; prisoner release tied to, 54–55; and settlements, 76, 77; Taba talks, 1, 3, 34, 201; two-state solution, 61, 196, 200

Place for Everyone, A (Ben-Ami), 101, 103

political parties, right-wing, 107

polls, Shamir and Shiqaqi, 13, 174–75, 199

Poraz, Avraham, 173

Powell, Colin, 31

power relations, 51, 142

prisoners, release of Palestinian, 45, 54–55

Prospect magazine, 196

Protective Wall operation, 65, 195

Pundak, Ron, 20, 21, 32, 33, 34, 43, 44, 52, 53, 72, 78

Qalandiya, 101

Qalandiya roadblock, 94, 180

Qassam rocket attacks, 210

Qassis, Nabil, 17, 22, 34, 55, 61, 119, 162

Quartet, 17

al-Quds (municipality), 29, 74, 101, 102, 111, 118, 119, 121, 122, 127, 135, 142, 144

al-Quds (newspaper), 14, 21

al-Quds University, 13

Qurei, Ahmed (Abu-'Ala), 4, 13, 47, 179

rabbis, extremist, 204

Rabin, Yitzhak, 82, 151, 161

Rabin-Pelosoff, Dalia, 35, 38

Rachel's tomb, 93, 94, 140

Rajoub, Jabril, 78

Ramallah, 41, 44, 56, 74, 75, 91, 94, 180

Ramallah-al-Bireh metro area, 74–75

Ramban Cave, 140

al-Ram meetings. See World Bank building meetings

reciprocity, principle of, 117

refugees: Algerian, 156; Jewish, 57–58

refugees of 1948, 2, 23, 26, 31, 38, 43, 45, 49, 57–62, 128, 149;

International Commission, 190; Israeli quota on return of, 190–91; legal status, 189–90; moral compensation for, 59, 60; responsibility for, 58–59, 184; territorial compensation for ("101 percent option"), 45, 62; video conference on, 38, 57, 61. *See also* Right of return

Republican party, American, 31

right of association, 141

right of return: Palestinian, 30, 37, 46, 61–62, 182, 188–92; Jewish, 189; PLO position on, 189–90, 192

roadblocks, Israeli, 19, 46, 57, 195; East Jerusalem, isolation of, 91, 94, 96; protection of settlements, 64

"Roadmap to a Permanent Two-State Solution to the Israeli-Palestinian Conflict," 17, 47, 48, 140, 161, 162, 178, 179, 180–81, 210–11

Ronal, Ayala, 34, 138

Ronen, Nechama, 12, 35, 37, 49, 76

Route 443, 37, 94

Rubenstein, Elyakim, 2

Sabra "new Jew," 82

Saharan nuclear testing site, 153, 155

Said, Edward, 196

Samuel, prophet, 75

Sarid, Yossi, 1, 2, 39

Schiff, Ze'ev, 177

security fence and wall, 15, 18, 39, 162, 174, 198, 200–201, 209, 210; through Jerusalem, 87, 93–96

security, Israeli: establishment, 158; ethic, 149; private, 64; subculture, 158

Seidemann, Daniel, 34

self-determination, right to, 59, 152, 192, 198–99

settlements, Israeli, 42, 62–65, 69, 74, 146, 152, 183, 185–86, 197, 198–99, 201, 203; annexation of, 53, 67, 69, 70–71, 73, 149, 154, 200; blocs, 67–68, 70; definition of, 67–68; evacuation of, 15, 65, 71, 76, 205, 209; as facts on the ground, 62, 96; financial support, 63; Israeli-Palestinian, 185; Israeli policy, 62; military defense, 63–65; military-settler complex, 204, 206; movement, 62, 204; national project, 63, 203, 205; "wildcat," unlicensed, 63, 201; World Zionist Organization Settlement Division plan, 62

settlers, French, 153–55

Sha'ath, Nabil, 32, 47, 179

Shahak, Amnon, 2, 4, 23, 31, 34, 37, 50, 52–53, 54, 55, 73

Shaked, Avi, 8

Shamir, Dr. Ya'akov, 13

Sharon, Ariel, 1, 3, 7, 9, 13, 15, 18, 21, 48, 161, 162, 179, 200, 201, 209; and Geneva initiative, 8, 10, 11, 173; al-Haram al-Sharif visit, 29; and Roadmap, 48, 178

Sharon government, 40, 65, 160, 175, 177, 200; Jerusalem, program for, 87

Shas party, 2, 9

Shefer, Gideon, 31, 50, 52, 54

Sher, Gilad, 2, 3, 4, 20, 35, 42

Shin Bet. *See* General Security Services

Shinui party, 35, 38

Shiqaqi, Dr. Khalil, 13

Sho'afat refugee camp, 90, 93

Shubaki, Jamal, 23

Shuk, 83, 120, 126, 136

Simon the Just, tomb of, 140

Solomon's Pools, 73

South Africa, 198
South African peace talks, 151–52.
   See also Cape Town seminar
sovereignty: divided, 104, 105, 118;
   and extraterritorial status, 103,
   105; full, principle of, 65, 156;
   functional, 103, 112, 127; of
   God, 106, 110; graduated, 108;
   indefinite, 105; joint, 104, 105; and
   sanctity, 116; subterranean, 110, 112,
   115; supreme, 109–10; symbolic,
   29, 33, 37, 116; and territorial
   powers, 127–28
Sternschuss, Dror, 7, 10, 13, 14
Stockholm, 38–39
Storrs, Sir Ronald, 100
suicide bombings, 16, 21, 199
Sukkah Tractate, 113
summit meetings, nature of, 164–65
Sweden, 19
Swiss foreign ministry, 18, 19, 57
Switzerland, 9, 12, 20
Syria, 5, 6, 66

Taba talks, 1–3, 6, 18, 34, 41, 52, 56,
   58, 68, 111–12, 201; Jerusalem
   issue, 118, 119, 126
Talmud, 113
Tamari, Salim, 26
Tamir, Yuli, 35, 38, 48
Tanzim party, 23, 41, 43–46, 77, 210
Technion, 138
Teddy Kollek sports stadium, 133, 135
Tel-Aviv–Jerusalem highway, 131, 135
Tel Aviv University, 53, 138, 149
Temple Mount, 103, 104–5, 106–7;
   access to, 90, 141; archeological
   excavations, 106, 113; cult of,
   88, 116; international body,
   commission, 106, 110, 111, 112;
   Jewish connection to, 116–17;
   Jewish prayer on, 104, 106, 110,
112, 113, 114, 115–16; Palestinian
   declaration, 116–17; ruins of
   second Temple, 110, 112–13, 115;
   security, 106–7; sovereignty over,
   28–30, 33, 36, 37, 105, 106, 116–17,
   118; sovereignty, subterranean,
   110, 112, 115; Third Temple, 88, 113,
   115, 116; Waqf administration of,
   90, 105, 106. *See also* al-Haram
   al-Sharif
Tenet, George, 181
territorial compensation, 45, 62, 66,
   71, 109, 134–35; ratios, 67
territorial negotiations, 31, 53, 62–79
Third Temple, 88, 113, 115, 116
Tomb of the Patriarchs, massacre at,
   16
Tosefot, 113
Tour of East–West Jerusalem seam,
   130, 131, 132, 134
Track-two talks, 33, 45, 49–50, 103,
   108, 117, 119, 158–77; experts,
   assistance of, 170; government
   cooptation of, 168–69; government disavowal of, 170–71; "hard"
   and "soft," 177–78; Jerusalem
   proposals, 103–7; leaders, 171–72;
   legitimacy of, 170–77; literature
   on, 169–70; Oklahoma track, 172–
   73; public exposure, 169; public
   opinion, 172, 176. *See also* Citizens'
   diplomacy
Tunisian national movement, 154
Tzaban, Dror, 63
Tzaban, Yair, 1, 21, 26, 27
Tzemach, Mina, 174
Tzur Hadassah, 128

unilateral disengagement plan, 15, 18,
   161, 162, 173, 174, 199, 200, 209,
   210
unilateral option, 200–202

unilateral withdrawal, 21, 40, 176, 200, 202

unilateralism, 35, 200, 210

United Nations, 146, 152, 176, 188; General Assembly Resolution 194, 188, 191–92; Relief and Works Agency, 131; Security Council Resolution 242, 147, 149, 191–92, 209; Security Council Resolution 338, 209

United States, 47, 147, 149, 178, 179

University of Geneva, 2001 conference at, 19

University of Haifa, 172

Usiskin, Paul, 13, 50

villages: Palestinian, ruins of, 72; Palestinian-Israeli, 185

Voice of Israel, 10, 11, 85

Wadi Fukin, 128–29

war crimes, 59, 186

Weisglass, Dov, 7, 161

West Bank, 75, 79, 96, 185, 200–202, 210; Israeli occupation, 14, 15, 59; Israeli flights over, 56; Jordanian rule, 42; Palestinian national institutions in, 86; Preventative Security force, 78

West Bank and Gaza Strip (1967 territories), 5, 13, 62, 64, 82, 137, 197, 204, 206, 207; negotiations, 65–66, 67, 69, 71–72; occupation, 188, 193; and Palestinian Author-

ity, 42, 46; and Palestinian state, 147, 154, 196

Western Europe, 176, 188

Western Wall: Israeli access to, 81, 119; Israeli paratroopers at, 81–82; Palestinian view of, 123; prayer compound, 124; sovereignty over, 28–30, 106, 110, 112, 114, 118, 124

Wolfowitz, Paul, 31

World Bank building meetings, 18–19, 26, 45, 48, 52, 77

World Bank report, 197

World Zionist Organization Settlement Division plan, 62

Wye agreement, 55

Yachad party, 18, 39, 40. See also Meretz party

Yediot Aharonat (newspaper), 10, 13, 174

Yehoshua, A. B., 21, 38, 60

Yesha settler's council, 173

Yeshivot, 204

Yisrael Beiteinu party, 173, 185

Yitzhaki, Rabbi Shlomo, 113

Zaki, Abbas, 46

Zaki, Uri, 10

Zakut, Jamal, 26

Zionism, Zionist, 115, 194, 202–6; ethos, 96; ideology, 62; Left, 20, 26, 27, 48; movement, 26, 83, 98, 203; project, 88